Collins

Student Book

CAMBRIDGE IGCSE® PHYSICS

Susan Gardner and Malcolm Bradley

GW00808304

William Collins' dream of knowledge for all began with the publication of his first book in 1819. A self-educated mill worker, he not only enriched millions of lives, but also founded a flourishing publishing house. Today, staying true to this spirit, Collins books are packed with inspiration, innovation and practical expertise. They place you at the centre of a world of possibility and give you exactly what you need to explore it.

Collins. Freedom to teach

Published by Collins
An imprint of HarperCollins *Publishers*
77 – 85 Fulham Palace Road
Hammersmith
London
W6 8JB

Browse the complete Collins catalogue at
www.collinseducation.com

© HarperCollins*Publishers* Limited 2012

10 9 8 7 6 5 4 3 2 1

ISBN 13 978 0 00 745444 0

The authors assert their moral rights to be identified as the authors of this work.

All rights reserved. No part of this publication may be reproduced, stored in a retrieval system, or transmitted in any form or by any means, electronic, mechanical, photocopying, recording or otherwise, without the prior written permission of the Publisher or a licence permitting restricted copying in the United Kingdom issued by the Copyright Licensing Agency Ltd., 90 Tottenham Court Road, London W1T 4LP.

British Library Cataloguing in Publication Data
A Catalogue record for this publication is available from the British Library

Commissioned by
Letitia Luff and Rebecca Richardson
Project edited by **Caroline Green**
Project managed by
Jim Newall and Lifelines Editorial Services
Edited by **Lauren Bourque and Elizabeth Jones**
Proofread by **Maggie Rumble and Mitch Fitton**
Indexed by **Michael Forder**
Designed by **Jouve India Private Limited**
New illlustrations by **Jouve India Private Limited**
Picture research by
Caroline Green and Grace Glendinning
Concept design by **Anna Plucinska**
Cover design by **Angela English**
Production by **Rebecca Evans**
Printed and bound by **L.E.G.O. S.p.A. Italy**

Fully safety checked but not trialled by CLEAPSS

The syllabus content is reproduced by permission of Cambridge International Examinations.

Acknowledgements

The publishers wish to thank the following for permission to reproduce photographs. Every effort has been made to trace copyright holders and to obtain their permission for the use of copyright materials. The publishers will gladly receive any information enabling them to rectify any error or omission at the first opportunity:

(t = top, c = centre, b = bottom, r = right, l = left)

Cover & p1 Irochka/Dreamstime, p8–9 Camellia/Shutterstock, p10 Rob kemp/Shutterstock, p11 Hung Chung Chih/Shutterstock, p16 wavebreakmedia ltd/Shutterstock, p25 Marcel Jancovic/Shutterstock, p31 Dorling Kindersley/Getty Images, p32 Alexander Chaikin/Shutterstock, p36 Andrea Danti/Shutterstock, p37 Michal Vitek/Shutterstock, p41 Charles D. Winters/Science Photo Library, p42 Jerritt Clark/Getty Images, p45 EcoPrint/Shutterstock, p48 Mark Thiessen/Alamy, p49 Kirk Geisler/Shutterstock, p50 Michael Wesemann/Shutterstock, p52 Martyn F. Chillmaid/Science Photo Library, p59 Peter Bernik/Shutterstock, p65 Andrew Barker/Shutterstock, p71 clearlens/Shutterstock, p72t Adrian Hughes/Shutterstock, p72l chatchai/Shutterstock, p72r sizov/Shutterstock, p80 Zoia Kostina/Shutterstock, p81 Ocean Power Delivery/Science Photo Library, p82 Rido/Shutterstock, p83 Peteri/Shutterstock, p88 NASA, p98t Marcel Jancovic/Shutterstock, p98b DenisNata/Shutterstock, p102 Charles D. Winters/Science Photo Library, p103 JonMilnes/Shutterstock, p104 Mike Heywood/Shutterstock, p118–119 Katrina Leigh/Shutterstock, p120 jele/Shutterstock, p121l Alan Freed/Shutterstock, p121r Geoffrey Kuchera/Shutterstock, p123 Mike Blanchard/Shutterstock, p126 goldenangel/Shutterstock, p133 Natursports/Shutterstock, p134 jan kranendonk/Shutterstock, p135 Dmitry Berkut/Shutterstock, p139 Khram/Shutterstock, p141 Dennis Donohue/Shutterstock, p148 PavleMarjanovic/Shutterstock, p153 Alexandra Lande/Shutterstock, p157 Ulrich Mueller/Shutterstock, p163 Vixit/Shutterstock, p166 Jim Lopes/Shutterstock, p170–171 Willyam Bradberry/Shutterstock, p172 Yuri Arcurs/Shutterstock, p178 Ensuper/Shutterstock, p181 Aija Lehtonen/Shutterstock, p182 Andrii Gorulko/Shutterstock, p183 Payless Images/Shutterstock, p189 Robert Pickett, p193 Nagy-Bagoly Arpad/Shutterstock, p197 Fedorov Oleksiy/Shutterstock, p198 Darren Pullman/Shutterstock, p200 Dario Sabljak/Shutterstock, p202 photoinnovation/Shutterstock, p208 Igor Klimov/Shutterstock, p209 Losevsky Photo and Video/Shutterstock, p210 Kick the beat/Shutterstock, p220–221 littlesam/Shutterstock, p222 Nadezhda Bolotina/Shutterstock, p224 REDAV/Shutterstock, p226 colematt/iStockphoto, p228 EPA/Alamy, p232 Tomasz Szymanski/Shutterstock, p236 Nir Levy/Shutterstock, p238 Mike Dunning/Getty Images, p241t Andrew Howe/iStockphoto, p241b Jhaz Photography/Shutterstock, p250 Richard Wareham Fotografie/Alamy, p258 Bart Coenders/iStockphoto, p261 Joshua Haviv/Shutterstock, p278t Papik/Shutterstock, p278b Marie C Fields/Shutterstock, p287 Alex Kuzovlev/Shutterstock, p288 Photoseeker/Shutterstock, p292 Slaven/Shutterstock, p295 oksana2010/Shutterstock, p296 M. Niebuhr/Shutterstock, p302 Paul Andrew Lawrence/Alamy, p304 SuriyaPhoto/Shutterstock, p306 xpixel/Shutterstock, p312l Trevor Clifford Photography/Science Photo Library, p312r Trevor Clifford Photography/Science Photo Library, p312b GIphotostock/Science Photo Library, p318 ermess/Shutterstock, p320 Rannev/Shutterstock, p326 BortN66/Shutterstock, p330–331 InnaFelker/Shutterstock, p332 Troy GB images/Alamy, p334 Gail Johnson/Shutterstock, p338 Toxicotravail/WikiMedia Commons, p339 Andrew Lambert Photogarphy/Science Photo Library, p346 Belmonte/Science Photo Library, p349t Ihervas/Shutterstock, p349b Robin Weaver/Alamy, p363 Ed Phillips/Shutterstock.

Contents

Getting the best from the book 4

Section 1
General physics 8
a) Length and time 10
b) Speed, velocity and acceleration 16
c) Mass and weight 31
d) Density 36
e) Forces 45
f) Energy, work and power 71
g) Pressure 98
h) Exam-style questions 110

Section 2
Thermal physics 118
a) Simple kinetic molecular model of matter 120
b) Thermal properties 133
c) Transfer of thermal energy 153
d) Exam-style questions 166

Section 3
Properties of waves 170
a) General wave properties 172
b) Light 181
c) Sound 208
d) Exam-style questions 217

Section 4
Electricity and magnetism 220
a) Simple phenomena of magnetism 222
b) Electrical quantities 232
c) Electric circuits 258
d) Dangers of electricity 287
e) Electromagnetic effects 295
f) Cathode-ray oscilloscopes 318
g) Exam-style questions 324

Section 5
Atomic physics 330
a) The nuclear atom 332
b) Radioactivity 338
c) Exam-style questions 354

Doing well in examinations 358
Introduction 358
Overview 358
Assessment objectives and weightings 358
Examination techniques 359
Answering questions 360

Developing experimental skills 362
Introduction 362
Using and organising techniques,
apparatus and materials 362
Observing, measuring and recording 364
Handling experimental observations
and data 367
Planning and evaluating investigations 369

Glossary 375
Answers 380
Index 389

Getting the best from the book

Welcome to *Collins Cambridge IGCSE Physics*.

This textbook has been designed to help you understand all of the requirements needed to succeed in the Cambridge IGCSE Physics course. Just as there are five sections in the Cambridge syllabus, there are five sections in the textbook: General physics, Thermal physics, Properties of waves - including light and sound, Electricity and magnetism and Atomic physics.

Each section is split into topics. Each topic in the textbook covers the essential knowledge and skills you need. The textbook also has some very useful features which have been designed to really help you understand all the aspects of Physics which you will need to know for this syllabus.

SAFETY IN THE SCIENCE LESSON

This book is a textbook, not a laboratory or practical manual. As such, you should not interpret any information in this book that related to practical work as including comprehensive safety instructions. Your teachers will provide full guidance for practical work and cover rules that are specific to your school.

A brief introduction to the section to give context to the science covered in the section.

Starting points will help you to revise previous learning and see what you already know about the ideas to be covered in the section.

The section contents shows the separate topics to be studied matching the syllabus order.

Knowledge check shows the ideas you should have already encountered in previous work before starting the topic.

Learning objectives cover what you need to learn in this topic.

Examples of investigations are included with questions matched to the investigative skills you will need to learn.

△ Fig. 5.1 This submarine gets its energy from a small nuclear reactor inside it.

The nuclear atom

INTRODUCTION
To understand radioactivity, you first need to know about the structure of the atom. Understanding of atomic structure has developed over time. The model that we use now was first developed as a result of an experiment by Geiger and Marsden in the 1910s. In this topic you will learn about the basic building blocks of atoms and about some uses of isotopes.

KNOWLEDGE CHECK
✓ Know that matter is made from atoms and molecules.

LEARNING OBJECTIVES
✓ Describe the structure of an atom in terms of a nucleus and electrons.
✓ EXTENDED Describe how the scattering of alpha particles by thin metal foils provides evidence for the nuclear atom.
✓ Describe the composition of the nucleus in terms of protons and neutrons.
✓ Use the term 'proton number Z'.
✓ Use the term 'nucleon number A'.
✓ Use the term 'nuclide' and use the nuclide notation $^A_Z X$.
✓ Use the term 'isotope'.
✓ EXTENDED Give and explain examples of practical applications of isotopes.

ATOMIC MODEL
All elements are made up of atoms, consisting of protons, neutrons and electrons. The protons and electrons have electrical charges that are exactly equal in size but opposite in sign. Because atoms generally do not have an electric charge, they usually contain the same number of protons and electrons.

The nucleus is made of protons and neutrons, bound together by an extremely strong force, far stronger than gravity, or electromagnetic forces, and completely different from any of them. The electrons form a loose cloud on the outside of the atom with the nucleus in the middle. Table 5.1 summarises this.

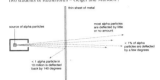

Particle:	proton	neutron	electron
Relative mass:	1.007	1.008	0.0005
Relative Charge:	+1	0	−1

△ Table 5.1 Atomic structure.

EXTENDED

Geiger and Marsden's experiment
In the first decade of the 20th century, scientists knew that the atom contained positive and negative charges but the structure was a great mystery. An experiment suggested by Rutherford discovered the strange scattering of **alpha particles** when they get close to atoms (Fig. 5.2), and this cast great light on the structure. (The actual work was done by two students of Rutherford's – Geiger and Marsden.)

△ Fig. 5.2 Rutherford's scattering experiment, which revealed the structure of the atom.

What they discovered was that almost all of the alpha particles got through the thin metal sheet with no difficulty, but maybe one particle in a million hit a relatively large object that sent it off at a wide angle – perhaps even back the way it had come. This 'back scattering' was very surprising as it went against the existing model of the atom, proposed by Thomson (the 'plum pudding' model). The results told them that the atom has a nucleus that contains almost all of the mass of the atom. Because so few alpha particles hit the nucleus, it must be extremely small, surrounded by a cloud of extremely light electrons.

Rutherford's nuclear model
We are left with the slightly disturbing thought that almost all of a solid object is actually empty space, loosely filled with **electrons**, with a tiny nucleus at the centre of each atom. In a neutron star, where all of the atoms collapse, the whole star can end up perhaps no more than 10 km across, with a density of 300 *million* tonnes per cubic centimetre.

END OF EXTENDED

Developing Investigative Skills

A student wants to investigate the factors that affect the strength of an electromagnet. He makes the electromagnet by winding a coil of wire around a large iron rod. He then holds the electromagnet vertically in a clamp attached to a clamp stand. He uses a low-voltage power supply to provide the current for the electromagnet.

The student decides to investigate the effect of changing the current in the coil. To measure the strength of the electromagnet he finds out how many paper clips he can hang from the end of the electromagnet. His measurements are shown in the table.

Current/A	Number of paper clips held
0	0
0.3	2
0.5	5
0.7	6
0.9	9
1.0	9

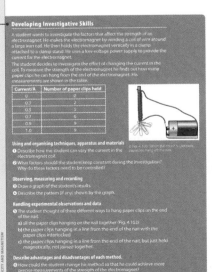

△ Fig. 4.103 When the current is switched off, the paper clips hang off the nail.

Using and organising techniques, apparatus and materials
❶ Describe how the student can vary the current in the electromagnet coil.
❷ What factors should the student keep constant during the investigation? Why do these factors need to be controlled?

Observing, measuring and recording
❸ Draw a graph of the student's results.
❹ Describe the pattern (if any) shown by the graph.

Handling experimental observations and data
❺ The student thought of three different ways to hang paper clips on the end of the nail.
a) all the paper clips hanging on the nail together (Fig. 4.103)
b) the paper clips hanging in a line from the end of the nail with the paper clips interlocked
c) the paper clips hanging in a line from the end of the nail, but just held magnetically, not joined together.

Describe advantages and disadvantages of each method.
❻ How could the student change his method so that he could achieve more precise measurements of the strength of the electromagnet?
❼ The student wants to continue making measurements with higher values of current. Suggest a difficulty he will have as the current increases further.

FORCE ON A CURRENT-CARRYING CONDUCTOR
When a wire carrying an electric current passes through a magnetic field, with the field at right-angles to the wire, the wire will experience a force at right-angles both to the wire and to the magnetic field. The size of the force depends on the magnitude of the current and the strength of the magnetic field. **Fleming's left-hand rule**, which is shown in Fig. 4.104, predicts the direction of the force. You can demonstrate this using the apparatus in Fig. 4.105.

Remember that the current direction is that of the conventional current, and that the electrons are travelling the opposite way.

△ Fig. 4.104 Fleming's left-hand rule predicts the direction of the force on a current-carrying wire.

△ Fig. 4.105 Apparatus that can be used to demonstrate that if a wire carrying an electric current passes through a magnetic field, with the field at right-angles to the wire, then the wire will experience a force at right-angles both to the wire and to the magnetic field.

When you try applying Fleming's left-hand rule, you should be able to confirm that if you reverse either the magnetic field or the current then the force will be applied in the opposite direction, but that if you reverse *both* the field *and* the current then the force stays unchanged.

It is useful to look at the magnetic field lines for this set-up (Fig. 4.106).

△ Fig. 4.106 How the magnetic field lines are changed by a wire in a uniform magnetic field.

The field lines from the magnet are dragged downwards by the direction of the field lines that are around the wire. If you imagine that the lines are made of stretched elastic, then it is clear why the wire feels an upwards force.

Getting the best from the book *continued*

Science in context boxes put the ideas you are learning into real-life context. It is not necessary for you to learn the content of these boxes as they do not form part of the syllabus. However, they do provide interesting examples of scientific application that are designed to enhance your understanding.

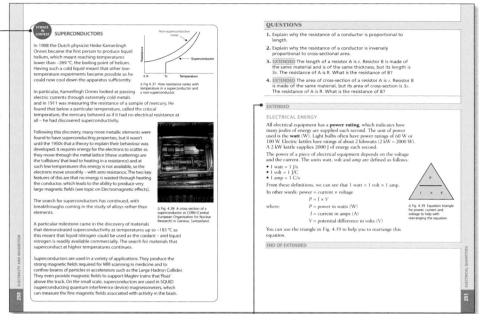

Clearly differentiated Extended material takes your learning even further.

Remember boxes provide tips and guidance to help you during your course and to prepare for examination.

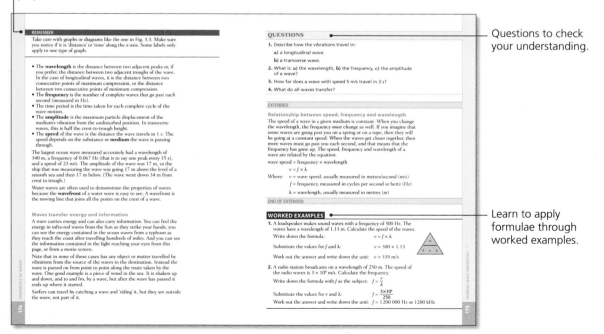

Questions to check your understanding.

Learn to apply formulae through worked examples.

End of topic questions allow you to apply the knowledge and understanding you have learned in the topic to answer the questions.

A full checklist of all the information you need to cover the complete syllabus requirements for each topic.

End of topic checklist

Key terms

absolute zero, Boyle's law, Brownian motion, Charles' law, evaporation, kelvin scale, kinetic molecular model, kinetic theory of gases, pressure law, vapour

During your study of this topic you should have learned:

○ About the distinguishing properties of solids, liquids and gases.

○ About the molecular structure of solids, liquids and gases.

○ EXTENDED How the motion of particles and the forces and distances between them relate to their properties.

○ How temperature affects the way gases behave.

○ How pressure affects the way gases behave.

○ About the effect of a change in temperature on the pressure of a gas at constant volume.

○ That the random motion of particles in a suspension gives evidence for the kinetic molecular model of matter.

○ About Brownian motion in terms of random molecular bombardment.

○ That massive particles may be moved by light, fast-moving molecules.

○ How evaporation can be described in terms of escape of more-energetic molecules from the surface of a liquid.

○ How evaporation is related to the consequent cooling of a liquid.

○ EXTENDED That evaporation is affected by temperature, surface area and draught over a surface.

○ How a change in the volume of a gas is related to a change in pressure applied to the gas at constant temperature.

○ EXTENDED To use the equation pV = constant at constant temperature.

End of topic questions

Note: The marks awarded for these questions indicate the level of detail required in the answers. In the examination, the number of marks awarded to questions like these may be different.

1. Give an example of a material for each state of matter that demonstrates the properties of that state. (3 marks)

2. Use ideas about particles to explain why:

   a) solids keep their shape, but liquids and gases don't (3 marks)

   b) solids and liquids have a fixed volume, but gases fill their container. (3 marks)

3. How does kinetic theory explain the existence of absolute zero? (3 marks)

4. Use the kinetic molecular model to explain the following observations in detail:

   a) It is possible to keep a bottle of drink cold by standing it in a bowl and covering it with a wet cloth. (3 marks)

   b) EXTENDED The drink gets even colder when you place the bowl in a strong draught. (3 marks)

5. How is the speed of a gas molecule linked to the temperature of the gas? (2 marks)

6. How does the kinetic theory explain the fact that gases exert a pressure on their container? (2 marks)

7. EXTENDED A student blows up a balloon. At room temperature, 20 °C, she measures the volume of the balloon as 1500 cm³. Then she puts the balloon in a freezer where the temperature is –13 °C. Assuming the pressure stays constant, work out the new volume of the balloon. (3 marks)

8. EXTENDED A sample of gas is sealed in a 20 cm³ metal container at a pressure of 1×10^5 Pa. Calculate the new pressure of the gas when the metal container is slowly crushed to a volume of 5 cm³ with the same temperature. (3 marks)

The first question is a student sample with teacher's comments to show best practice.

Each section includes exam-style questions to help you prepare for your exam in a focussed way and get the best results.

Exam-style questions

Note: The questions, sample answers and marks in this section have been written by the authors as a guide only. The marks awarded for these questions indicate the level of detail required in the answers. In the examination, the number of marks awarded to questions like these may be different.

Sample student answers

Question 1

This question is about electrostatics.

a) There are two kinds of electric charge.

   Write down the names of both types of electric charge.

   positive and negative ✓ ① (1)

b) Leon wants to charge his plastic comb.

   Write down one way he could do this.

   He could rub it. ✓ ① (2)

c) Leon holds his charged comb near some small pieces of paper.

   Suggest what might happen to the papers.

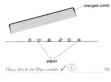

   charged comb

   paper

   They stick to the comb. ✓ ① (1)

TEACHER'S COMMENTS

a) The correct response has been given. The symbols '+' and '–' would also be acceptable.

b) 'He could rub it' scores one mark, although 'by friction' would have been a stronger phrase to use. There is a second mark for saying that the comb should be rubbed against an insulator (or you could give an example of an insulator, such as cloth). Always check the number of marks available.

c) One mark has been awarded for the correct response. The student indicates correctly that there will be an attraction between the comb and the pieces of paper.

d) This is a very vague answer. There are three marks available. The correct response needs to state that Leon has become charged (perhaps by friction against a carpet) and that these charges move when he touches the radiator, from Leon to the radiator. The third mark is for using correct scientific words. Relevant words here are: charging, electrons, earth, earthing.

e) i) One mark has been awarded. Alternative correct responses would include inkjet printers, dust precipitators or crop spraying.

   ii) Two marks have been awarded. The student seems to have an idea of what is happening, but has failed to use the correct scientific terms accurately. One mark has been awarded for the idea that opposite charges attract, but saying that the paint 'sticks' to the car is not accurate enough to gain a second mark – the student needed to say that the paint is attracted to the car. In a similar way, saying that paint covers 'much better' is too vague. At this level, the student should refer to the paint being attracted to the whole object, even parts not in direct line, or that less paint is wasted. Another approach would be to state that like charges repel (one mark), which produces an even coat (one mark).

d) Leon touches a metal radiator. He gets an electric shock.

   Describe how Leon gets an electric shock. (One mark would be awarded for the correct use of scientific words.)

   The metal radiator is electric and gives Leon a shock. ✗ ✗ ✗ (3)

e) Leon paints cars.

   Static electricity is useful in spraying paint.

   i) Write down **one other** use of static electricity.

   A photocopier ✓ ① (1)

   ii) Explain why static electricity is useful in spraying cars.

   Use ideas about electric charge in your answer. (One mark is for linking ideas.)

   The paint is charged when it comes out of the sprayer. The car is also charged with the opposite charge. ✓ *This makes the paint stick to the car much better.* ✓ ② (4)

   ⑥⁄₁₂

   (Total 12 marks)

GETTING THE BEST FROM THE BOOK

7

This section covers concepts that will be important throughout your course. First, you will look at how to measure quantities such as length and time. Then you will look at speed, velocity and acceleration before considering mass, weight and density. You will then consider forces and their different effects, before looking at energy, work, power and pressure.

STARTING POINTS

1. What would you use to measure: a) the width of this book; b) the length of the school playing field; c) the amount of milk needed to make a dessert?

2. How could you find the time taken to: a) finish your physics homework; b) run 100 metres?

3. What do we mean when we say a car is travelling at 30 kilometres per hour?

4. If an object is stationary, What must be true about the forces acting on a stationary object?

5. In physics, what do we mean when we say an object is accelerating?

6. How are mass and density related?

7. List four different forms of energy.

CONTENTS

a) Length and time

b) Speed, velocity and acceleration

c) Mass and weight

d) Density

e) Forces

f) Energy, work and power

g) Pressure

h) Exam-style questions

1 General physics

△ In this chapter you will learn about the forces at work on this parachutist.

Δ Fig. 1.1 Using a micrometer.

Length and time

INTRODUCTION

Making measurements is very important in physics. Without numerical measurements, physicists would have to rely on descriptions, which could lead to inaccurate comparisons. Imagine trying to build a house if the only descriptions were 'big' and 'small'.

You also need to make sure that you are consistent in your use of units. For example, the Mars Climate Orbiter mission failed in 1999 because not all of the scientists were using the same units.

KNOWLEDGE CHECK

✓ Know how to use a rule to measure lengths to the nearest millimetre.
✓ Know how to use a stopwatch to measure time to the nearest second.
✓ Know how to use a measuring cylinder to measure volume.

LEARNING OBJECTIVES

✓ Be able to use and describe the use of rules and measuring cylinders to calculate a length or volume.
✓ Be able to use and describe the use of clocks and devices for measuring an interval of time.
✓ **EXTENDED** Be able to use and describe the use of a mechanical method for the measurement of a small distance.
✓ **EXTENDED** Be able to measure and describe how to measure a small interval of time.

MAKING MEASUREMENTS

When making measurements, physicists use different instruments, such as rules to measure lengths, measuring cylinders to measure volume and clocks to measure time.

A physicist always takes care to make the measurements as accurate as possible. If she is using a rule, she will place the rule along the object to be measured, and read off the scale the positions of the beginning and the end of the object. The length is the difference between these two readings. When the rule is nearer to her eye than the object being measured, the reading will appear to change as she moves her eye. The correct reading is obtained when her eye is directly above the point being measured.

End of topic questions

Note: The marks awarded for these questions indicate the level of detail required in the answers. In the examination, the number of marks awarded for questions like these may be different.

1. Rules that are 30 cm long are often made of wood or plastic that is thicker in the middle and thinner along the edges where the scale is printed. Explain why the user is less likely to make an error if the rule is thinner at the edge, and suggest reasons why the rule is thicker in the middle. **(3 marks)**

2. A plastic measuring cylinder is filled with water to the 100 cm^3 mark. A student measures the column of water in the cylinder with a rule and finds that it is 20 cm high.

   a) The student pours 10 cm^3 of the water out of the cylinder. How high will the column of water be now? **(2 marks)**

   b) The student then refills the cylinder back to the 100 cm^3 mark by holding it under a dripping tap. She finds that it takes 180 drops of water to do this. What is the volume of one of these drops? **(3 marks)**

   c) What is the cross-sectional area of the cylinder? (Hint: The volume of a cylinder is given by the equation: volume = cross-sectional area × length.) **(3 marks)**

   d) From your answer to part c), what is the internal diameter of the measuring cylinder? **(3 marks)**

3. EXTENDED A student tries to measure the period of a pendulum that is already swinging left and right. At the moment when the pendulum is fully to the left, she counts 'one' and starts a stopwatch. She counts successive swings each time that the pendulum returns to the left. When she counts 'ten' she stops the stopwatch, and sees that it reads 12.0 s.

   a) What was her mistake? **(2 marks)**

   b) What is the period of swing of this pendulum? **(3 marks)**

   c) In this particular experiment, explain the likely effect of her reaction time on her answer. **(3 marks)**

Speed, velocity and acceleration

△ Fig 1.5 You can use a stopwatch to measure the time taken to run a certain distance.

INTRODUCTION

To study almost anything about the world around us or out into Space, we will need to describe where things are, where they were and where we expect them to go. It is even better if we are able to measure these things. Only when we have an organised system for doing this will we be able to look for the patterns in the way things move – the laws of motion – before going a step further and suggesting *why* things move as they do – using ideas about forces.

Think about being a passenger in a car travelling at 90 kilometres per hour. This, of course, means that the car (if it kept travelling at this speed for 1 hour) would travel 90 km. During 1 second the car travels 25 metres, so its speed can also be described as 25 metres per second. Scientists prefer to measure time in seconds and distance in metres. So they prefer to measure speed in metres per second, usually written as m/s.

KNOWLEDGE CHECK

✔ Know how to measure distances and times accurately.
✔ Know how to calculate the area of a rectangle and a triangle.
✔ Know how to plot a graph given particular points.
✔ Know how to substitute values into a given formula.

LEARNING OBJECTIVES

✔ Define speed and calculate speed from total distance/total time.
✔ Be able to plot and interpret a speed/time graph or a distance/time graph.
✔ Recognise from the shape of a speed/time graph when a body is at rest, moving with constant speed or moving with changing speed.
✔ Be able to calculate the area under a speed/time graph to work out the distance travelled for motion with constant acceleration.
✔ Demonstrate some understanding that acceleration is related to changing speed.
✔ State that the acceleration of free fall for a body near to the Earth is constant.

✔ EXTENDED Distinguish between speed and velocity.

✔ EXTENDED Recognise linear motion for which the acceleration is constant and calculate the acceleration.

✓ **EXTENDED** Recognise motion for which the acceleration is not constant.

✓ **EXTENDED** Be able to describe qualitatively the motion of bodies falling in a uniform gravitational field with and without air resistance (including reference to terminal velocity).

CALCULATING SPEED

The **speed** of an object can be calculated using the following formula:

$$\text{speed} = \frac{\text{distance}}{\text{time}}$$

$$v = \frac{s}{t}$$

Where: v = speed in m/s,

$\quad\quad\quad$ s = distance in m, and

$\quad\quad\quad$ t = time in s.

Most objects speed up and slow down as they travel. An object's 'average speed' can be calculated by dividing the total distance travelled by the total time taken.

REMEMBER

Make sure you can explain *why* this is an average speed. You need to talk about the speed not being constant throughout, perhaps giving specific examples of where it changed. For example, you might consider a journey from home to school. You know how long the journey takes and the distance between home and school. From these, you can work out the average speed using the formula. However, you know that, in any journey, you do not travel at the same speed at all times. You may have to stop to cross the road, or at a road junction. You may be able to travel faster on straight sections of the journey or round corners.

WORKED EXAMPLES

1. Calculate the average speed of a motor car that travels 500 metres in 20 seconds.

Write down the formula: $\quad\quad\quad\quad\quad\quad\quad\quad\quad\quad$ $v = s / t$

Substitute the values for s and t: $\quad\quad\quad\quad\quad$ $v = 500 / 20$

Work out the answer and write down the units: $\quad$ $v = 25$ m/s

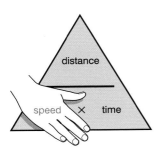

◁ Fig. 1.6 Cover speed to find that speed = distance/time.

2. A horse canters at an average speed of 5 m/s for 2 minutes. Calculate the distance it travels.

Write down the formula in terms of s: $s = v \times t$

Substitute the values for v and t: $s = 5 \times 2 \times 60$

Work out the answer and write down the units: $s = 600$ m

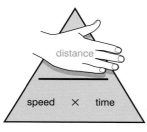

◁ Fig. 1.7 Cover distance to find that distance = speed × time.

EXTENDED

ARE SPEED AND VELOCITY THE SAME?

We often want to know the direction in which an object is travelling. For example, when a space rocket is launched, it is likely to reach a speed of 1000 km/h after about 30 seconds. However, it is extremely important to know whether this speed is upwards or downwards. You want to know the speed *and* the direction of the rocket. The **velocity** of an object is one piece of information, but it consists of two parts: the speed and the direction. In this case, the velocity of the rocket is 278 m/s (its speed) upwards (its direction).

A velocity can have a minus sign. This tells you that the object is travelling in the opposite direction. So a velocity of −278 m/s upwards is actually a velocity of 278 m/s downwards.

The diagram shows two cars with the same speed but opposite velocities.

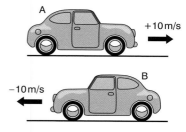

△ Fig. 1.8 Both cars have the same speed. Car A has a velocity of +10 m/s and car B has a velocity of −10 m/s.

END OF EXTENDED

QUESTIONS

1. Imagine two cars travelling along a narrow road where it is not possible to pass each other. Describe what would happen when:

   a) both cars have a velocity of +15 m/s

   b) one car has a velocity of +15 m/s and the other −15 m/s

   c) both cars have a velocity of −15 m/s.

2. You walk to school and then walk home again. What is your average velocity for the whole journey? Be careful!

3. A journey to school is 10 km. It takes 15 minutes in a car. What is the average speed of the car?

4. How far does a bicycle travelling at 1.5 m/s travel in 15 s?

5. A person walks at 0.5 m/s and travels a distance of 1500 m. How long does this take?

USING GRAPHS TO STUDY MOTION

Journeys can be summarised using graphs. The simplest type is a **distance/time graph** where the distance travelled is plotted against the time of the journey.

At the beginning of any measurement of motion, time is usually given as 0 s and the position of the object 0 m. If the object is not moving, then time increases but distance does not. This gives a horizontal line. If the object is travelling at a steady speed, then both time and distance increase steadily, which gives a straight line. If the speed is varying, then the line will not be straight. In Fig. 1.9, which shows a bicycle journey, the graph slopes when the bicycle is moving. The slope gets steeper when the bicycle goes faster. The slope is straight (has a constant gradient) when the bicycle's speed is constant. The cyclist falls off at about 142 metres from the start. After this, the graph is horizontal because the bicycle is not moving.

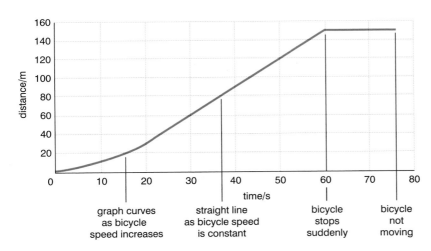

△ Fig. 1.9 A distance/time graph for a bicycle journey.

QUESTIONS

1. How can you tell from a distance/time graph whether the object was moving away from you or towards you?

2. Very often we use sketch graphs to illustrate motion. Describe the main differences between a sketch graph and a graph.

3. Sketch a distance/time graph for a bicycle travelling downhill.

WHAT IS ACCELERATION?

The speedometer of a car displays 50 km/h and then a few seconds later it displays 70 km/h, so the car is accelerating. When a car is slowing down, this is called negative acceleration, or deceleration. **Acceleration** is a change in speed or velocity. On a distance/time graph, acceleration is shown by a smooth curve.

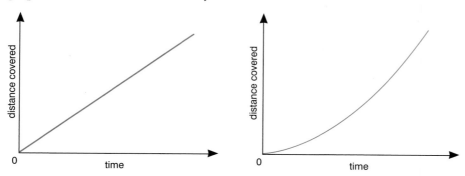

△ Fig. 1.10 Steady speed is shown by a straight line. Acceleration is shown by a smooth curve of increasing gradient.

Imagine that the car is initially travelling at 15 m/s, and that 1 second later it has reached 17 m/s, and that its speed increases by 2 m/s each second after that. Each second its speed increases by 2 metres per second. We can say that its speed is increasing at '2 metres per second *per second*'. This can be written, much more conveniently, as an acceleration of 2 m/s².

Our planet Earth attracts all objects towards its centre with the force of **gravity**. The strength of the force decreases slowly with increasing distance from the surface of the Earth, but for objects within a few km of the surface, all objects that are falling freely will have the same constant acceleration of just under 10 m/s². If a coconut falls from a tree, then after 1 s it will be falling at 10 m/s (though it will only have travelled 5 m because, of course, it started with zero velocity). After 2 s it will be falling at 20 m/s, if it does not hit the ground first.

How much an object's speed or velocity *changes* in one second is its acceleration.

Acceleration can be calculated using the following formula:

$$acceleration = \frac{change\ in\ velocity}{time\ taken}$$

$$a = \frac{(v - u)}{t}$$

Where: a = acceleration

v = final velocity in m/s

u = starting velocity in m/s

t = time in s

A negative acceleration shows that the object is slowing down.

Make sure that you are clear what the word 'acceleration' means in physics. It does *not necessarily* mean 'gets faster'. Neither does it measure *how much* the velocity changes.

Acceleration measures *how quickly* the velocity changes, i.e. the *rate of change* of velocity.

WORKED EXAMPLE

Calculate the acceleration of a car that travels from 0 m/s to 28 m/s in 10 seconds.

Write down the formula: $a = (v - u) / t$

Substitute the values for v, u and t: $a = 28 - 0 / 10$

Work out the answer and write down the units: $a = 2.8$ m/s^2

END OF EXTENDED

QUESTIONS

1. As a stone falls, it accelerates from 0 m/s to 20 m/s in 2 seconds. Calculate its acceleration and the state the unit.

2. A racing car slows down from 45 m/s to 0 m/s in 3 seconds. Calculate its acceleration and the state the unit.

USING VELOCITY/TIME GRAPHS

A **velocity/time graph** provides information on speed or velocity, acceleration and distance travelled. Steady speed is shown by a horizontal line. Steady acceleration is shown by a straight line sloping up.

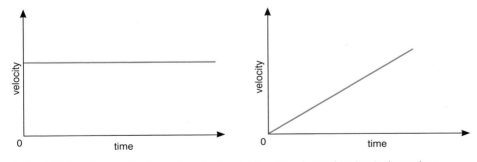

△ Fig. 1.11 Steady speed is shown by a horizontal line. Steady acceleration is shown by a straight line sloping up.

In the left-hand graph, the object is already moving when the graph begins. In the right-hand graph, the object starts with a velocity of zero, and the line therefore starts from the origin.

Note that the object may not move to begin with. In this case the line will start by going along the x-axis, showing that the velocity stays at zero for a while.

1. An athlete and a fun runner complete a 400 m race. The athlete takes 50 s and the fun runner takes 64 s.

   a) Calculate the average speed for each runner.

   b) Sketch a speed/time graph for the two runners.

Finding distance from a velocity/time graph

The area under a velocity/time graph gives the distance travelled because distance = velocity × time. Always make sure the units are consistent, so when the velocity is in km/h you must use time in hours too.

The graph in Fig. 1.12 shows how the velocity of a car varies as it travels between two sets of traffic lights. The graph can be divided into three regions.

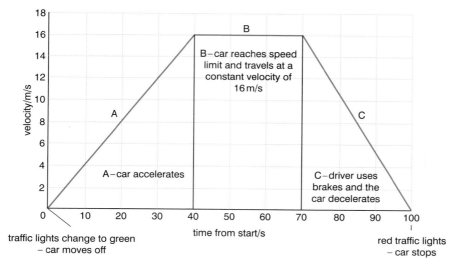

△ Fig. 1.12 The velocity of a car travelling between two sets of traffic lights.

In region A, the car has constant acceleration (the line has a constant positive gradient). The distance travelled by the car can be calculated as follows:

average velocity in region A = (16 + 0) / 2 = 8 m/s

time = 40 s

so distance = $v \times t$ = 8 × 40 = 320 m

This can also be calculated from the area under the line:

½ base × height = ½ × 40 × 16 = 320 m

In region B, the car is travelling at a *constant velocity* (the line has a gradient of zero). The distance travelled by the car can be calculated:

velocity in region B = 16 m/s

time = 30 s

so, distance = $v \times t$ = 16 × 30 = 480 m

This can also be calculated from the area under the line (base × height = 30 × 16 = 480 m).

In region C, the car is *decelerating at a constant rate* (the line has a constant negative gradient). The distance travelled by the car can be calculated:

average velocity in region C =

(16 + 0) / 2 = 8 m/s

time = 30 s

so, distance = $v \times t$ = 8 × 30 = 240 m

This can also be calculated from the area under the line:

½ base × height = ½ × 30 × 16 = 240 m

Total distance travelled in 100 s = 320 + 480 + 240 = 1040 m

EXTENDED

In the earlier worked example the acceleration and deceleration were constant and the lines in regions A and C were straight. This is very often not the case. You will probably have noticed that a car can accelerate much more quickly when it is travelling at 30 km/h than when it is travelling at 120 km/h.

A people-carrying space rocket does exactly the opposite. If you watch one being launched you can see that it has a small acceleration as it leaves the ground. As it is burning several tonnes of fuel per second, it quickly becomes less massive and its acceleration increases.

END OF EXTENDED

Developing Investigative Skills

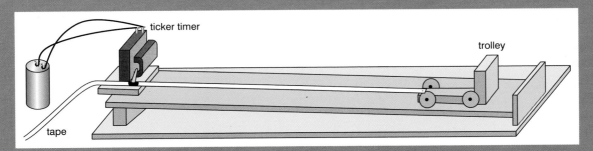

△ Fig. 1.13 Apparatus needed for the investigation.

A student investigated the motion of a trolley rolling down a ramp. To measure the distance travelled by the trolley at different times, she used a ticker timer and ticker tape. A ticker timer has a moving arm that bounces up and down 50 times each second. When the arm moves down and hits the tape it makes a small dot on the tape.

The student attached the tape to the trolley and released the trolley to roll down the ramp.

After that she divided the tape into strips with five dots in each strip – at 50 dots per second this meant that a five-dot strip had taken 0.1 s.

She measured the length of each five-dot strip with a ruler. Her results are shown in the table.

Time/s	Distance from start/cm	Distance covered in the last 0.1 s/cm	Average speed for last 0.1 s/cm/s
0.0		0.0	
0.1		1.8	
0.2		3.4	
0.3		5.2	
0.4		6.0	
0.5		7.7	
0.6		11.1	
0.7		9.9	
0.8		11.9	
0.9		12.5	
1.0		14.0	

Using and organising techniques, apparatus and materials

❶ Suggest how using this method might change the motion of the trolley as it rolls down the ramp.

❷ How else could the student measure the position of the trolley every 0.1 s?

Observing, measuring and recording

❸ Copy the table and complete the second column, showing the total distance travelled up to that time.

❹ Draw a distance/time graph using the data in the first two columns. Use your graph to describe the motion of the trolley.

❺ Use the equation speed = distance/time to complete the final column.

❻ Draw a speed/time graph using the data in the first and fourth columns. Does this graph support the description of the motion you gave in question 4? Explain your answer.

Handling experimental observations and data

❼ The student thought she had made a mistake in measuring the strips. Is there any evidence for this on either of the graphs?

Planning and evaluating investigations

❽ Would repeating the experiment make the data more reliable? Justify your answer.

FALLING OBJECTS

When you drop an object it falls towards the ground. The force of gravity acts on the object and causes it to accelerate. The acceleration due to gravity acts downwards and has a value of approximately 10 m/s².

Falling objects and terminal velocity

As a skydiver jumps from a plane, the weight will be much greater than the opposing force caused by air resistance. Initially she will accelerate downwards at 10 m/s².

The skydiver's speed will increase rapidly – and the force caused by the air resistance increases as the skydiver's speed increases. Eventually the resistive force will exactly match the weight, the forces will be balanced and the speed of the skydiver will remain constant. This speed is known as the **terminal velocity**, typically 180 km/h.

In Fig. 1.14, the skydiver has her arms outstretched so the air resistance force is fairly high. If the skydiver makes herself streamlined by going head first, with her arms by her side, then the air resistance force will be reduced and she will cut through the air more easily. She will then accelerate again, until the force of air resistance increases again to equal her weight. She will now be travelling at almost 300 km/h.

A parachute has a very large surface area and produces a very large resistive force, so the terminal velocity of a parachutist is quite low. This means that he or she can land relatively safely.

△ Fig. 1.14 The forces on the skydiver are balanced so the speed is the terminal velocity.

△ Fig. 1.15 The terminal velocity of this parachutist is quite low so he will be able to land safely.

REMEMBER

Make sure you think carefully about the *two* opposing forces that lead to terminal velocity. The force causing the motion (such as gravity or the force from a car engine) usually remains constant. It is the drag force (such as air or water resistance) that increases as the velocity increases, until the two are balanced and the velocity stays constant.

Developing Investigative Skills

Two students are investigating terminal velocity. They use a tall tube filled with wallpaper paste and drop a steel ball into it. The weight of the ball pulls it down through the paste. As it gets faster, the drag from the paste increases until the two forces are balanced.

The students mark every 10 cm along the tube using tape.

One of the students releases the ball carefully from the surface of the paste.

At the same time, the other student starts a stop clock.

As the ball passes each mark, the first student calls out and the second student makes a note of the time.

Since the marks on the tube are 10 cm apart, the students can calculate the speed of the ball in each section of the tube. Their results are shown in the table.

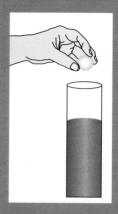

△ Fig. 1.16 Dropping the ball bearing into the tall tube filled with wallpaper paste.

Distance fallen through paste/cm	Time/s	Speed/cm/s
0	0	0.0
10	4	2.5
20	4.5	4.4
30	5.3	5.7
40	6.6	6.1
50	7.8	6.4
60	9.4	6.4

Using and organising techniques, apparatus and materials

❶ What advantage is there for the students to work together on this investigation?

❷ What factors should the students keep constant during this investigation?

Observing, measuring and recording

❸ Draw a graph of speed against time for this experiment. Describe the pattern (if any) in the results.

❹ Add a second line to your graph to indicate the expected results for a slightly larger ball with a slightly higher mass.

Planning and evaluating investigations

❺ Suggest how the method could be improved to gain more accurate measurements.

QUESTIONS

1. What is terminal velocity?

2. A skydiver jumps from a plane. How fast will he be travelling after 1 s?

3. The air resistance force on the skydiver in question 2 = 0.15 × v^2. What will the magnitude and direction of this force be after 1 s?

4. The skydiver has mass 60 kg. What will be the magnitude and direction of the resultant force on him after 1 s?

5. EXTENDED Graphs can be drawn to show how the force, acceleration and velocity of a falling object vary with time. The two graphs in Fig. 1.17 show two of these variables but the labels have been missed from the y-axis in each case. State the correct label for each y-axis. Explain the curve of each graph.

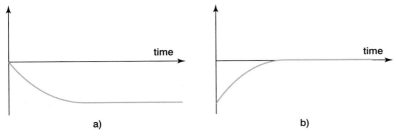

a)   b)

△ Fig. 1.17 Graphs can be used to show how force, acceleration and velocity of falling objects vary with time.

End of topic checklist

Key terms
acceleration, distance/time graph, gravity, speed, terminal velocity, velocity

During your study of this topic you should have learned:

○ How to define speed and calculate speed from total distance/total time.

○ How to plot and interpret a speed/time graph or a distance/time graph.

○ How to recognise from the shape of a speed/time graph when a body is:

- at rest
- moving with constant speed
- moving with changing speed.

○ How to work out the distance travelled from a speed/time graph by calculating the area under the speed/time graph for motion with constant acceleration.

○ That acceleration is related to changing speed.

○ That the acceleration of free fall for a body near the Earth is constant.

○ **EXTENDED** How to distinguish between speed and velocity.

○ **EXTENDED** How to recognise linear motion for which the acceleration is constant and calculate the acceleration.

○ **EXTENDED** How to recognise motion when the acceleration is not constant.

○ **EXTENDED** How to describe the motion of bodies falling in a uniform gravitational field with and without air resistance (including reference to terminal velocity).

End of topic questions

Note: The marks awarded for these questions indicate the level of detail required in the answers. In the examination, the number of marks awarded for questions like these may be different.

1. A student's journey to school takes 10 minutes and is 3.6 kilometres. What is his average speed in km/min? **(1 mark)**

2. **a)** A runner runs 400 metres in 1 minute 20 seconds. What is her speed in m/s? **(1 mark)**

   b) At one point she is running due west at 6 m/s. Later she is running due east at 4 m/s. How could we write her velocities to show that they are in opposite directions? **(2 marks)**

3. A train moves away from a station along a straight track, increasing its velocity from 0 to 20 m/s in 16 s. What is its acceleration in m/s^2? **(1 mark)**

4. A rally car accelerates from 100 km/h to 150 km/h in 5 s. What is its acceleration in:

   a) km/h per second **(1 mark)**

   b) m/s^2? **(1 mark)**

5. **a)** On a distance/time graph, what does a horizontal line indicate? **(2 marks)**

   b) A car is travelling at constant speed. What shape would the corresponding distance-time graph have? **(2 marks)**

6. **a)** EXTENDED Describe the difference between speed and velocity. **(2 marks)**

   b) Explain the significance of a positive or negative sign for a velocity. **(2 marks)**

   c) Define acceleration. **(2 marks)**

   d) State an everyday name for negative acceleration. **(1 mark)**

   e) Explain how to calculate the distance travelled from a velocity/time graph. **(3 marks)**

7. A student cycles to his friend's house. In the first part of his journey, he rides 200 m from his house to a road junction in 20 s. After waiting for 10 s to cross the road, he cycles for 20 s at 8 m/s to reach his friend's house.

   a) What is his average speed for the first part of the journey? **(3 marks)**

   b) How far is it from the road junction to his friend's house? **(2 marks)**

   c) What is his average speed for the whole journey? **(2 marks)**

End of topic questions continued

8. The graph shows a distance/time graph for a car journey.

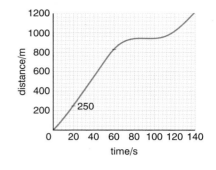

a) What does the graph tell us about the speed of the car between 20 and 60 seconds?　**(2 marks)**

b) How far did the car travel between 20 and 60 seconds?　**(3 marks)**

c) Calculate the speed of the car between 20 and 60 seconds.　**(3 marks)**

d) What happened to the car between 80 and 100 seconds?　**(2 marks)**

9. Look at the velocity/time graph for a toy tractor.

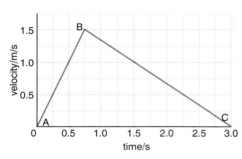

Calculate the total distance travelled by the tractor from A to C.　**(3 marks)**

10. **EXTENDED** The diagram shows the stages in the descent of a skydiver.

a) Describe and explain the motion of the skydiver at each stage.　**(10 marks)**

b) In stage 5, explain why the parachutist does not sink into the ground.　**(2 marks)**

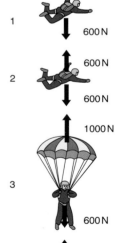

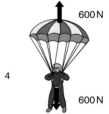

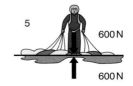

Mass and weight

Scientists use the words 'mass' and 'weight' with special meanings. By the **mass** of an object we mean how much material is present in it. **Weight** is the force on the object due to gravity. It is measured in **newtons**. The weight of an object depends on its mass and **gravitational field strength**. Any mass near the Earth has weight due to the Earth's gravitational pull.

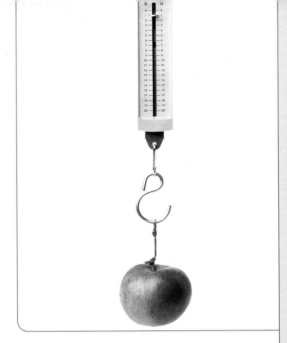

△ Fig. 1.18 An apple being weighed using a Newton meter.

✓ Know the acceleration due to the Earth's gravitational field.

✓ Show familiarity with the idea of the mass of a body.
✓ State that weight is a force.
✓ Demonstrate understanding that weights (and hence masses) may be compared using a balance.
✓ EXTENDED Demonstrate an understanding that mass is a property that 'resists' change in motion.
✓ EXTENDED Be able to describe, and use the concept of, weight as the effect of a gravitational field on a mass.

THE EARTH'S GRAVITATIONAL FIELD

Scientists often use the word 'field'. We say that there is a 'gravitational field' around the Earth, and that any object that enters this field will be attracted to the Earth.

The value of the gravitational field strength on Earth is 9.8 N/kg, though we usually round it up to 10 N/kg to make the calculations easier. A gravitational force of 10 N acts on an object of mass 1 kg on the Earth's surface.

Note that gravity does not stop suddenly as you leave the Earth. Satellites go around the Earth and do not escape, because the Earth is still pulling them, even if less strongly than before the satellites were launched. The Earth is even pulling the Moon, and this is why it orbits the Earth once every month. And the Earth goes around the Sun because the Sun's gravity is pulling the Earth.

If you could stand on the Moon you would feel the gravity of the Moon pulling you down. Your mass would be the same as on Earth, but your weight would be less. This is because the gravitational field strength on the Moon is about one-sixth of that on the Earth, and so the force of attraction of an object to the Moon is about one-sixth of that on the Earth. The gravitational field strength on the Moon is 1.6 N/kg, so a force of 1.6 N is needed to support a 1 kg mass. Weight is the effect of a gravitational field on a mass.

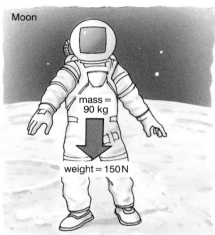

△ Fig. 1.19 Though your mass remains the same, your weight is greater on Earth than it would be on the Moon.

If two astronauts played football on the Moon, it would be just as difficult to halt a tackle by one of them as it would be on the Earth, and any collision between them would hurt just as much. The reason for this is that the mass of an object resists any change in the motion of the object, and the mass of each astronaut is the same in both places.

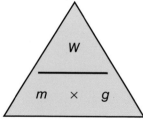

△ Fig. 1.20 The equation triangle for weight, mass and acceleration due to gravity.

It is harder to get a massive object moving, and it is harder to stop it once it is moving. In Fig. 1.21 the supertanker, which is laden with oil and travelling at 18 km/h, takes over 12 km to stop. In contrast, a speedboat, which has much less mass, takes less than 100 m to stop if it is travelling at the same speed as the supertanker.

Mass is a property that 'resists' change in motion.

△ Fig. 1.21 A supertanker will take very much longer to stop than a speedboat travelling at the same speed.

HOW DO YOU FIND THE MASS OF SOMETHING?

A balance is level when the forces pulling down on both sides are the same. In the balance shown in Fig. 1.22, the forces of 10 N and 20 N on one side balance the force of 30 N on the other side. If the balance is on the surface of the Earth, then the masses of these objects are 1 kg and 2 kg on one side, and 3 kg on the other. If the balance could be taken to the Moon, the forces on each side would become 4.8 N instead of 30 N, but they would still be balanced. So a balance allows you to compare masses.

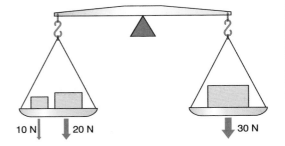

△ Fig. 1.22 The total force is the same on each side of the balance.

HOW DO YOU WEIGH SOMETHING?

A spring balance can also be used for weighing things, but works in a different way.

The top of the spring is hung from a hook, and the spring is stretched by the weight of the pan attached to its lower end. The scale can then be adjusted so that the pointer is aligned with the 'zero' mark.

When a known mass is placed in the pan, the spring stretches further due to the extra weight and the new pointer position can be marked. In the spring balance shown in Fig. 1.23, the pointer should be at the 30 N mark when the scale is set correctly. If this balance were moved to the Moon, the weight would be less and the spring would not stretch so far. In fact the pointer would indicate a weight of 4.8 N.

So the spring balance measures the weight of the object in newtons. For non-scientific use, these balances are often given a scale that indicates the mass of the object in kg, without the need for any calculations. This scale gives the correct mass on the surface of the Earth, but would definitely not give the correct mass if the spring balance were moved to the Moon.

See the topic on Forces for more about springs.

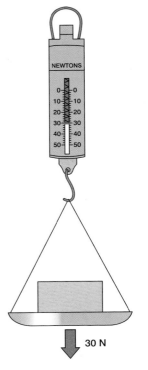

△ Fig. 1.23 A spring balance.

End of topic checklist

Key terms

gravitational field, mass, weight

During your study of this topic you should have learned:

○ That mass is the amount of matter in a body.

○ That weight is a force.

○ That weights (and hence masses) may be compared using a balance.

○ EXTENDED That mass is a property that 'resists' change in motion.

○ EXTENDED How to describe, and use the concept of, weight as the effect of a gravitational field on a mass.

End of topic questions

Note: The marks awarded for these questions indicate the level of detail required in the answers. In the examination, the number of marks awarded for questions like these may be different.

1. **a)** Explain the difference between 'mass' and 'weight'. **(2 marks)**

   b) Explain why your weight would change if you stood on the surface of different planets. **(3 marks)**

2. A balance has 30 N on the left-hand side and 50 N on the right-hand side. What weight must be added so that the sides are balanced, and to which side? **(3 marks)**

3. The height that you can jump has an inverse relationship to the gravitational field strength. When the field strength doubles, the height halves. The gravitational field strength on the surface of Mars is 3.8 N/kg. If the Olympic Games were held on Mars in a large dome to provide air to breathe, what would happen to the records for:

   a) weightlifting (weight in N) **(2 marks)**

   b) high jump (height) **(2 marks)**

   c) pole vault (height) **(2 marks)**

   d) throwing the javelin (distance) **(2 marks)**

   e) the 100 m race (time)? **(2 marks)**

   In each case, explain if the record will increase, stay similar or decrease.

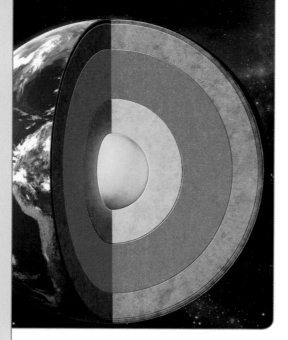

△ Fig. 1.24 The density of the different layers of the Earth varies.

Density

INTRODUCTION

Which is heavier, a tonne of feathers or a tonne of iron?

That is a trick question, of course – they have the same weight (a tonne). But there would be a noticeable difference if you loaded each one onto a truck: the feathers would take up more space. Knowledge of density helps to describe the difference between the feathers and the iron, and knowledge about pressure helps to describe the effect on the truck.

Density and pressure are useful measures that give an insight into other areas of physics. For example, they help to explain why objects float. They also explain convection currents, which can lead on to the movement of the continents on the surface of the Earth and the very structure of the Earth itself.

The density of the Earth's structure varies. The solid core (yellow in the picture) has a much higher density than the liquid mantle (red in the picture). It is in the liquid mantle that convection currents occur, and these currents are responsible for the movement of continents.

KNOWLEDGE CHECK

✓ Know how to calculate areas of regular shapes, such as squares and rectangles.

LEARNING OBJECTIVES

✓ Be able to describe an experiment to determine the density of a liquid and of a regularly shaped solid and make the necessary calculation.

✓ EXTENDED Be able to describe the determination of the density of an irregularly shaped solid by the method of displacement and make the necessary calculation.

WHAT IS DENSITY?

You must have noticed that the weight of objects can vary greatly. A plastic teaspoon weighs less than a metal one, and a gold ring weighs twice as much as a silver one, even if the objects are exactly the same size.

The **density** of a material is a measure of how 'squashed up' it is, and a dense object contains more mass than a light object of the same size. The density of a material is defined as the mass per unit **volume**.

The density of a material is calculated using this formula:

$$d = m \,/\, V$$

Where: m = mass in g or kg

V = volume in cm³ or m³

d = density in g/cm³ or kg/m³

Note that in this equation you must use g and cm throughout, or you must use kg and m. Also note that if you measure the weight in N you must convert it into mass in g or kg.

△ Fig. 1.25 Gold is one of the densest metals. A block of gold the size of a one-litre carton of milk would have a mass of almost 20 kg.

THE DENSITY OF A REGULARLY SHAPED OBJECT

	Density/g/m³	Density/g/m³
Vacuum	0	0
Helium gas	0.00017	0.17
Air	0.00124	1.24
Oil (petroleum)	0.88	880
Water	1.0	1000
Sea water	1.03	1030
Plastic	0.9–1.6	900–1600
Wood	0.5–1.3	500–1300
Magnesium	1.74	1740
Aluminium	2.7	2700
Titanium	4.5	4500
Steel	7.8	7800
Mercury (liquid)	13.6	13 600
Silver	10.5	10 500
Gold	19.3	19 300

△ Table 1.1 Some useful densities.

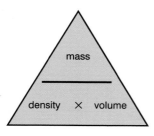

△ Fig. 1.26 The equation triangle for mass, density and volume.

The density of water is 1.0 g/cm³, and the rule is that an object of greater density will sink in a liquid of lower density. So, perhaps not surprisingly, the brick will sink in water. But will it sink in mercury? To decide whether it will sink in mercury, you need to compare the density of the brick (1.90 g/cm³) with the density of mercury using the same units. From Table 1.1, you can see that the density of mercury is 13.6 g/cm³, which is very much greater than that of the brick, so the brick will float on liquid mercury.

WORKED EXAMPLE

A brick has the dimensions 20 cm × 9 cm × 6.5 cm.

Weight of brick = 22.2 N.

What is the density of the brick?

Mass of brick, m $= W / g$

$= 22.2 / 10$ kg

$= 2.22$ kg

$= 2220$ g

(Remember that 1 kg = 1000 g)

Volume of brick, V $= 20 × 9 × 6.5$ cm³

$= 1170$ cm³

Density of brick, ρ $=$ mass / volume

$= 2200 / 1170$ g/cm³

$= 1.90$ g/cm³

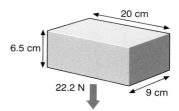

△ Fig. 1.27 Finding the density of a brick.

Developing Investigative Skills

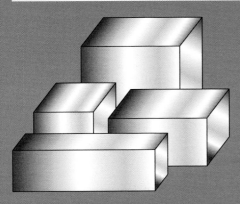

△ Fig. 1.28 Regular shapes for use in the investigation.

A student is finding the density of some different materials. The samples she has are all regular shapes.

The student has a ruler, marked in mm, and an electronic balance that measures to the nearest 0.1 g. The student finds the mass and the volume of each sample. Her data is shown in the table.

Sample	Mass/g	Volume/cm³	Density/?
Aluminium	97.2	36	
Brass	302.4	36	
Copper	321.5	36	
Iron	282.6	36	

Using and organising techniques, apparatus and materials

❶ Describe how the student should use the ruler to find the volume of each sample.

❷ If the student checks that the balance reads zero before she puts the sample on, will this improve the accuracy or the precision of the experiment? Explain your answer.

Observing, measuring and recording

❸ Copy the table and use the equation density = mass / volume to complete it. Include the units at the top of the 'density' column.

❹ How many significant figures should you give your values of density? Explain your answer.

Planning and evaluating investigations

❺ How could the method be changed to find the density of objects with an irregular shape?

MEASURING THE DENSITY OF A LIQUID

The density of a liquid can be measured using an instrument called a **hydrometer**. The hydrometer measures the ratio of the density of the liquid to the density of water and is usually made of glass. It has a cylindrical stem and a bulb, which contains mercury or lead shot to make it float upright. The liquid that is being tested is poured into a measuring cylinder and the hydrometer is lowered into the liquid until it floats. There is a scale on the stem of the hydrometer and the point on the scale at which the surface of the liquid touches the stem of the hydrometer is noted. The scale usually allows the density to be read directly. The type of scale used depends on what the hydrometer is used for.

DID YOU KNOW?

The first hydrometer is credited to the Greek scholar Hypatia, and was probably made sometime in the late 4th or early 5th century. An early description of such a device appears in a letter from Synesius of Cyrene, who asked Hypatia to make one for him.

QUESTIONS

1. A small rectangular block of steel measures 2 cm by 4 cm by 5 cm and has a mass of 312 g. Calculate:

   a) its volume

   b) its density.

2. Why is bread usually less dense than a root vegetable such as a potato or onion?

3. A block of wood floats on sea water. What can you say about the density of the block of wood?

EXTENDED

MEASURING THE DENSITY OF AN IRREGULAR OBJECT

This method involves submerging an object in a liquid and measuring the volume of the liquid that is displaced. It only works when the object is denser than the liquid used so that it sinks, although the method can be modified to measure a less dense object by attaching a 'sinker' to the object to hold it beneath the surface. It does not work when the object absorbs the liquid, or if it is damaged by the liquid.

1. A balance is used to weigh the object in question, as shown in Fig. 1.30, and find its mass, m.

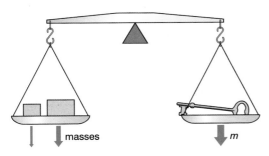

△ Fig. 1.29 Using a balance to find the mass of an object.

2. A measuring cylinder is chosen that is wide and deep enough to hold the object. A narrower cylinder will give a more accurate answer than a wider one. Liquid is added to fill the cylinder to a deep enough level so that the object will be completely submerged. The volume of liquid, V_1, is then measured (see Fig. 1.30). The exact amount of liquid that you use is not at all critical. Water is the liquid normally used.

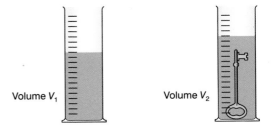

△ Fig. 1.30 Measuring the volume of an object.

3. The object is lowered into the liquid (without splashing) and the new reading v_2 is measured (Fig. 1.31). This is the volume of the object and the liquid. The volume of the object is therefore $v_2 - v_1$.

4. The density of the object can now be calculated from the mass and the volume.

WORKED EXAMPLE

The mass of a small metal statue, like the one in Fig. 1.32, is found to be 90 g.

A measuring cylinder is filled with water to the 82 cm³ mark. The statue is lowered into the measuring cylinder and the water rises to the 91 cm³ mark.

What metal is the statue made of?

Volume of the statue: $V = 91 - 82$

$= 9 \text{ cm}^3$

Write down the formula: $\rho = m / v$

Substitute the values for m and V: $\rho = 90 / 9$

Work out the answer and write down the units: $\rho = 10 \text{ g/cm}^3$

△ Fig. 1.31 Measuring the volume of an irregular metal object by displacing water.

So, from the Table 1.1, what metal could the statue be made of?

An experiment of this type is never perfectly accurate, so the density that you measure will never be exactly the same as the values given in tables.

END OF EXTENDED

SCIENCE IN CONTEXT

DENSITY IN ACTION

In January 2009, an aircraft took off from LaGuardia Airport, New York, bound for Charlotte/Douglas International Airport in North Carolina. About three minutes into the flight, it struck a flock of Canada geese, which resulted in a complete loss of thrust from both engines. The pilot realised that they could not safely reach any airfield, so he decided to ditch the aircraft on the Hudson River – in the middle of New York City! The aircraft ditched safely about three minutes after losing power. The pilot said later that he had chosen the ditching location to be as close as possible to boats to maximise the chance of rescue.

△ Fig. 1.32 The ditched aircraft floating in the Hudson River.

Immediately after the aircraft ditched, the crew began to evacuate the passengers. A panicking passenger opened a rear door, which could not be resealed. This made the aircraft fill with water more quickly than it would otherwise have done. All 155 passengers and crew safely evacuated the aircraft, which was almost completely intact but partially submerged and slowly sinking, and nearby ferries and other watercraft quickly rescued them all.

The successful outcome was due to all involved knowing what they had to do and doing it, and to the fact that the density of the aircraft allowed it to stay afloat long enough for the evacuation to take place.

End of topic checklist

Key terms

density, hydrometer, volume

During your study of this topic you should have learned:

○ About an experiment to determine the density of a liquid and of a regularly shaped solid and how to make the necessary calculation.

○ EXTENDED How to describe the determination of the density of an irregularly shaped solid by finding its mass and then determining the volume of water that it will displace, and how to make the necessary calculation.

End of topic questions

Note: The marks awarded for these questions indicate the level of detail required in the answers. In the examination, the number of marks awarded for questions like these may be different.

1. For each of the following objects, state whether they will sink or float or whether the outcome depends on the sample of material chosen:

    a) wood in oil (1 mark)

    b) wood in mercury (1 mark)

    c) plastic in oil (1 mark)

    d) steel in mercury (1 mark)

    e) silver in air (1 mark)

    f) gold in mercury (this experiment must be done rapidly as the gold will dissolve very quickly) (1 mark)

    g) helium balloon in air. (1 mark)

2. Write out the worked example given earlier in this topic for the case of a student who measures all the lengths of the brick in m and calculates with the mass in kg. Give the answer in kg/m^3. (3 marks)

3. A king who has studied physics believes that his jeweller has given him a crown that is a mixture of gold and silver, not the 1.93 kg of pure gold that he paid for. He weighs the crown in a balance and finds that it has the correct mass of 1.93 kg. He then immerses it in a measuring jug where the water level was originally 800 cm^3.

    a) If the crown is pure gold, what will the new water level be? (2 marks)

    b) What will happen to the water level if the jeweller has cheated? (2 marks)

Forces

INTRODUCTION

We live in a dynamic universe. There is constant motion around us all the time, from the vibrations of our atoms to the sweep of giant galaxies through space, and the motion is constantly changing. Objects themselves do not remain constant – some change size, others change shape. Atoms arrange and rearrange themselves into many different chemicals. Energy moves about through the motion of objects and through transfer by waves. All of this motion and change is driven by forces. This topic explores the forces behind the movement of objects.

△ Fig. 1.33 These people are applying forces to drag the net from the sea.

KNOWLEDGE CHECK

✓ Be able to explain that mass is how much matter is contained in a body.
✓ Be able to distinguish between mass and weight and know that weight is a force.
✓ Know that acceleration is a rate of change of speed.

LEARNING OBJECTIVES

✓ State that a force may produce a change in size and shape of a body.
✓ Be able to plot extension/load graphs and describe the associated experimental procedure.

✓ EXTENDED Be able to interpret extension/load graphs.

✓ EXTENDED State Hooke's Law and recall and use the expression $F = kx$.

✓ EXTENDED Recognise the significance of the term 'limit of proportionality' for an extension/load graph.
✓ Be able to describe the ways in which a force may change the motion of a body.
✓ Be able to find the resultant of two or more forces acting along the same line.

✓ EXTENDED Recall and use the relation between force, mass and acceleration (including the direction).

✓ EXTENDED Describe qualitatively motion in a curved path due to a perpendicular force.
✓ Be able to describe the moment of a force as a measure of its turning effect and give everyday examples.
✓ Be able to describe qualitatively the balancing of a beam about a pivot.

✓ EXTENDED Be able to perform and describe an experiment (involving vertical forces) to show that there is no net moment on a body in equilibrium.

✓ EXTENDED Be able to apply the idea of opposing moments to simple systems in equilibrium.

✓ State that, when there is no resultant force and no resultant turning effect, a system is in equilibrium.

✓ Be able to perform and describe an experiment to determine the position of a centre of gravity of a plane lamina.

✓ Describe qualitatively the effect of the position of the centre of gravity on the stability of simple objects.

✓ **EXTENDED** Demonstrate an understanding of the difference between scalars and vectors and give common examples.

✓ **EXTENDED** Be able to add vectors by graphical representation to determine a resultant.

✓ **EXTENDED** Be able to determine graphically the resultant of two vectors.

WHAT ARE FORCES?

A **force** is a push or a pull. The way that an object behaves depends on all of the forces acting on it. A force may come from the pull of a chain or rope, the push of a jet engine, the push of a pillar holding up a ceiling, or the pull of the gravitational field around the Earth.

Effects of forces

It is unusual for a single force to be acting on an object. Usually there will be two or more. The sizes and directions of these forces determine whether the object will move and the direction it will move in.

Forces are measured in newtons (N). They take many forms and have many effects, including pushing, pulling, bending, stretching, squeezing and tearing. Forces can:

• change the speed of an object
• change the direction of movement of an object
• change the shape of an object.

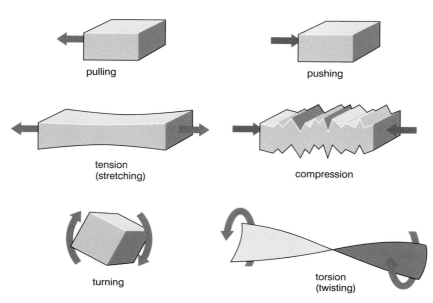

pulling

pushing

tension
(stretching)

compression

turning

torsion
(twisting)

Δ Fig. 1.34 Different types of force.

There are several different types of force. All objects in the Universe attract each other with the extremely feeble force of gravity. The strength of the attraction depends on the mass of the two objects and the distance between their centres. You may think that gravity is strong, but you are, after all, close to the Earth, which is a very massive object! The gravitational attraction between everyday objects is very small.

Electricity and **magnetism** both generate forces that are far stronger than gravity. You see **magnetic** forces and electric forces combining as an electromagnetic force used every day when an electric motor turns. A current in a magnetic field experiences a force. A motor has a coil of wire moving in a magnetic field. One side of the coil experiences an upwards force in the magnetic field, the other side experiences a downward force, and the coil turns in the magnetic field.

Electrostatic forces are the most important in our everyday lives. Electrostatic forces are those between charges such as electrons. Like charges repel (so an electron will repel another electron) and unlike charges attract (so a negatively charged electron will attract a positively charged proton). The reason that you are not sinking into the floor at the moment is that the electrons on the outside of the atoms of your shoes are being repelled by the electrons on the outside of the atoms of the floor (Fig. 1.35).

The same force is used when your hand lifts something up, or when friction slows down a car. In fact, all of the forces in this section are either gravitational or – ultimately – electrostatic.

And when you consider that it is an electrostatic force that allows a bulletproof coat to stop a speeding bullet, you'll probably agree that electrostatic forces are much stronger than gravity.

△ Fig. 1.35 Electrons on the surface of the floor repel electrons on the surface of the sole of the shoe.

There are a few other types of force apart from these three – for example, the 'strong' force that holds the nucleus of the atom together. But most of the forces that we feel or notice around us are one of the three: gravitational, electrostatic or magnetic.

QUESTIONS

1. a) Describe three effects of a force.

   b) Describe three types of force.

2. a) What is the force that causes all the objects in the Universe to attract?

   b) What two factors does the strength of this force depend on?

3. Where do we find the 'strong' force?

4. What force is seen in a motor?

LINKING THE FUNDAMENTAL FORCES

Scientists are working to find a theory that links all the fundamental forces: gravity, electromagnetism, strong nuclear force and weak nuclear force. Particle accelerators, in which high-energy collisions take place, are useful tools in this search. In 1963, Glashow, Salam and Weinberg predicted that the electromagnetic force and the weak nuclear force might combine (in what would be called the electroweak force) at energies of about 100 GeV or temperatures of about 10^{15} K, which would have occurred shortly after the Big Bang. This prediction was confirmed 20 years later in a particle accelerator.

Δ Fig. 1.36 Inside the Large Hadron Collider.

There are theories that predict that the electroweak and strong forces would combine at energies greater than 10^{15} GeV and that all the forces may combine at energies greater than 10^{19} GeV. At present, the largest particle accelerator is the Large Hadron Collider, at the European Organization for Nuclear Research (CERN) in Switzerland. It is able to accelerate protons to 99.99% of the speed of light, and they can reach energies of 1.4×10^4 GeV, so it is still some way short of the energies needed to test the theory about combining the electroweak and strong forces, and all four forces.

However, science never stands still and it may be that these energies are reached in your lifetime!

ADDING FORCES

When two or more forces are pulling or pushing an object in the same direction, then the effect of the forces will add up; when they are pulling it in opposite directions, then the backwards forces can be subtracted.

△ Fig. 1.37 These husky dogs are able to pull the sledge due to the low level of friction between the sledge and the snow.

Twelve husky dogs are pulling a sledge. The sledge is travelling to the right and each dog is pulling with a force of 50 N. There is a friction force of 250 N that is trying to slow the sledge, and therefore must be pointing to the left.

The total force to the right is (12 × 50) N = 600 N.

The total force to the left is 250 N.

The **resultant** force (the total added-up force) = 600 – 250 N to the right
= 350 N to the right.

Note that you must give the direction of the resultant force.

REMEMBER

Think very carefully about this. Having zero resultant force does *not* mean the object is stationary. What it *does* mean that the object is not *accelerating* – if it is already moving it will continue to so at constant speed in a straight line.

HOW ARE MATERIALS AFFECTED BY STRETCHING?

When weights are added to a length of wire, the wire will stretch. The top graph in Fig. 1.38 shows how the amount that the wire stretches (the extension) varies with the load attached to it (the force). The wire will stretch in proportion to the load up to a certain point, which depends on the material from which the wire is made. Beyond this point, the extension is no longer proportional to the load, and so this point is called the **limit of proportionality**.

A string on a musical instrument, such as a guitar string, will behave as shown in the graph for wire, but will break shortly after the limit of proportionality is reached. This means that, when tuning a string on a musical instrument, we need to take care that we do not tighten the string too much or we risk it breaking.

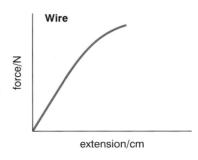

△ Fig. 1.38 Force/extension graph for a wire.

REMEMBER

A material shows elastic behaviour if it returns to its original length when any deforming forces have been removed. During elastic behaviour, the particles in the material are pulled apart a little, so they return to their original positions when the forces are removed. A material shows plastic behaviour if it remains deformed when a load is removed. During plastic behaviour the particles slide past each other and the structure of the material is changed permanently.

SCIENCE IN CONTEXT **THE BEGINNINGS OF PLASTICS**

In 1862, at the Great Exhibition in London, Alexander Parkes demonstrated an organic material that was derived from cellulose that, once it was heated, could be moulded and kept its moulded shape when it was cooled. This was the first plastic material, which was called Parkesine.

Six years later, John Wesley Hyatt invented celluloid, which again is derived from cellulose, as an alternative to ivory, which was then used to make billiard balls. Celluloid became more famous as the first flexible photographic film used for still photographs and moving pictures. By 1900 it had an expanding market in movie films.

The first fully synthetic resin to be commercially successful was Bakelite, which was invented in 1907 by Leo Hendrik Baekeland.

△ Fig. 1.39 Many early telephones were made from Bakelite.

Hooke's law

For a wire, there is a section of the force/extension graph that is linear. Like a wire, when a spring stretches, the extension of the spring is proportional to the force stretching it, provided the limit of proportionality (see Fig. 1.38) of the spring is not exceeded. This is **Hooke's law** and is shown by a straight line on a force–extension graph (Fig. 1.40).

The gradient of the line is a measure of the stiffness of the spring.

An experiment to show Hooke's law:

1. Assemble the apparatus (Fig. 1.41) and allow the spring to hang down. Measure the starting position of the bottom end of the spring on the ruler.

2. Take the first mass, which consists of the hook and base plate, typically of mass 100 g (a weight of 1 N), and hang it on the spring (take care to ensure that the mass can't fall onto anyone's feet). Measure the new position of the bottom end of the spring on the ruler. The difference in the readings is the extension of the spring.

3. Add masses one by one to the first one. Typically each mass is C-shaped, and adds an additional 100 g. Add the masses carefully so that the spring stretches slowly.

4. You should then reverse the experiment to see what happens as the masses are removed.

5. Calculate the extension (Table 1.2) and plot a graph of extension against force (Fig. 1.42).

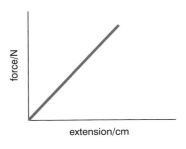

△ Fig. 1.40 Hooke's law in a spring is shown by a straight line.

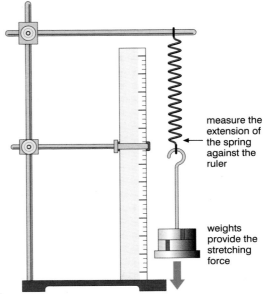

measure the extension of the spring against the ruler

weights provide the stretching force

△ Fig. 1.41 Apparatus to investigate Hooke's law.

Mass/g	Force/N	Reading/ cm	Calculate the extension/ cm	Extension/ cm
0	0	15.2	–	–
100	1.0	16.8	16.8–15.2	1.6
200	2.0	18.5	18.5–15.2	3.3
300	3.0	19.9	19.9–15.2	4.7
400	4.0	21.6	21.6–15.2	6.4
etc.	etc.			

△ Table 1.2. Results of experiment.

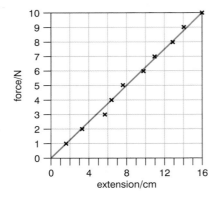

△ Fig. 1.42 Graph of results.

A spring that obeys Hooke's law shows '**proportional**' **behaviour**: the extension of the spring increases in proportion to the load on the spring. It also shows **elastic behaviour** – when the force is removed, the spring returns to its original length provided the elastic limit (the point at which the spring returns to its original length after the load is removed) has not been exceeded.

△ Fig. 1.43 Carrying out the experiment.

SCIENCE IN CONTEXT

HOOKE'S LAW IN ACTION

Hooke's law applies to springs that are both extended and compressed by a load, so whenever a spring is used it is an application of Hooke's law. Examples are toys that use springs such as jack-in-the boxes, and trampolines, which rely on springs returning to their original length and then stretching again to give the 'bounce' required. Anyone who sleeps on a mattress that contains springs also experiences Hooke's law in action on a nightly basis – a mattress with springs that do not return to their original length after being compressed would be rather uncomfortable to sleep on!

Developing Investigative Skills

A student assembled the apparatus as in Fig. 1.41, allowing the spring to hang vertically. Wearing safety glasses, the student measured the initial length of the spring and then measured it again after hanging an additional 100 g onto it. The student continued adding 100 g masses, measuring the length of the spring after each one. His measurements are shown in the table.

Mass added/g	Force/N	Length of spring/cm	Extension of spring/cm
0		2.0	
100		6.0	
200		10.0	
300		14.0	
400		18.0	
500		22.0	
600		26.0	
700		30.0	
800		34.0	
900		38.0	
1 000		42.0	
1 100		46.0	
1 200		52.0	
1 300		59.0	
1 400		77.0	

Using and organising techniques, apparatus and materials

❶ Why should the student wear eye protection during this experiment?

❷ Describe how any other safety risks can be minimised.

❸ The student carried out a preliminary experiment before deciding to use 100 g masses. Why is a preliminary experiment valuable?

Observing, measuring and recording

❹ The force stretching the spring is equal to the weight of the 100 g masses that have been added. Use the equation: $W = mg$ to calculate the values for the 'force' column.

❺ Use the equation: extension of spring = length – original length, to calculate the values for the 'extension' column.

❻ Plot a graph of force (on the y-axis) against extension (on the x-axis).

Handling experimental observations and data

❼ EXTENDED Use your graph to justify whether or not the spring obeyed Hooke's Law.

Planning and evaluating investigations

❽ The student could not repeat the experiment using this spring. Explain why not.

❾ The student found it difficult to judge the 'end' of the spring. How could this be improved?

LIMIT OF PROPORTIONALITY

When you stretch a spring too far, the line is no longer straight and Hooke's law is no longer true. This point at the end of the straight line is known as the 'limit of proportionality'.

The spring may (if you do not stretch it too far) be elastic and go back to its original length.

However, as you stretch the material beyond the limit of proportionality, different materials can behave in widely different ways.

As we have seen, the equation for Hooke's law is:

force = spring constant × extension of spring

$$F = kx$$

Where: F = force in newtons

k = spring constant in N/m

x = extension of the spring in m

Note that it is acceptable to use a spring constant in N/cm or N/mm, so long as the extension is measured in the same units.

This equation works for springs that are being stretched or compressed. The value of k will be the same for both, but note that some springs cannot be compressed (if, for example, the turns of the spring are already in contact).

You can use the triangle in Fig. 1.44 to help you to rearrange the equation. Cover the quantity you want to find and the form of the other two will show you how to write the equation. For example, to find x, cover it and you will see that the equation should be written as $x = F/k$.

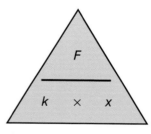

△ Fig. 1.44 The equation triangle for Hooke's law.

WORKED EXAMPLE

A motorbike has a single compression spring on the rear wheels. When the cyclist sits on the bike, she pushes on the rear wheel with 60 per cent of her weight. Her mass is 50 kg, and the spring constant is 60 N/cm. How much does the spring compress when she sits on the bike?

The formula for the weight of the cyclist: $W = mg$

Substitute the values for m and g: $W = 50 \times 10$

Work out the answer and write down the units: $W = 500$ N

The force on the rear spring   = 60 per cent of 500 N

          = 0.6×500 N

          = 300 N

Write down the formula for the compression of the spring: $x = F / k$

Substitute the values for F and k: $\qquad x = 300 / 60$

Work out the answer and write down the units: $\qquad x = 5$ cm

The spring compresses by 5 cm.

QUESTIONS

1. EXTENDED What force is required to stretch a spring with spring constant 0.2 N/m a distance of 5 cm?

2. EXTENDED A vertical spring stretches 5 cm under a load of 100 g. Determine the spring constant.

3. EXTENDED A force of 600 N compresses a spring with spring constant 30 N/cm. How far does the spring compress?

END OF EXTENDED

BALANCED FORCES

Usually there are at least two forces acting on an object. When these two forces are **balanced** then the object will either be stationary or moving at a constant speed. Two forces are balanced when their magnitude is the same but they act in opposite directions.

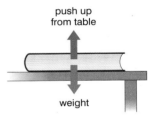

△ Fig. 1.45 The forces on this book are balanced.

The book in Fig. 1.45 is stationary because the push upwards from the table is equal to the weight downwards. If the table stopped pushing upwards, the book would fall.

This aircraft in Fig. 1.46 is flying 'straight and level' because the lift generated by the air flowing over the wings is equal and opposite to the weight of the aircraft. This diagram shows that the plane will neither climb nor dive, as it would if the forces were not equal.

△ Fig. 1.46 The balanced forces on this aircraft mean that its direction of motion will not change.

This is **Newton's first law of motion**, which simply says you need a resultant force to change the way something is moving.

UNBALANCED FORCES

For an object's speed or direction of movement to change, the forces acting on it must be **unbalanced**. You can find the resultant of two unbalanced forces by adding them up, taking into account their direction. So, when the driving force on a car is 100 N to the left but the friction force is 50 N to the right, the resultant force is 50 N to the left.

WORKED EXAMPLES

1. Find the resultant force when a skydiver of mass 60 kg jumps from a plane and the air resistance is 10 N.

Force downwards $= m \times g$
$= 60 \times 10$
$= 600$ N

Force upwards $= -10$ N (if you take downwards direction as positive)

Resultant force $= 600 - 10$ N
$= 590$ N downwards

2. Find the resultant force on a car when the driving force in 1500 N to the left and the friction force is 100 N to the right.

Resultant force $= 1500 - 100$
$= 1400$ N to the left

As a gymnast first steps on to a trampoline, his weight is much greater than the opposing supporting force of the trampoline, so he moves downwards, stretching the trampoline. (Note that we are not talking about the gymnast jumping onto the trampoline – if that were the case, the physics would be different!) As the trampoline stretches, its supporting force increases until the supporting force is equal to the gymnast's weight. When the two forces are balanced, the trampoline stops stretching. If an elephant stood on the trampoline, it would break because it could never produce a supporting force equal to the elephant's weight.

You see the same effect when you stand on snow or soft ground. When you stand on quicksand, the supporting force will not equal your weight, and you will continue to sink.

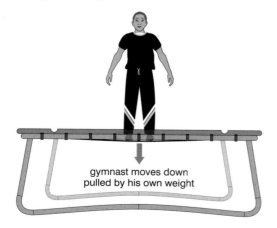
gymnast moves down pulled by his own weight

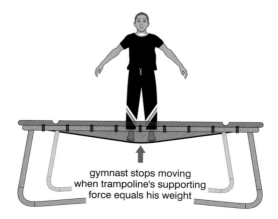
gymnast stops moving when trampoline's supporting force equals his weight

Δ Fig. 1.47 A trampoline stretches until it supports the weight on it.

QUESTIONS

1. Describe the motion of an object when the forces on it are balanced.

2. Describe the motion of an object when the forces on it are unbalanced.

3. In Fig. 1.47, if the gymnast is standing at rest on the trampoline, what must the supporting force of the trampoline be equal to?

EXTENDED

HOW ARE MASS, FORCE AND ACCELERATION RELATED?

A relationship between these factors is given by the formula:

force = mass × acceleration

$F = ma$

Where: F = force in newtons

m = mass in kg

a = acceleration in m/s^2

This equation comes from **Newton's second law of motion,** which links acceleration (the rate of change of velocity, remember) to the *resultant* force that is causing the change. In this form we can only use the equation if the mass stays constant.

This equation explains the definition of the newton. 'One newton is the force that will accelerate a mass of 1 kg at 1 m/s^2.'

The equation is perhaps easier to understand when we rearrange it into the form $a = F / m$. This shows us that when we use a big force we will get a larger acceleration, but when the object has more mass then we get a smaller acceleration.

END OF EXTENDED

Fig. 1.48a shows that, for a constant force, as mass increases acceleration decreases (they are inversely proportional). Fig. 1.48b shows that, for a constant mass, as force increases, acceleration also increases (they are directly proportional).

So, a light object with a large force applied to it will have a large acceleration. For example, an athlete with a racing bicycle applies a large force to the pedals of the light bicycle, so the bicycle will have a large acceleration. However, a massive object with a small force applied to it will have a small acceleration. For example, a small child trying to pedal a large bicycle rickshaw will only be able to apply a small force to the pedals of the heavy rickshaw, and so the acceleration will be small.

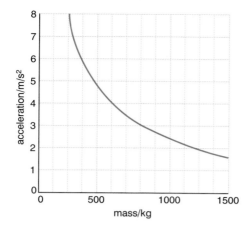

a)

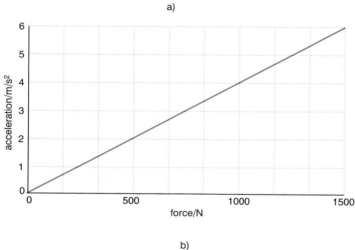

b)

◁ Fig. 1.48 a) For a constant force, acceleration is inversely proportional to mass. b) For a constant mass, acceleration is directly proportional to force.

The equation $F = ma$ shows that the acceleration of an object is directly proportional to the force acting (when its mass is constant) and is inversely proportional to its mass (when the force is constant). The gradient of a graph of force (on the y-axis) against acceleration (on the x-axis) is equal to the mass of the object.

WORKED EXAMPLES

1. What force would be required to give a mass of 5 kg an acceleration of 10 m/s²?

Write down the formula: $F = ma$
Substitute the values for m and a $F = 5 \times 10$
Work out the answer and write down the units: $F = 50$ N

2. A car has a resultant driving force of 6000 N and a mass of 1200 kg. Calculate the car's initial acceleration.

Write down the formula in terms of a: $a = F / m$
Substitute the values for F and m: $a = 6000 / 1200$
Work out the answer and write down the units: $a = 5$ m/s²

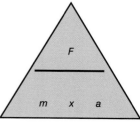

△ Fig. 1.49 The equation triangle for force, mass and acceleration.

QUESTIONS

1. **EXTENDED** **a)** Write down the equation linking force, mass and acceleration.

   b) For the equation to apply, what conditions must the 'force' and 'mass' meet?

2. **EXTENDED** What force is acting when a 60 kg bungee jumper is accelerating at 10 m/s^2?

3. **EXTENDED** The resultant force on an object of mass 3.2 kg is 2560 N. What is the acceleration of the object?

END OF EXTENDED

NEWTON'S THIRD LAW

Newton's Third Law refers to forces that are: equal in size, opposite in direction, of the same type and acting on different bodies. All four conditions must be satisfied. If you lean your body against a wall, your body is exerting a contact force on the wall. The wall is also exerting a contact force on your body. The force exerted by the wall on you is equal and in the opposite direction to the force exerted by your body on the wall. If the wall did not exert a force on your body, you would fall through the wall!

This is an example of Newton's third law. The law says that forces always come in pairs. If a body A exerts a force on body B, then body B also exerts a force on body A. The two forces are of the same type, are equal in size, opposite in direction, and act on different bodies.

For example, look at the sprinter's blocks in Fig. 1.50. When the race starts the sprinter's feet exert a pushing force against the blocks. The blocks exert a pushing force on the sprinter's feet of the same size and in the opposite direction, propelling the sprinter forward. Another example would be a falling brick. Ignoring air resistance, there is one force acting on the brick – its weight, or the gravitational pull of the Earth on the brick. The other half of Newton's Third Law pair is the gravitational pull of the brick on the Earth. This fulfils all four conditions.

◁ Fig. 1.50 The forces exerted by the sprinter's feet and the blocks are the same size but in opposite directions.

ANALYSING THE FORCES ON AN OBJECT

An excellent method of observing forces in action is to consider the forces acting on an aircraft from take-off to landing. The aircraft will have several different forces acting on it at any one time – some will balance one another but others will be unbalanced. In this example, all the forces considered act on the same object (the plane).

Your task is to produce a storyboard to illustrate these forces at certain parts of the aircraft's journey. For each section, you should draw force arrows on the aircraft to represent the direction and the size of the forces acting on it.

Your storyboard should include the following stages of the journey:

1. The aircraft is sitting on the runway, ready for take-off.

2. The aircraft is accelerating down the runway.

3. The aircraft has taken off and is rising through the air.

4. The aircraft has reached its maximum height and is travelling at a steady speed.

5. The pilot decides to decrease the altitude of the aircraft because of turbulence.

6. The aircraft is slowing down as it approaches the runway.

7. The aircraft has landed, but is decelerating to try and stop.

8. The aircraft has stopped on the runway.

For each section, you should write a line to describe what is happening.

MOTION IN A CURVED PATH DUE TO A PERPENDICULAR FORCE

When a moving object has no forces acting on it, it will continue to move in a straight line at constant velocity (Fig. 1.51).

no force

constant velocity
in a straight line

△ Fig. 1.51 This object is moving in a straight line at constant velocity and has no forces acting on it.

So, when an object is moving in a circle, or along the arc of a circle, there must be a force acting on it to change its direction (Fig. 1.52). Moving in a circle means that the direction of motion is constantly changing, so this in turn means that the direction of the force is constantly changing.

This force, which always acts towards the centre of the circle, is given the name **centripetal force**. The force also acts perpendicularly to the

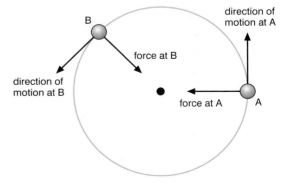

direction of
motion at A

B

force at B

direction of
motion at B

force at A

A

△ Fig. 1.52 In order for an object to move on a circular path, the force must always be acting towards the centre of the circle.

direction of motion of the object at any instant. It changes the direction of motion of the object but does not change its speed.

The centripetal force is not a new and different force from any you have come across before, but is one or more of the forces already acting on the object that is moving in a circle. Table 1.3 gives some examples.

Example	How is the centripetal force supplied?
A stone on the end of a string, being whirled in a horizontal circle	By the tension force in the string
The Moon, orbiting the Earth	By the gravitational force of the Earth on the Moon
A car turning a corner	By the sideways friction force of the road on the tyres
A train going round a bend	By the sideways force of the rails on the wheels
A person standing on the Earth, which is spinning rapidly	By the gravitational force of the Earth on the person

△ Table 1.3 Examples of centripetal force in action

See if you can think of other examples of things moving around arcs of circles, and work out what force is providing the centripetal force. Remember that the centripetal force is always towards the centre of the arc and perpendicular to the direction in which the object is travelling at that instant.

Consider a stone being whirled in a horizontal circle on the end of a string (Fig. 1.53).

What happens if the string breaks?

In this case, the centripetal force is suddenly removed. There is now no force acting on the stone, so it continues to move in a straight line in whatever direction it had when the string broke (i.e. along the tangent to the circle at that point; Fig. 1.54), but falls vertically under gravity.

It is important to note that the stone does *not* fly outwards along a radius. (A common mistake some people make is to say that there is a centrifugal [note: not centripetal] force pulling the stone outwards, which leads to the conclusion that when the string breaks, the stone flies out along a radius. This idea is incorrect.)

Suggest what would happen:

1. to the Moon if gravity suddenly ceased

2. to a car turning a corner when the road was very slippery

3. to a person on Earth if gravity suddenly ceased.

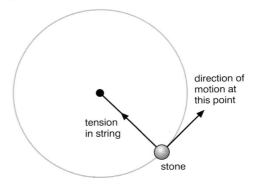

△ Fig. 1.53 A stone being whirled in a horizontal circle on the end of a string, just before the string breaks.

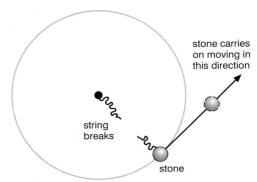

△ Fig. 1.54 When the string breaks, the stone flies off along a tangent until the force of gravity takes over, and the stone falls to the ground.

TURNING EFFECT

If you have used a spanner to tighten a nut, or you have turned the handle of a rotary beater, you have used a force to turn something. But turning applies to less obvious examples, such as when you push the door handle to close a door, or when a child sits on the end of a see-saw to push her end of it down.

The turning effect of a force is called the **moment** of the force. The moment of a force depends on two things:

- the size of the force
- the perpendicular distance between the line of the force and the turning point, which is called the **pivot**.

When moments balance

The principle of moments says that when a system of forces is not turning, then the sum of the clockwise moments equals the sum of the anticlockwise moments about any point.

So, for example, when the following system of forces is balanced:

sum of clockwise moments = sum of anticlockwise moments

$$\text{moment of } F_3 = \text{moment of } F_1 + \text{moment of } F_2$$
$$(F_3 \times c) = (F_1 \times b) + (F_2 \times a)$$

An experiment to verify the principle of moments

1. Drill a hole at the 50 cm mark of a metre rule.

2. Support the rule on a pivot through the drilled hole.

3. Using two loops of thread and two mass hangers and some slotted masses, suspend different weights, W_1 and W_2, at different distances, a and b, from the pivot. Carefully adjust the distances a and b until the rule balances horizontally.

4. Record the values of W_1, W_2, a and b.

5. Repeat stages 3 and 4 several times, with different values of W_1, W_2, a and b.

6. For each set of results, calculate $(W_1 \times a)$ and $(W_2 \times b)$.

You will find that, within the limits of experimental accuracy, $(W_2 \times a)$ and $(W_2 \times b)$ will be equal for each set of readings.

	W_1/N	W_2/N	a/cm	b/cm	$(W_1 \times a)$/ Ncm	$(W_2 \times b)$/ Ncm
a)	0.5	1.0	41.6	20.4	20.8	20.4
b)	1.5	1.0	25.7	38.8	38.6	38.8
c)	1.5	0.5	15.8	47.8	23.7	23.9
d)	2.0	2.5	44.4	35.4	88.8	88.5

You will see that for each set of readings, the last two columns are equal, within the limits of the accuracy of the experiment. So the results verify the principle of moments.

The name we use in physics to describe a set of balanced forces is **equilibrium**. When the system of forces is in equilibrium then the sum of the anticlockwise moments are balanced by the sum of the clockwise moments. In other words, there is no net moment on a body in equilibrium.

END OF EXTENDED

QUESTIONS

1. What two things does the moment of a force depend on?

2. EXTENDED Two children are sitting on a see-saw. The child to the left of the pivot is sitting x m from the pivot and has a weight of 400 N. The child on the right of the pivot is sitting 2 m from the pivot and has a weight of 300 N. What is the distance x?

Conditions for equilibrium

The word 'system' describes a collection of objects working together. So in the example of a see-saw, the two children and the see-saw form a system. We say that a system is in equilibrium when it is not moving in any direction and it is *not* rotating. You already know that for a system not to be moving, the forces on it must be equal and opposite. So:

For a system to be in equilibrium, there must be no resultant force and no resultant turning effect.

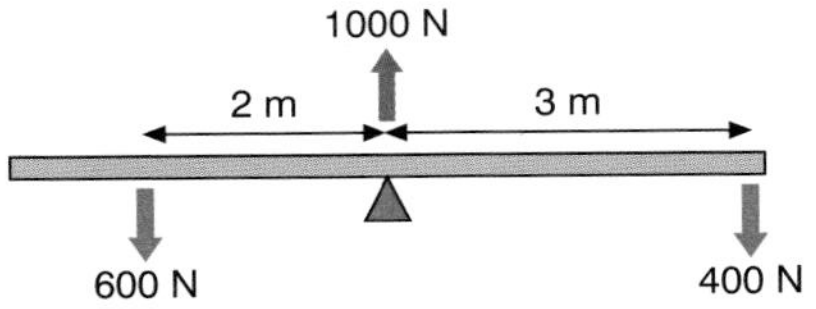

△ Fig. 1.55 This beam is balanced because the moments around the pivot are equal and opposite, and the downwards and upwards forces are equal and opposite.

In the case of the balanced see-saw, there is no resultant turning effect on the see-saw because the clockwise and anticlockwise turning effects are equal and opposite. In addition, the downward weight of the two children on the see-saw is 1000 N, and the upward force on the see-saw from the pivot must also be 1000 N (Fig. 1.55).

CENTRE OF MASS AND STABILITY

When considering the motion of objects, it is useful to be able to make some assumptions. One assumption we can make is to assume that all the mass of the body is concentrated at one point, which we call the **centre of mass**. This is a useful simplification because we can pretend gravity only acts at a single point in the object, so a single arrow on a diagram can represent the weight of an object. For this reason, the centre of mass is sometimes called the centre of gravity.

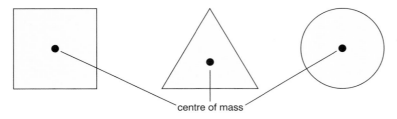

△ Fig. 1.56 The centre of mass for objects with a regular shape is in the centre.

To find the centre of mass of simple objects, such as a piece of card, follow these steps:

1. Hang up the object.

2. Suspend a mass from the same place.

3. Mark the position of the thread.

4. The centre of mass is somewhere along the line of the thread.

5. Repeat steps 1 to 3 with the object suspended from a different place.

6. The centre of mass is where the two lines meet.

The idea of centre of mass is useful when predicting whether or not an object will fall over – whether or not it is stable.

When displaced, the conical object shown in Fig. 1.58 will fall back into place – the centre of mass is inside the pivot, so the weight of the object pulls it back onto its base. The moment of the force produced by its weight returns the object to its base. An object that is difficult to topple is said to be in **stable equilibrium**.

The object in Fig. 1.59 will topple over – the centre of mass is outside the pivot so the weight of the object tips it over the rest of the way.

When the object in Fig. 1.60 is displaced it will move to a new, similar position. It is in neutral equilibrium.

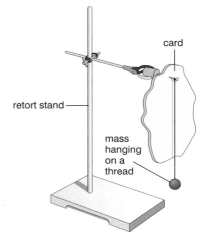

△ Fig. 1.57 Finding the centre of mass of a plane object.

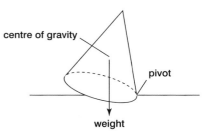

△ Fig. 1.58 This object has its centre of mass inside its pivot so it is stable.

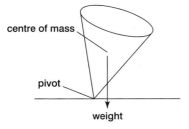

△ Fig. 1.59 This object is not stable as its centre of mass is outside its pivot.

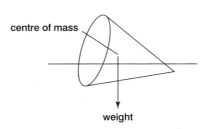

△ Fig. 1.60 This object is in neutral equilibrium.

CENTRE OF MASS AND FLYING

The concept of centre of mass is important in determining whether or not an aircraft is safe to fly. For an aircraft to be safe, its centre of mass must fall within limits that are set by the manufacturer. The area between these limits is called the CG range for the aircraft. The centre of mass needs to be calculated before each flight and, if it is not within the CG range, weight must be removed, added (which is rare) or redistributed until the centre of mass falls within the range.

Part of the calculation of the centre of mass involves the weights within the aircraft. The weights of fixed parts of the aircraft, such as engines and wings, do not change and are provided by the manufacturer. The manufacturer will also provide information about the effect of different fuel loads. The operator is responsible for allowing for removable weight such as passengers, crew and luggage, in the calculation.

△ Fig. 1.61 An aeroplane taking off.

All aircraft have a maximum weight for flight. If this maximum is exceeded, then the aircraft may not be able to fly in a controlled, level flight. It may be impossible to take off with a given length of runway. Excess weight may make it impossible to climb beyond a particular altitude (so the aircraft may not be able to take its proper course determined by air traffic control).

QUESTIONS

1. What is the centre of mass of an object?

2. Explain why a vase of flowers is less likely to fall over if it has a wide, heavy base.

EXTENDED

SCALARS AND VECTORS

You know that speed and velocity are not the same – velocity has a direction associated with it. Physical quantities can be divided into two groups – those that have direction associated with them and those that do not.

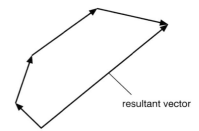

△ Fig. 1.62 The resultant vector represents the combined effect of the individual vectors.

Force, velocity and acceleration are examples of **vector** quantities. A vector has a specific direction as well as a size, with a unit.

Speed and mass are examples of **scalar** quantities. A scalar quantity has size only, with a unit. There are many more scalar quantities to be met: temperature, work, power and electrical resistance are all scalars.

To add vectors, draw them to scale, joining them in turn 'head to tail'. The final, or resultant, vector is drawn from the 'tail' of the first vector to the 'head' of the last one (Fig. 1.62).

REMEMBER

Displacement is the vector quantity linked to distance, which is a scalar quantity. Displacement is the distance travelled *in a particular direction*.

QUESTIONS

1. **EXTENDED** Explain the difference between a *scalar* quantity and a *vector* quantity.

2. **EXTENDED** Explain why force is a vector.

3. **EXTENDED** Describe how you would find the resultant of two forces.

Drawing a graph to find the resultant

Earlier, you saw what happens when two husky dogs are pulling a sledge in the same direction, but what if they were pulling in different directions? It is clear that the sledge will move in a direction that is some sort of average of these directions. To find out exactly what will happen, we replace the two forces with a single force (the resultant) that will have just the same effect.

To calculate this single force you draw the two forces in the correct direction and to a scale length that is suitable. In the case of the husky dogs, a suitable scale might be 1 cm per 10 N, or perhaps 1 cm per 5 N.

You then find the resultant by completing a parallelogram. The resultant is the diagonal line across the parallelogram between the two forces. This gives the direction of the resultant force. You can calculate the magnitude of the resultant force by measuring its length, and using the scale that we chose to begin with.

If one of the dogs is not working very hard, the sledge will start to go in the direction in which the stronger dog is pulling.

The vector nature of force

To describe a force fully, you must state the size of the force and also the direction in which it is trying to move the object. The direction can be described in many different ways such as 'left to right', 'upwards' or 'north'. Sometimes it is useful to describe all of the forces in one direction as positive, and all of the forces in the other direction as negative. For two forces to be identical they must have the same size and the same direction.

END OF EXTENDED

End of topic checklist

Key terms

balanced force, centre of mass, centripetal force, elastic behaviour, electricity, electromagnetic force, electrostatic force, force, friction, Hooke's law, limit of proportionality, magnetism, moment, newton, Newton's first law of motion, pivot, plastic flow, principle of moments, proportional behaviour, resultant force, scalar, stable equilibrium, unbalanced force, vector

During your study of this topic you should have learned:

○ That a force may produce a change in size and shape of a body.

○ How to plot load/extension graphs and describe the associated experimental procedure.

○ EXTENDED How to interpret extension/load graphs.

○ EXTENDED That Hooke's law can be summarised as $F = kx$ where F is the load, k is the spring constant and x is the extension.

○ EXTENDED The significance of the term 'limit of proportionality' for an extension/load graph.

○ EXTENDED About the relationship between force, mass and acceleration (including the direction).

○ EXTENDED About motion in a curved path due to a perpendicular force.

○ That the moment of a force is a measure of its turning effect and be able to give everyday examples.

○ About the balancing of a beam about a pivot.

○ EXTENDED About an experiment to show that there is no net moment on a body in equilibrium.

○ EXTENDED About the idea of opposing moments to simple systems in equilibrium.

○ That, where there is no resultant force and no resultant turning effect, a system is in equilibrium.

○ About an experiment to determine the position of the centre of mass of a plane lamina.

○ About the effect of the position of the centre of mass on the stability of simple objects.

○ EXTENDED About the difference between scalar and vector quantities and be able to give common examples.

○ EXTENDED How to add vectors by graphical representation to determine a resultant.

○ EXTENDED How to determine graphically the resultant of two vectors.

End of topic questions

Note: The marks awarded for these questions indicate the level of detail required in the answers. In the examination, the number of marks awarded to questions like these may be different.

1. A student performed an experiment stretching a spring. She loaded masses onto the spring and measured its extension. Here are her results.

Extension/cm	0	4	8	12	16	20	24
Load/N	0	2.0	4.0	6.0	7.5	8.3	8.6

   According to checklist this should be core and parts b) and c) are extended.

   a) On graph paper, plot a graph of load (vertical axis) against extension (horizontal axis). Draw a suitable line through your points. **(3 marks)**

   b) EXTENDED Mark on the graph the limit of proportionality, and indicate the region where proportional behaviour occurs and the region where the behaviour is probably plastic. **(3 marks)**

   c) EXTENDED How does she check whether the spring, after being loaded with 8.6 N, has shown plastic behaviour or purely elastic behaviour? **(1 mark)**

2. The manufacturer of a car gave the following information:

   Mass of car: 1000 kg. The car will accelerate from 0 to 30 m/s in 12 seconds.

   a) Calculate the average acceleration of the car during the 12 seconds. **(2 marks)**

   b) Calculate the force needed to produce this acceleration. **(2 marks)**

3. Two tug boats have ropes attached to a ship and are about to start moving it very carefully. One tug is north of the ship and is pulling with a force of 3000 N, and the other tug is east of the ship and is pulling with a force of 4000 N.

   a) EXTENDED By means of a diagram, calculate the total force with which the ship will be pulled, and show the direction in which it will be pulled. **(3 marks)**

   b) The ship has a mass of 500 tonnes (1 tonne = 1000 kg).

   i) Calculate the acceleration of the ship. **(2 marks)**

   ii) Calculate the speed of the ship after 10 s. **(2 marks)**

4. Which of these containers is the most stable? Explain your answer. **(2 marks)**

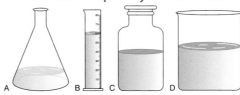

5. EXTENDED Find the resultant of a force of 3 N acting vertically and a force of 4 N acting horizontally. **(4 marks)**

Energy, work and power

INTRODUCTION

The study of energy, how it moves about, what it does when it is transferred, is at the heart of physics. Energy is that 'stuff' that allows things to happen. But what actually *is* 'energy'?

Energy is surprisingly hard to pin down. We have an intuitive 'feel' that when we have lots of energy, we can get lots of things done. When we are feeling 'drained' of energy, then it is much harder.

△ Fig. 1.63 These trams take electrical energy from the overhead wires and convert some of it into kinetic energy.

Being able to track where the energy is moving, in all its 'disguises', it a key skill that will help you explain many aspects of physics.

KNOWLEDGE CHECK

✓ Know some everyday uses of energy.
✓ Be able to describe devices that transform energy from one form to another.

LEARNING OBJECTIVES

✓ Demonstrate an understanding that an object may have energy due to its motion or its position, and that energy may be transferred and stored.
✓ Be able to give examples of energy in different forms, including kinetic, gravitational, chemical, strain, nuclear, internal, electrical, light and sound.
✓ Give examples of the conversion of energy from one form to another, and of its transfer from one place to another.
✓ Apply the principle of energy conservation to simple examples.
✓ EXTENDED Recall and use the expressions k.e. = ½ mv^2 and p.e. = mgh.
✓ Distinguish between renewable and non-renewable sources of energy.
✓ Be able to describe how electricity or other useful forms of energy may be obtained.
✓ Be able to give advantages and disadvantages of each method in terms of cost, reliability, scale and environmental impact.
✓ Show a qualitative understanding of efficiency.
✓ EXTENDED Show an understanding that energy is released by nuclear fusion in the Sun.
✓ EXTENDED Recall and use the equation: efficiency = $\dfrac{\text{useful energy output}}{\text{energy input}} \times 100\%$
✓ Be able to relate (without calculation) work done to the magnitude of a force and the distance moved.
✓ EXTENDED Be able to describe energy changes in terms of work done.
✓ EXTENDED Recall and use $\Delta W = Fd = \Delta E$.

✓ Be able to relate (without further calculation) power to work done and time taken, using appropriate examples.

✓ **EXTENDED** Recall and use the equation $P = E / t$ in simple systems.

ENERGY

A car will not move without using fuel. At present this fuel could be petrol or alcohol or diesel fuel or liquefied petroleum gas (LPG). In the past the fuel could, just possibly, have been coal; and in the future it could be hydrogen, or electricity stored in a battery. However, whatever fuel you use, you are buying something with the ability to make that car move. This stored ability is known as **potential energy**.

△ Fig. 1.64 Fuel, whatever form it comes in, gives a car the ability to move.

A clock needs energy to make the hands move, and this energy can be stored in a spring that you wind up with a key, in an electrical battery, or in weights that are raised up.

Potential energy is stored or hidden energy. In this context 'potential' means 'containing power'. When a spring is stretched or compressed, the spring will have elastic potential energy as shown in Fig. 1.65.

When a load is raised above the ground, it will have **gravitational potential energy**, as shown in Figure 1.66. Gravitational potential energy is energy due to an object's position.

△ Fig. 1.66 This cuckoo clock stores gravitational potential energy in two weights: one to run the mechanism that turns the hands, and one to make the cuckoo sing on each hour.

△ Fig. 1.65 The spring in this vehicle suspension system stores elastic potential energy.

If the spring is released or the load moves back to the ground, the stored potential energy is transferred to movement energy, which is called **kinetic energy**.

Potential energy can be used to make an object move, and so give it kinetic energy. Kinetic energy can also be transferred into potential energy, and this can be seen most clearly in the action of a pendulum, where at each end of its swing (AT A AND C) the pendulum has a maximum amount of gravitational potential energy, and at the middle of its swing (AT B) some of the potential energy has been transferred into kinetic energy (the pendulum is moving fastest), as shown in Figure 1.67.

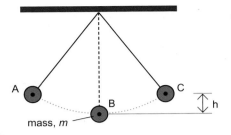

△ Fig. 1.67 Energy changes in the swing of a pendulum.

REMEMBER

An object gains gravitational potential energy as it gains height. Work has to be done to increase the height of the object above the ground. Therefore: gain in gravitational potential energy of an object = work done on that object against gravity.

EXTENDED

You can use the expression p.e. = *mgh* to calculate the amount of potential energy an object has. In this expression, *m* is its mass, *g* is acceleration due to gravity (usually taken as 10 m/s²) and *h* is its height above the ground (zero level).

WORKED EXAMPLE

A skier has a mass of 70 kg and travels up in a ski lift a vertical height of 300 m. Calculate the change in the skier's gravitational potential energy.

Write down the formula: p.e. = $m \times g \times h$

Substitute values for *m, g* and *h*: p.e. = $70 \times 10 \times 300$

Work out the answer and write
down the unit: p.e. = 210 000 J or 210 kJ

WORKED EXAMPLE

An ice skater has a mass of 50 kg and travels at a speed of 5 m/s. Calculate the ice-skater's kinetic energy.

You can use the expression k.e. = ½ mv^2 to calculate the amount of potential energy an object has. In this expression, m is its mass and v is its velocity.

Write down the formula: k.e. = ½ mv^2

Substitute the values for m and v: k.e. = ½ × 50 × 5 × 5

Work out the answer and write down the unit: k.e. = 625 J

QUESTIONS

1. EXTENDED Calculate the gravitational potential energy gained when a 5 kg mass is lifted 2 m.

2. EXTENDED Calculate the kinetic energy of a 2 kg ball rolling at 2 m/s.

END OF EXTENDED

DIFFERENT FORMS OF ENERGY

As shown by the pendulum, energy can either be stored or can be seen as a form of motion. The different types of stored energy are all forms of potential energy. Here are some important examples:

- **Gravitational potential energy:** This is energy stored by an object being raised up in a gravitational field, for example a ball at the top of a hill.
- **Elastic strain energy:** The word 'strain' means stretched. 'Strain energy' can be stored in springs (in clocks, for example) and in bows when they are drawn back before the arrow is released.
- **Chemical energy:** The energy stored in fuels such as petrol and diesel is usually called 'chemical energy'. In any object the atoms are held together by forces that are called bonds. These bonds behave like springs. In some materials, such as fuels and explosives, the bonds are forced to be shorter or longer than they wish. This stores energy in the bonds that can be transferred by breaking up the structure of the fuel or the explosive.
  A battery is ready to turn 'chemical energy' into 'electrical energy', and a rechargeable battery is so called because every time that it is discharged it can be recharged by forcing electricity through it backwards. The 'electrical energy' that is transferred is stored as 'chemical energy'.
- **Nuclear energy:** The energy in a nucleus of an atom is stored in the extremely strong bonds between the particles of which the nucleus is made. Some of this energy can be released, in the case of uranium (and a couple of other metals) by splitting the nucleus of the atom into two smaller nuclei. This can be done either slowly and for good purposes in a nuclear power station, or very rapidly in an atomic bomb.

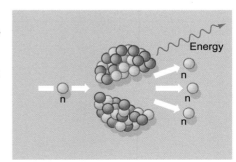

△ Fig. 1.68 Splitting a nucleus can release a lot of energy.

Forms of kinetic energy

Here are some other important types of energy. They are actually all different sorts of kinetic energy, but this is far from obvious in some cases:

When people just use the words 'kinetic energy', then they are referring to the energy of a visible moving object with k.e. $= \frac{1}{2} mv^2$.

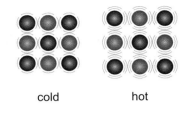

cold   hot

△ Fig. 1.69 The atoms in a hot object vibrate more because they have more energy.

- **Internal energy (heat):** This is contained within an object and makes the difference between the object being hot or cold. A hot object contains atoms that are moving fast or vibrating strongly.
- **Electrical energy:** Electrical currents carry electrical energy from one place to another. Electrical energy can easily be turned into kinetic energy in a motor or internal energy in a resistor, perhaps used as a heater.

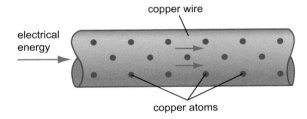

△ Fig. 1.70 Electrical energy in a wire.

- **Light energy:** A light wave carries 'light energy' as it travels, and this will be turned into internal energy in most objects when it strikes them. If the light hits a solar panel it can be made to generate electrical energy.
- **Sound waves:** These carry a very small amount of energy from the source of the noise. The source vibrates, setting air particles around it into vibration. These vibrations are passed through the air as a **longitudinal wave**. When the wave reaches the ear it sets the eardrum into vibration. (Do not confuse the 2000 W of electricity consumed by a band performing on stage with the 100 W of sound being emitted by the loudspeakers. The ear is extremely good at detecting sound.)

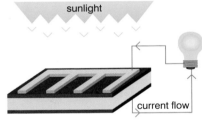

△ Fig. 1.71 A solar cell transfers light energy into electrical energy.

TRANSFER OF ENERGY

Any type of energy can be transferred into any other type of energy. In some cases this transfer can be done efficiently, such as between kinetic energy and electrical energy. In other cases the transfer is inefficient. One example of inefficient transfer of energy is the power station Fig. 1.74.

In every case of transfer of energy, some of the energy is converted to internal energy. A light bulb transfers electrical energy to light energy but also gets hot; an electric motor transfers electrical energy to kinetic energy but also gets hot; a diesel engine transfers chemical energy to kinetic energy but also gets hot; a battery that is being charged gets hot. Even a pendulum eventually stops swinging because the movement of the pendulum through the air heats up the air due to resistance.

SCIENCE IN CONTEXT — ENERGY AND THE EARTH

Energy and matter are constantly interacting on our planet. Part of this interaction produces volcanoes, glaciers, mountain ranges, oceans and continents. The energy comes from two sources: energy from the Sun, which keeps the oceans and the atmospheric cycles (such as the water cycle) going; and the internal energy, which comes from radioactive decay in the Earth's core and is the driving force behind plate tectonics.

The amount of energy that moves through the system is huge: it is of the order of 1.74×10^{17} W. Most of this comes from the Sun. Fig. 1.72 shows the energy transfers that take place in the Earth's system.

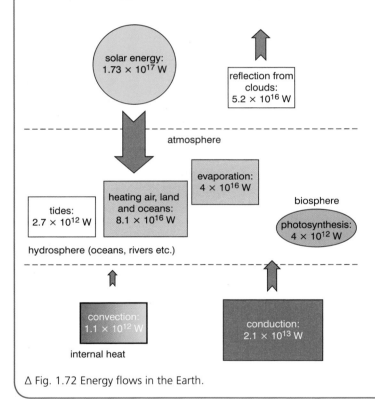

△ Fig. 1.72 Energy flows in the Earth.

QUESTIONS

1. Describe the energy changes that take place as a pendulum swings from one side to the other.

2. Where can elastic strain energy be found?

3. What is the source of chemical energy?

CONSERVATION OF ENERGY

The law of conservation of energy says that energy cannot be created or destroyed. Often the words 'conversion' and '**conservation**' are misused.

Energy *conversion* is transferring one form of energy to another (such as electrical to light in a light bulb). In another example, a streetcar takes electrical energy and converts it mainly into kinetic energy, but also into internal energy and sound. Likewise, as a pendulum swings, some of its energy is transferred between kinetic and gravitational potential energy: but when you add up its total energy, you will find that the total stays almost the same. The movements of the pendulum slowly die away as energy is transferred to the air in the room and the air heats up slightly.

REMEMBER

You may need to describe how energy is transferred in different situations, but remember that total energy is always conserved: the energy at the start and at the end must have the same total value. So you must account for all of the energy converted, and that includes the energy that will have been transferred as internal energy, as well perhaps as light or sound. For example, the amount of electrical energy that is put into a light bulb will all come out of the light bulb in the form of light (useful output) and some internal energy (heat), which is wasted output.

EXTENDED

You can use the principle of the conservation of energy to calculate what happens when kinetic energy and potential energy are converted from either one to the other.

So long as negligible energy is lost in the conversion, $mgh = \frac{1}{2}mv^2$.

QUESTIONS

1. State the law of conservation of energy.

2. Describe the energy transfers that take place in a light bulb.

3. Consider a street car.

    a) What form of energy is its input?

    b) What form of energy is its useful output?

    c) What form of energy is its 'waste' output?

A stone is thrown vertically upwards and reaches a height of 6 m above the hand of the thrower. What speed was the stone travelling at when it left the person's hand?

The decrease in k.e. of the stone as it rises = the increase in the p.e. of the stone.

As the final k.e. of the stone = 0, the initial k.e. of the stone = the increase in the p.e. of the stone at the top of its flight.

Write down the formula: $\frac{1}{2} mv^2 = mgh$
$$\frac{1}{2} v^2 = gh$$

Note that the mass has cancelled out; the mass does not matter in this case.

Substitute values for g and h: $v^2 = gh \times 2$
$$= 10 \times 6 \times 2$$
$$= 120$$

Work out the answer and write down the unit:
$$v = \sqrt{120}$$
$$= 10.95 \text{ m/s}$$

△ Fig. 1.73 The path of a stone when it is thrown.

REMEMBER

Note that in this worked example, the answer has been given to four significant figures. In most physics examples at this level, you should remember to use three or four significant figures, not the 10 or more digits that your calculator might give! You may be penalised in an exam if you give too many.

The kinetic energy given to the stone when it is thrown is transferred to potential energy as it gains height and slows down. At the top of its flight a large part of the kinetic energy will have been converted into gravitational potential energy. A small amount of energy will have been lost due to friction between the stone and the air.

END OF EXTENDED

REMEMBER

As a skier skis down a mountain the loss in potential energy should equal the gain in kinetic energy (assuming no other energy transfers take place, as a result of friction, for example). Calculations can then be performed using: loss in p.e. = gain in k.e. ($mgh = \frac{1}{2} mv^2$).

ENERGY RESOURCES

Fossil fuels

Most of the energy we use is obtained from **fossil fuels** – coal, oil and natural gas.

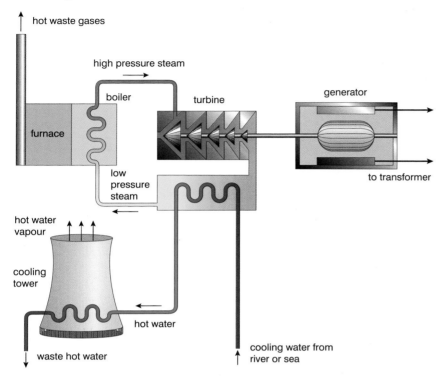

△ Fig. 1.74 How a power station works. The most common fuels used in power stations are coal, oil and gas.

Many power stations use fossil fuels (coal, oil, natural gas) to produce electricity that is supplied to homes and factories. Other power stations burn alternative fuels to produce this electricity, but the basic method of producing power is generally the same:

• Fuel is burned and steam is produced in a boiler.
• The steam turns a turbine.
• The turbine drives a generator.
• The generator produces electricity.
• The electricity is supplied to homes, industry, etc.

Once supplies of fossil fuels have been used up they cannot be replaced – they are **non-renewable**. At current levels of use, oil and gas supplies will probably last for about another 40 years, and coal supplies for no more than a few hundred years from now. The development of **renewable** sources of energy is therefore becoming increasingly important.

Wind power

The wind is used to turn windmill-like turbines that generate electricity directly from the rotating motion of their blades. Modern wind turbines are efficient, but it takes about one thousand of them to produce the same amount of energy as a modern gas, coal or oil-burning power station, and that is only when the wind is blowing favourably.

△ Fig. 1.75 On a windy day a very large wind turbine generates 2000 kW of electricity. That's enough to meet the needs of about 1200 families.

Developing Investigative Skills

You are going to plan an investigation to evaluate wind power as an energy source. You have the following equipment:

- model wind turbine
- multimeter to measure the voltage generated
- anemometer to measure wind speed
- hair dryer to generate wind power (note: set hair dryer setting to cold)
- metre rule to measure distance.

Using and organising techniques, apparatus and materials

❶ Plan your experiment, describing clearly the following:

   a) the aim of your investigation

   b) what you will measure

   c) the number and range of readings that you will take

   d) the independent variable

   e) the dependent variable

   f) the control variables

   g) how you will make your experiment a fair test.

❷ Draw out a results table that you would use in your investigation.

Planning and evaluating investigations

❸ Write an evaluation identifying aspects of your experiment where modifications are possible.

Water power

The motion of waves can be used to move large floats and generate electricity. Similarly, a very large number of floats are needed to produce a significant amount of electricity.

◁ Fig. 1.76 A wave generator.

Dams on tidal estuaries trap the water at high tide. When the water is allowed to flow back at low tide, **tidal power** can be generated. This obviously limits the use of the estuary for shipping and can cause environmental damage along the shoreline.

EXTENDED

The River Severn Barrage is a proposed project to build a huge dam on the estuary of the River Severn in the UK. The project is expected to cost around $20 billion and if completed will produce a clean, sustainable source of electricity for the next 120 years.

In the area behind the dam are huge areas of mud that are exposed at low tide. These mud flats contain many small animals and are a significant source of food for many species of birds. If the dam is built, these mud flats could be disrupted and it may not be easy for the birds to feed on the small animals in the mud.

Imagine that you are called as an expert witness as part of an environmental group to evaluate the benefits, disadvantages and environmental impact of constructing the barrage. Write a report in preparation for a press release. It should be approximately 200 words long.

END OF EXTENDED

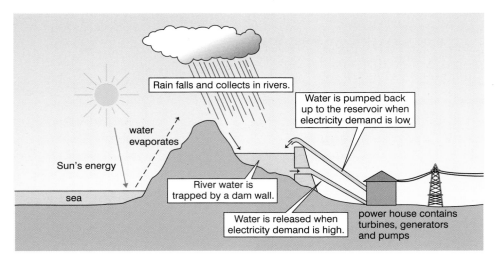

Rain falls and collects in rivers.

Water is pumped back up to the reservoir when electricity demand is low.

water evaporates

Sun's energy

River water is trapped by a dam wall.

sea

Water is released when electricity demand is high.

power house contains turbines, generators and pumps

△ Fig. 1.77 A pumped storage hydroelectric power station.

Dams can be used to store water, which is allowed to fall in a controlled way that generates electricity. This is particularly useful in hilly regions for generating **hydroelectric power**. When demand for electricity is low, surplus electricity can be used to pump water back up into the high dam for use in times of high demand.

Solar power

Solar cells can be used to convert light energy from the Sun directly into electricity. This electricity can be stored, often in batteries, to be used when convenient. Electricity generated in this way uses a renewable source. These panels are commonly referred to as solar PV (photovoltaic) panels to distinguish them from solar heating panels.

In **solar panels**, the energy from the Sun is used simply to heat water that is pumped through black pipes in a panel, often on the roof of a house. Heating the water in this way reduces the demand on other energy resources. Again, the energy can be stored in the water for later use.

△ Fig. 1.78 Solar (photovoltaic) panels on a roof.

REMEMBER

Make sure you don't confuse the two systems for using the Sun's energy. One heats water; the other generates electricity.

Solar power is energy from the Sun, which itself is powered by nuclear fusion reactions (where the small nuclei of hydrogen atoms join to make larger nuclei that are, in fact, helium) and an enormous amount of energy is released.

Although there have been several attempts to reproduce this continuous release of energy on Earth, so far they have been unsuccessful.

Geothermal power

Geothermal power is obtained using the heat of the Earth. In certain parts of the world, water forms hot springs that can be used directly for heating. Water can also be pumped deep into the ground to be heated.

Nuclear fission

A **nuclear power** station uses the heat generated by a controlled fission process to convert water to steam. This drives a turbine as in a conventional power station. However, a typical power plant produces 3 m³ of waste per year. People disagree over whether this radioactive waste is more hazardous than the gases emitted by coal-fired power stations.

Δ Fig. 1.79 A nuclear power station in the Czech Republic.

1. What energy transfers take place in a solar cell?

2. What energy transfers take place in a wind turbine?

3. Describe the process used to generate electricity in fossil-fuelled power stations.

4. How is electricity produced from geothermal sources?

EFFICIENCY OF ENERGY TRANSFER

Energy is always conserved – the total amount of energy after the transfer must be the same as the total amount of energy before the transfer. Unfortunately, in nearly all energy transfers some of the energy will end up as 'useless' heat.

EXTENDED

In a power station only some of the energy originally produced from the fuel is transferred to useful electrical output. Energy efficiency can be calculated from the following formula:

$$\text{efficiency} = \frac{\text{useful energy output}}{\text{energy input}} \times 100\%$$

For example, the electric motor that is used to power a train may take in 10 kW of electricity, and give out 9.5 kW of kinetic energy.

The useful energy output is therefore 9.5 kJ and the energy input is 10 kJ.

Using $\text{efficiency} = \dfrac{\text{useful energy output}}{\text{energy input}} \times 100\%$

we find that $\dfrac{9.5}{10} \times 100\% = 95\%$

The other 5% of energy ends up increasing the temperature of the motor and passes to the surrounding air. This energy is wasted, and in fact the motor will need cooling fans to prevent it from overheating.

A diesel engine is more efficient than a petrol engine, and can give out 200 kW of kinetic energy while it is consuming diesel fuel at a rate of 500 kW. This equates to an efficiency of 40. You will note that the engine will have to lose 300 kW of heat, much of it down the exhaust pipe, but it still needs a large radiator as well.

END OF EXTENDED

In a power station, as much as 70% of the energy transfers may not produce useful energy. This would mean that the power station was only 30% efficient.

Scientists are working hard to increase the efficiency of power stations. Many power stations are now trying to make use of the large amounts of energy 'lost' in the hot water. In some cities, the houses of whole regions of the city are heated by hot water from a nearby power station. Some of the most modern fossil-fuelled power stations have had efficiencies nearer to 40%. This may not seem much, but if all power stations in the world could use 25% less fuel, it would save millions of tonnes of coal or gas per year. Combined cycle gas-fired power stations can have efficiencies of almost 50%, whilst combined heat and power installations may be over 70% efficient.

Developing Investigative Skills

A student investigates the efficiency of a small electric motor. She uses a motor to lift a mass through a constant distance of 1 m. She times how long it takes to lift the masses and makes a record of the potential difference and the current of the motor. The student's data is shown in the table.

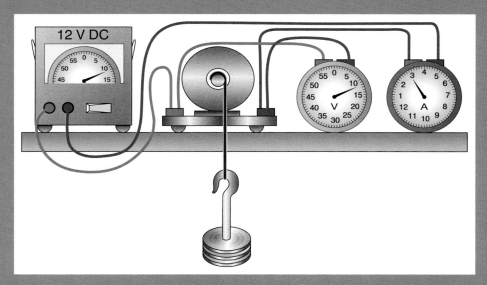

△ Fig. 1.80 Apparatus for the investigation.

Mass lifted/g	Distance lifted/m	Useful work done/J	Voltage of motor/V	Current in motor/A	Time to lift the mass/s	Electrical energy supplied/J
0.01	1.0		2.4	0.20	22.0	
0.03	1.0		2.4	0.22	24.4	
0.05	1.0		2.4	0.25	26.5	
0.07	1.0		2.3	0.28	27.6	
0.09	1.0		2.3	0.29	28.7	

Using and organising techniques, apparatus and materials

❶ What quantities would be measured and what measuring instruments would the student need to measure them for this investigation?

❷ The timer measured to 0.01 s, but the student decided to record values to a precision of 0.1 s. Suggest why she did this. Was the student correct to do this?

Observing, measuring and recording

❸ Copy and complete the table to show the useful energy output and the total energy input. (Take $g = 10$ N/kg.)

❹ Use your data to plot a graph of useful energy out (y-axis) against total energy in (x-axis).

❺ Describe the pattern (if any) shown by the graph.

Planning and evaluating investigations

❻ If you were to take more measurements with this equipment, what value(s) of mass would you choose? Explain your answer.

WORK

Work is done when the application of a force results in movement. Work can only be done when the object or system has energy. When work is done energy is transferred.

Look at Fig. 1.82. In this position the gymnast is not doing any work against his body weight – he is not moving (he will be doing work pumping blood around his body though).

The gymnast in Fig. 1.81 is doing work. He is moving upwards against his weight. Energy is being transferred as he does the work.

△ Fig. 1.81 A gymnast doing work against his own body weight.

△ Fig. 1.82 A gymnast.

Work done is equal to the amount of energy transferred. It can be calculated using the following formula:

work done = force × distance moved in the direction of the force
　　　　　= energy transferred

$$W = F \times d = E$$

Where: W = work done in joules (J)

F = force in newtons (N)

d = distance moved in the direction of the force in metres (m)

E = energy transferred in joules (J)

1 joule of energy (or work) will move a weight of one newton a distance of one metre.

Delta notation

We use the Greek letter Δ (delta) to stand for 'the change in'. For example, ΔE means 'the change in the energy'. When you are using ΔE in an equation, treat them as one symbol meaning 'the change in energy'; so don't even think of separating them.

WORKED EXAMPLES

1. A cyclist pedals along a flat road. He exerts a force of 60 N on the road surface and travels 150 m. Calculate the work done by the cyclist.

Write down the formula: $\qquad W = F \times d$

Substitute the values for F and d: $\qquad W = 60 \times 150$

Work out the answer and write down the unit: $\quad W = 9000$ J

2. A person does 3000 J of work in pushing a supermarket trolley 50 m across a level car park. What force was the person exerting on the trolley?

Write down the formula with F as the subject: $\quad F = W / d$

Substitute the values for W and d: $\qquad F = 3000 / 50$

Work out the answer and write down the unit: $\quad F = 60$ N

When something slows down because of friction, work is done. The kinetic energy of the motion is transferred to heat as the frictional forces slow the object down. For example, if you are riding your bike and you brake, the energy from your motion is converted to heat in the brake blocks.

QUESTIONS

1. Calculate the work done when a 50 N force moves an object 5 m.

2. Calculate the force required to move an object 8 m by transferring 4000 J of energy.

3. Calculate the work done when a force of 40 N moves a block 2 m.

4. How far does an object move when the force on it is 6 N and the work done is 300 J?

5. What force is needed to move a piano a distance of 2 m when the work done is 800 J?

6. EXTENDED The space shuttle uses friction to do work on its motion upon re-entry into the Earth's atmosphere.

△ Fig. 1.83 The space shuttle in orbit.

The shuttle has 8.45×10^{12} J of energy to transfer over an 8000 km flight path. What force is applied by the atmosphere?

7. EXTENDED Use the internet or books to research the shuttle landing and answer the following questions.

a) What happens to the transferred energy?

b) What temperatures are generated by the work being done, and how does this relate to the material used for the underside of the shuttle surface, such as why is it not made from aluminium or iron?

SIMPLE MACHINES

A machine is a device that makes it easier to do work. The law of conservation of energy tells us that no machine can produce *more* work that you put in. Going further, no machine will even produce *the same* amount of work as you put in, since there will always be non-useful energy transfers – efficiency will always be less than 100%.

However, machines are still useful since they can:

● increase the magnitude of the force

● increase the distance that an object (the 'load') moves

● change the direction of a force.

Notice, of course, that no machine can increase the magnitude of the force *and* the distance the load moves.

An example of a simple machine is the **inclined plane**.

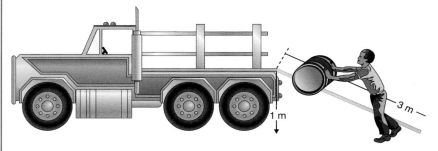

△ Fig. 1.84 An example of an inclined plane.

Suppose the load has a mass of 120 kg, so its weight will be 1200 N. To lift it directly onto the back of the truck, the work required would be:

work done = force × distance moved = 1200 N x 1 m = 1200 J

In pushing the load up the inclined plane (the ramp) the same work must be done altogether since the load ends up in the same place. To find the force required, we can use:

force = work done / distance moved
     = 1200 J / 3 m
     = 400 N

So using the inclined plane has made it three times easier (three times less force) to move the load onto the truck. In reality the force will be more than 400 N because of friction on the ramp, but this is reduced if the load can roll, like a barrel or by putting it on wheels, rather than sliding it.

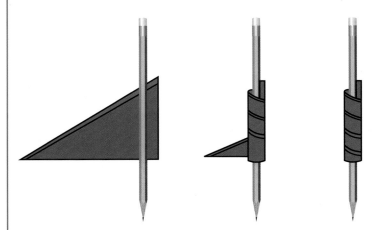

△ Fig. 1.85 Rolling a triangular piece of paper round a pencil.

If you imagine 'rolling' an inclined plane around a cylinder you will make a screw. This is another machine that reduces the force you have to exert – compare the difference in force required to hammer in a nail with screwing in a screw. Of course, the *distance* you have to move is much larger for the screw – you need to turn the screwdriver around a number of times, just like pushing all the way up the ramp – but the *force* you need is much less.

△ Fig. 1.86 A screw and screwdriver

POWER

There are many situations where it is important to know how *quickly* the energy is being transferred – a kettle is no use if it takes 5 hours to deliver the energy to heat some water. For this we need to introduce the concept of **power**.

A powerful engine in a car can take you up a road to the top of a mountain more quickly than a less-powerful engine. Both engines can do the same amount of work, given enough time, but the powerful engine can do the work more quickly. In the same way, a powerful electric motor on a cooling fan will move the air in the room more quickly; and a 'powerfully built' athlete will, by transferring more kinetic energy to it as it is launched, throw a javelin further.

Power is defined as the rate of doing work or the rate of transferring energy. The more powerful a machine is, the quicker it does a fixed amount of work or transfers a fixed amount of energy.

Since power is the rate of doing work or the rate of transferring energy, power can be calculated using the formula:

power = work done / time taken = energy transferred / time taken

$P = W / t$ or $P = E / t$

Where: P = power in joules per second or watts (W)

E = energy transferred in joules (J)

W = work done in joules (J)

t = time taken in seconds (s)

1 watt of power is 1 joule of work being done every second.

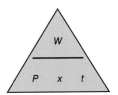

△ Fig. 1.87 the equation triangle for work done, power and time, You can use this triangle to help you rearrange the formula.

WORKED EXAMPLES

1. A crane lifts a 100 kg girder for a skyscraper by 20 m in 40 s. Hence it does 20 000 J of work in 40 s. Calculate its power over this time. Note: this calculation tells you the power of the electric motor that the crane needs.

Write down the formula: $P = W / t$

Substitute the values for W and t: $P = 20\ 000\ /\ 40$

Work out the answer and write down the unit: $P = 500$ W

2. A student with a weight of 600 N runs up the flight of stairs, a distance of 5 m, shown in the diagram (right) in 6 s. Calculate the student's power.

Write down the formula for work done: $W = F\ d$

Substitute the values for F and d: $W = 600 \times 5 = 3000$ J

△ Fig. 1.88 A student running up a flight of stairs.

Write down the formula for power: $P = W / t$

Substitute the values for W and t: $P = 3000\ /\ 6$

Work out the answer and write down the unit:
$P = 500$ W

REMEMBER

The student is lifting his body against the force of gravity, which acts in a vertical direction. The distance measured must be in the direction of the force (that is, the vertical height).

QUESTIONS

1. A man (70 kg) and a boy (35 kg) run up a set of stairs in the same time. Explain why the man is twice as powerful.

2. When a machine is called 'powerful', what does it mean?

3. EXTENDED What is the unit of power?

4. EXTENDED Calculate the power of a motor that transfers 1200 J of energy every 5 s.

5. EXTENDED a) A crane lifts a mass of 60 kg to a height of 5 m. How much work does it do?

   b) The crane takes 1 minute to do this. Calculate the power of the crane.

End of topic checklist

Key terms

(law of) conservation of energy, efficiency, fossil fuel, gravitational potential energy, kinetic energy, non-renewable resource, potential energy, renewable resource, work

During your study of this topic you should have learned:

○ That an object may have energy due to its motion or its position, and energy may be transferred and stored.

○ About examples of energy in different forms, including kinetic, gravitational, chemical, strain, nuclear, internal, electrical, light and sound.

○ EXTENDED That k.e. $= \frac{1}{2}mv^2$ and p.e. $= mgh$.

○ How to disinguish between renewable and non-renewable sources of energy.

○ EXTENDED That energy is released by nuclear fusion in the Sun.

○ That electricity or other useful forms of energy may be obtained from:

  ● chemical energy stored in fuel

  ● water, including the energy stored in waves, in tides, and in water behind hydroelectric dams

  ● geothermal resources

  ● nuclear fission

  ● heat and light from the Sun (solar cells and panels).

○ About the advantages and disadvantages of each method in terms of cost, reliability, scale and environmental impact.

○ About efficiency.

○ EXTENDED That efficiency = useful energy output / energy input × 100%

○ That work done is related to the magnitude of a force and the distance moved.

○ EXTENDED How to describe energy changes in terms of work done.

○ EXTENDED $\Delta W = Fd = \Delta E$

○ That power is related to work done and time taken and be able to give appropriate examples.

○ EXTENDED That $P = E/t$ in simple systems.

End of topic questions

Note: The marks awarded for these questions indicate the level of detail required in the answers. In the examination, the number of marks awarded to questions like these may be different.

1. EXTENDED 50 000 J of work are done as a crane lifts a load of 400 kg. How far did the crane lift the load? (Gravitational field strength, g, is 10 N/kg.) **(3 marks)**

2. EXTENDED A student is carrying out a personal fitness test. She steps on and off the 'step' 200 times. She transfers 30 J of energy each time she steps up. Calculate the energy transferred during the test. **(3 marks)**

3. EXTENDED A child of mass 35 kg climbed a 30 m high snow-covered hill.

   a) Calculate the change in the child's potential gravitational energy. **(3 marks)**
   b) The child then climbed onto a lightweight sledge and slid down the hill. Calculate the child's maximum speed at the bottom of the hill. (Ignore the mass o f the sledge.) **(3 marks)**
   c) Explain why the actual speed at the bottom of the hill is likely to be less than the value calculated in part b. **(3 marks)**

4. EXTENDED Use the relationship between the work done, force and distance to complete the table.

Work done/J	Force/N	Distance/m
	100	2
750		375
9 000	120	
	450	200
3 000		30
60 000	150	

(6 marks)

5. EXTENDED Calculate the potential energy of a piano of mass 300 kg lifted through a vertical height of 9 m. **(3 marks)**

6. EXTENDED Calculate the height climbed up a ladder when the person's mass is 70 kg and the gravitational potential energy gained is 2800 J. **(3 marks)**

7. EXTENDED A 1500 kg helicopter gains potential energy of 1.35 MJ in climbing from the ground. Calculate its height. **(3 marks)**

8. EXTENDED Use the relationship between kinetic energy, mass and velocity to complete the table.

Kinetic energy/J	Mass/kg	Speed/m/s
	84	9
196		1.4
50	1	
	950	13
62 500		250
6000	3000	

(6 marks)

9. EXTENDED What is the kinetic energy of a bird of mass 200 g flying at 6 m/s?

(3 marks)

10. EXTENDED What is the speed of a car of mass 1500 kg with a kinetic energy of 450 kJ?

(3 marks)

11. EXTENDED a) A skateboarder of mass 60 kg is 3.15 m above ground level travelling at 1 m/s. What is his kinetic energy?

(3 marks)

b) What is the gravitational potential energy of the skateboarder in part a)?

(3 marks)

c) What is the total energy (kinetic + gravitational) of the skateboarder in parts a) and b)?

(2 marks)

d) Assuming that no energy is lost in the descent, show that the skateboarder is travelling at about 8 m/s on reaching ground level after the descent down the 3.15 m slope.

(3 marks)

12. a) What is meant by a non-renewable energy source?

(2 marks)

b) Name three non-renewable energy sources.

(2 marks)

c) Which non-renewable energy source is likely to last the longest?

(2 marks)

13. Draw up a table to compare renewable energy resources and non-renewables. Add columns to your table to describe at least one advantage and one disadvantage for each energy resource when it is used to provide large-scale electricity production.

(6 marks)

14. Compare the effects on the environment of coal-fired power stations and nuclear power stations.

a) Which of these power stations releases greenhouse gases?

(1 mark)

b) Which of the fuels used in these power stations, will run out first?

(1 mark)

15. Power stations need to be located on suitable sites. Write down *three* factors that a company may consider before choosing a site for a coal-fired power station.

(3 marks)

16. EXTENDED The input to an electric motor is 5000 J. 1500 J of the output heats the engine and the surrounding air.

  a) How much energy is usefully transferred? (3 marks)

  b) EXTENDED What is the efficiency of the motor? (3 marks)

17. EXTENDED A fan has 50 J input, 30 J used to spin the fan, 15 J output as heat and 5 J as sound. How much energy does it waste? (3 marks)

18. EXTENDED Some energy is useful and some energy is wasted in energy transformations. Copy the table and fill in the gaps.

Object	Input energy/J	Useful energy/J	Wasted energy as heat/J	Efficiency/%
Light bulb	100	10		
Torch	70	55		
Radio	250	210		

(6 marks)

19. EXTENDED State the equation used to calculate efficiency. (2 marks)

20. EXTENDED A crane does 650 J of useful work for every 1000 J of energy put in. What is its efficiency? (3 marks)

21. EXTENDED An engine has 1000 J energy input. It produces 400 J of useful energy. What is its efficiency? (3 marks)

22. EXTENDED 1000 J is put into a device that is 40% efficient. How much energy is wasted? (3 marks)

23. EXTENDED Which is the least efficient of these two engines: a petrol engine that wastes 70 J for every 100 J input, or a steam–diesel hybrid engine that gives 20 J useful energy for every 80 J input? (3 marks)

24. EXTENDED Jumana and Maria went up the hill. Jumana's weight is 500 N and Maria's weight is 450 N. Who did the most work? (3 marks)

25. EXTENDED Explain why, however long you have been sitting writing, you have hardly done any work at all. (3 marks)

26. EXTENDED A man pushes a wheelbarrow up a 5 m long ramp onto a surface 1.6 m higher than his starting level. The weight of the barrow is 300 N.

  a) How much work has been done in raising the barrow 1.6 m? (3 marks)

  b) The force he needed to push the barrow along the ramp is 100 N. How much work did he do? (3 marks)

c) Why are the numbers in parts a and b different? (2 marks)

d) Why are ramps useful? (1 mark)

27. EXTENDED Peter and Paul walk home from school together up a hill. Peter is heavier than Paul.

   a) Who does most work? (2 marks)

   b) Who produces most power? (2 marks)

28. EXTENDED A crane takes 10 s to left a load of 5000 N a distance of 20 m. What is its power? (4 marks)

29. EXTENDED Calculate the work done by a 75 kW tractor in 20 s. (3 marks)

Pressure

△ Fig. 1.89 The skis underneath stop the snowmobile from sinking into deep snow.

INTRODUCTION

A snowmobile can travel over soft snow because its weight is spread over a large area of snow by the skis. If the rider got off and stood on the snow, he would probably sink into it up to his knees, even though he is much lighter than the snowmobile.

If a pair of shoes has narrow (stiletto) heels, the wearer can easily damage a wooden floor by making indentations in it. You can push a drawing pin into a notice board by the pressure your thumb exerts on the sharp end.

In this topic you will find out why these things happen. In each case, the question is not just what force is used, but also what area it is spread over.

KNOWLEDGE CHECK

✓ Know how to calculate areas of regular shapes, such as squares and rectangles.
✓ Know how to calculate the volume of regular objects, such as cubes and cylinders.
✓ Understand the concept of force.

LEARNING OBJECTIVES

✓ Be able to relate (without calculation) pressure to force and area, using appropriate examples.
✓ Be able to describe the simple mercury barometer and its use in measuring atmospheric pressure.
✓ Be able to relate (without calculation) the pressure beneath a liquid surface to depth and to density, using appropriate examples.
✓ Be able to use and describe the use of a manometer.
✓ EXTENDED Recall and use the equation $p = F / A$.
✓ EXTENDED Recall and use the equation $p = h\rho g$.

MEASURING PRESSURE

Pressure is the ratio of force to area. Where we have a large force over a small area we have a high pressure, and a small force over a large area gives us a low pressure.

Pressure is measured in newtons per square metre (N/m^2), usually called pascals (Pa). So 1 Pa = 1 N/m^2.

△ Fig. 1.90 When a drawing pin is placed pin-side down, the pressure on the surface is much greater than when it is placed head-side down.

In order to measure how 'spread out' a force is, use this formula:

pressure = force / area

$$p = F / A$$

Where: p = pressure in pascals, Pa (or newtons per square metre, N/m²)

F = force in newtons, N

A = area in m²

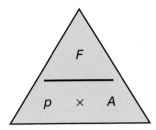

△ Fig. 1.91 the equation triangle for force, pressure and area.

WORKED EXAMPLE

What pressure on the snow does a snowmobile make when it has a weight of 800 N and the runners have an area of 0.2 m²?

Write down the formula: $p = F / A$

Confirm that F is in N and A is in m².

Substitute the values for F and A: $p = 800 / 0.2$

Work out the answer and write down the units: $p = 4000$ Pa or 4 kPa

Note that 4 kPa is a very low pressure. When you stand on the ground in basketball shoes, the pressure on the ground will be around 20 kPa. The wheel of a car generates a pressure on the ground of around 200 kPa. Pressures can be quite high, so the kPa is often used.

QUESTIONS

1. Why can you push a drawing pin into a surface using your thumb when you can't push your thumb into the same surface?

2. EXTENDED Calculate the pressure exerted by a 100 N force acting on an area of 0.2 m².

3. EXTENDED A pressure of 40 Pa is exerted over an area of 2 m². Calculate the force involved.

4. EXTENDED A force of 500 N produces a pressure of 640 Pa. Over what area is the force acting?

Developing Investigative Skills

A student has been reading about how scientists can gain information about the mass of dinosaurs from the depth of their fossilised footprints. He decides to investigate how far a wooden block sinks into sand when the pressure on it changes. The student loads 100 g masses onto the block one at a time (to a maximum of six masses) and measures how deeply the block is pushed into some sand.

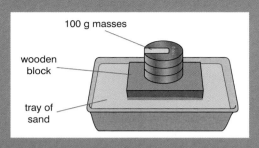

△ Fig. 1.92 Apparatus for the investigation.

The student finds very little evidence of a pattern in his measurements. He feels this is because the block tends to tip over, rather than standing straight, which means that the sand is not equally pushed down. He also feels that the sand does not push down very much anyway – it just gets pushed to the side.

To extend his experiment, the student has an idea about investigating if the 'wetness' of the sand makes a difference to the way the block behaves, but he has not yet devised a plan to test this.

Using and organising techniques, apparatus and materials

❶ Explain how using the block in different ways and using different numbers of 100 g masses allows the student to test a variety of different pressures.

❷ Devise a method to measure the depth to which the block sinks in the sand. You should name any equipment needed. Remember that the block may not sink equally in all directions.

❸ What is the independent variable in this investigation? What is the dependent variable?

Observing, measuring and recording

❹ Use ideas about particles to explain the student's observation that the sand 'just gets pushed to the side'.

Handling experimental observations and data

❺ Suggest how the student could measure the 'wetness' of the sand in a reliable way.

❻ Give an example of a situation where the idea of pressure can be used to explain why an object does not sink into a material such as sand.

PRESSURE IN FLUIDS

Because particles in a liquid or gas (a **fluid**) are constantly in **random motion**, they are constantly colliding with each other and the walls of the container.

This causes a force on the other particles and the container walls. Usually this force is described in terms of the pressure it causes on a particular area. The pressure at a point in a gas or liquid which is at rest acts equally in all directions.

A mercury barometer is a thick-walled glass tube with a height of at least 84 cm, which is closed at one end and has an open mercury-filled reservoir at the base.

The weight of the mercury creates a vacuum in the top of the tube. The height of mercury in the tube adjusts until the weight of the mercury column balances the atmospheric pressure exerted on the reservoir. High atmospheric pressure places more force on the reservoir, forcing mercury higher in the column. Low pressure allows the mercury to drop to a lower level in the column by lowering the force placed on the reservoir.

Torricelli (who is credited with the original design of a barometer in 1643) observed that the height of the mercury in a barometer changed slightly each day and concluded that this was due to the changing atmospheric pressure. He wrote: 'We live submerged at the bottom of an ocean of elementary air, which is known by incontestable experiments to have weight'.

The mercury barometer's design gives rise to the expression of **atmospheric pressure** in inches or millimetres (torr): the pressure is quoted as the level of the mercury's height in the vertical column. 1 atmosphere is equivalent to about 760 mm of mercury.

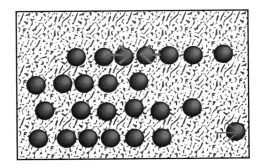

△ Fig. 1.93 The particles in a fluid are constantly colliding with each other and the walls of the container.

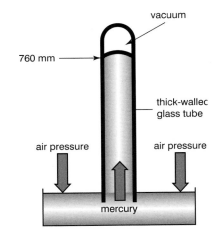

△ Fig. 1.94 A mercury barometer.

ATMOSPHERIC PRESSURE

Because we have spent all of our lives living in the atmosphere of the Earth, we seldom think that we have 20 km or so of air pressing on us. We do not feel the pressure because it does not just push down, it pushes us inwards from all sides. Our lungs do not collapse, because the same air pressure flows into our lungs and presses outwards. It would be a very different story if our lungs did not contain any air and there was a **vacuum** inside them.

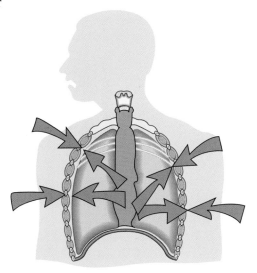

△ Fig. 1. 95 Because the pressure inside is the same as the pressure outside, our lungs do not collapse.

An aluminium soft drink can is filled with 1 tablespoon of water and heated over a Bunsen burner until the water boils, then the can is grasped with tongs, turned upside down, and dipped into a beaker of cold water. The can will collapse almost instantaneously due to the change in air pressure. (See Fig. 1.96.) Boiling the water drives the air out of the can and replaces it with water vapour. When the water vapour condenses, the pressure inside the can is much less than the air pressure outside, causing the can to collapse.

△ Fig. 1.96 Collapsing can experiment.

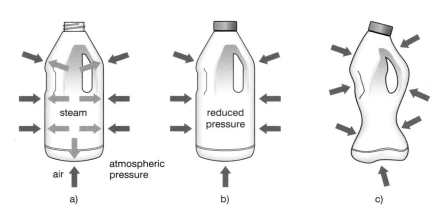

△ Fig. 1.97 How a bottle filled with steam collapses when it cools down.

Similarly, when a plastic bottle has same pressure inside and out as shown in Fig. 1.97a, the bottle will be as normal. If the pressure inside the bottle is reduced, so that the pressure outside is greater, as shown in Fig. 1.97b, then the bottle will start to collapse. If the pressure inside is completely removed, as shown in Fig. 1.97c, then the bottle will collapse.

Atmospheric pressure is approximately 100 kPa. This value is a pure coincidence. In fact it is around 101.3 kPa, though it increases and decreases by 5 per cent or so depending on the weather. But in the same way that we often take g to be 10 m/s² on the Earth when it is more accurately 9.8 m/s², we often choose to take atmospheric pressure to be 100 kPa.

Pressure may also be measured in bars and millibars. Normal atmospheric pressure is approximately 1 bar. The pressure on a scuba diver's cylinder of air can easily be 200 bar. You will see millibars used in some weather forecasts. Atmospheric pressure is approximately 1000 mbar.

PRESSURE DIFFERENCE, HEIGHT AND DENSITY

If you dive below the water, the height of the water above you also puts pressure on you. At a depth of 10 m of water, the pressure has increased by 100 kPa, and for each further 10 m of depth the pressure increases by another 100 kPa. The rapid increase in pressure explains why scuba divers cannot go down more than 20 m without taking extra precautions.

The increase in pressure below the surface of a liquid depends on a) the depth below the surface and b) the density of the liquid. So the pressure will be much higher at a certain depth below the surface of mercury than it is below the surface of water. Note in particular that the pressure does not depend on the area of the water. When a diver goes to inspect a well, the pressure 10 m below the surface is the same as the pressure 10 m below the surface of a large lake. This explains why an engineer who is designing a dam needs to make it the same thickness whether the lake that will be made is going to be 100 m² or 100 km².

Scuba divers breathe compressed air at high pressure to prevent their lungs collapsing due to the high pressure from the water above them. This is a safe sport, but only because first-time divers are trained to a very high standard before they are allowed to dive.

Δ Fig. 1.98 These scuba divers breathe compressed air at high pressure to prevent their lungs collapsing due to the high pressure from the water above them.

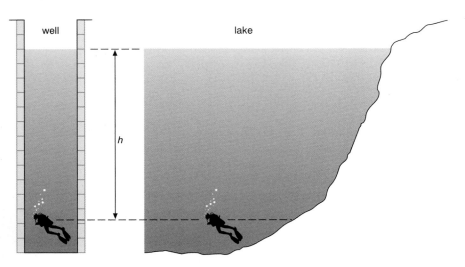

△ Fig. 1.99 The pressure on the diver is the same in the well and in the lake. In both cases it depends only on the density of the liquid and the depth of the diver.

SCIENCE IN CONTEXT **PRESSURE AND SUBMARINES**

Early military submarines had underwater endurance limited by battery capacity, so these submersibles actually spent most of their time on the surface, with hull designs that balanced the need for a relatively streamlined structure with the ability to move on the surface. Late in World War II, the invention of the air-breathing Snort mast meant that longer and faster submerged operations were possible.

△ Fig. 1.100 Submarines have two hulls to withstand the water pressure at depths down to about 300 m.

Submarines actually have two hulls. The external hull, which forms the visible shape of the submarine, is called the casing, which hides external ballast tanks to give buoyancy on the surface, and is free-flooding when dived. It is made of steel only 2 to 4 millimetres thick. The pressure hull, which is inside the casing, is designed to withstand the pressure outside it from the water around the submarine, and has normal atmospheric pressure inside it, which allows the crew of the submarine to breathe normally. The dive depth (the maximum depth at which the submarine can operate) is dependent on the strength of the hull. Submarines used in World War I had hulls made of carbon steel and could not dive below 50 m. In World War II, high-strength alloyed steel was used, and the dive depth increased to 150 m. This is still the main material used today, with a current limit of 450–550 m dive depth. A few submarines have been built with titanium hulls reach 700 m and the US Deep Submergence research Vehicle *Alvin* has dived 4000 m.

The pressure below the surface of a fluid, and in fact between any two points in the fluid, can be calculated by the following equation:

pressure difference = height × density × gravitational field strength

$$p = h \times \rho \times g$$

Where: p = pressure difference in pascals (Pa)

h = height in metres

ρ = density in kilograms per cubic metre (kg/m³)

g = gravitational field strength (N/kg)

Note that the density ρ must be in kg/m³. When it is quoted in g/cm³, you must convert it. Remember that 1 g/cm³ = 1000 kg/m³.

There is one major cause of confusion: the difference between total pressure and additional pressure. Consider the pressure on scuba divers. Before they jump in, the pressure on them is already 100 kPa (or 1 bar). When they have dived down 10 m, the pressure on them increases by 100 kPa, so the total pressure is now 200 kPa (2 bar). The pressure is a combination of 100 kPa from the air above and 100 kPa from the water above them. At 20 m, the total pressure on them is 300 kPa, and so on.

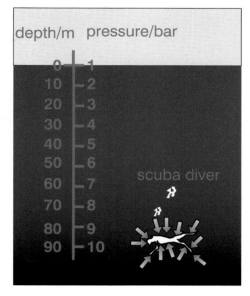

△ Fig. 1.101 How the pressure on a diver varies with depth.

WORKED EXAMPLE

An aquarium has a tunnel through a tank of water at a depth of 5 m below the surface. The manufacturer guarantees the tunnel to a pressure difference of 200 kPa. Is the tunnel safe? (The density of water = 1000 kg/m³.)

Write down the equation: $p = h \times \rho \times g$

Substitute the values into the equation: $p = 5 \times 1000 \times 10$

Work out the answer and write down the unit: $p = 50\,000$ Pa or 50 kPa

The tunnel is safe.

Note that the total pressure on the outside of the tunnel is 50 kPa from the water, plus 100 kPa from the air pushing on top of the water, giving 150 kPa. However, the tunnel is also full of air, which is pushing outwards with a pressure of 100 kPa. So the tunnel only has to withstand a pressure difference of 50 kPa.

QUESTIONS

1. What two factors does the pressure in a fluid depend on?

2. **EXTENDED** Calculate the increase in pressure as you dive from the surface of a lake to a depth of 8 m. (density of water = 1000 kg/m³ and g = 10 N/kg).

3. **EXTENDED** What is the pressure difference at 100 m below sea level? (Density of sea water = 1030 kg/m³)

4. **EXTENDED** What is the pressure on a scuba diver at a depth of 30 m?

5. **EXTENDED** What is the total pressure at the bottom of a column of mercury of height 15 cm? (Density of mercury = 13 600 kg/m³)

Pressure can also be measured using a **manometer**. A simple manometer consists of a U-shaped tube of glass filled with some liquid, which is often mercury because of its high density. The manometer compares the pressure of the gas in each arm of tube.

P_{air} = 740 mm Hg

30 mm

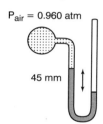
P_{air} = 0.960 atm

45 mm

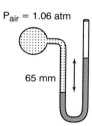
P_{air} = 1.06 atm

65 mm

△ Fig. 1.102 The pressure measured by each of these manometers is different, which is indicated by the difference in height of the liquid between the two tubes shown in each one.

End of topic checklist

Key terms
atmospheric pressure, manometer, pressure, vacuum

During your study of this topic you should have learned:

- ○ That pressure is related to force and area and be able to give appropriate examples.
- ○ About the simple mercury barometer and its use in measuring atmospheric pressure.
- ○ That pressure beneath a liquid surface is related to depth and density and be able to give appropriate examples.
- ○ How to use a manometer.
- ○ EXTENDED That $p = F / A$.
- ○ EXTENDED That $p = h\rho g$.

End of topic questions

Note: The marks awarded for these questions indicate the level of detail required in the answers. In the examination, the number of marks awarded to questions like these may be different.

1. **a)** Calculate the pressure on the floor caused by:

    i) an ordinary shoe heel (person of mass 40 kg, heel 5 cm × 5 cm) when all the person's weight is on one heel   **(2 marks)**

    ii) an elephant (mass 500 kg, area of one foot 300 cm^2) when all four feet are on the ground   **(2 marks)**

    iii) a high-heeled shoe (worn by a person of mass 40 kg, heel area 0.5 cm^2) when all the person's weight is on one heel.   **(2 marks)**

   b) Which of the situations described in part a will damage a wooden floor that starts to yield at a pressure of 4000 kPa?   **(2 marks)**

   (Note: to convert from cm^2 to m^2 you need to divide by 10 000.)

2. The density of fresh water is 1000 kg/m^3. The pressure gauge on a submarine in a river was reading 100 kPa when it was at the surface. A sailor notices that the gauge is now reading 250 kPa. How deep is he? How would this answer change if the sailor were diving in sea water that is slightly denser than fresh water? **(3 marks)**

3. A diver on Saturn's moon Titan is 50 m below the surface of a lake of liquid methane.

   a) What is the increase in pressure on him due to his depth in the methane? The density of liquid methane is 420 kg/m^3. The gravitational field strength on Titan is 1.4 N/kg.   **(2 marks)**

   b) We are told that the pressure of the atmosphere on Titan is 1600 mbar. What is the total pressure on the diver (in kPa)?   **(2 marks)**

4. A skater glides on one skate. The mass of the skater is 65 kg and the area of the skate is 9×10^{-4} m^2. What pressure is exerted on the ice by the skate? **(2 marks)**

5. EXTENDED An oil well is 1500 m deep and is filled with a fluid of density 960 kg/m^3. What is the pressure due to the fluid at the bottom of the well?   **(2 marks)**

6. EXTENDED A diver is exploring a sunken ship and notes that the pressure is 2.96×10^5 Pa at the ship compared to 1.00×10^5 Pa at the surface. Taking the density of water to be 1000 kg/m^3, calculate the depth that the diver is at.   **(3 marks)**

7. **a)** EXTENDED How does the pressure in a liquid depend on the depth of the liquid and the density of the liquid?   **(2 marks)**

   b) A container has an area of 4 m^2 and is filled with water of density 1000 kg/m^3. What is the pressure of the water at a point 0.5 m below the surface?   **(2 marks)**

8. <u>EXTENDED</u> The air pressure at the base of a mountain is 1.01×10^5 Pa. At the top of the mountain, the air pressure is measured at 0.80×10^5 Pa. Given that the density of air is 1.2 kg/m^3, calculate the height of the mountain. **(2 marks)**

9. <u>EXTENDED</u> The density of water in a lake is 1.02×103 kg/m^3. Atmospheric pressure is 1.01×10^5 Pa. What is the total pressure at a depth of 12 m below the surface of the lake? **(2 marks)**

10. <u>EXTENDED</u> A fish is swimming at a depth of 10.4 m in water of density 1.03×10^3 kg/m^3. Calculate the pressure at this depth caused by the water. **(2 marks)**

Exam-style questions

Note: The questions, sample answers and marks in this section have been written by the authors as a guide only. The marks awarded for these questions indicate the level of detail required in the answers. In the examination, the number of marks awarded to questions like these may be different.

Sample student answers

Question 1

The diagram shows a car travelling to the right.

The arrows represent four forces on the car as it moves.

The arrows are **not** drawn to scale.

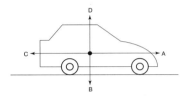

a) i) Which arrow represents the weight of the car?

B ✓ ①   **(1)**

ii) Which arrow represents the driving force acting on the car?

A ✓ ①   **(1)**

b) The horizontal forces on the car are unbalanced.

i) State the equation linking unbalanced force, mass and acceleration.

$F = ma$ ✓ ①   **(1)**

The car accelerates at 2 m/s^2 and it has a mass of 1500 kg.

ii) Calculate the magnitude of the unbalanced force on the car.

$1500 \times 2 = 3000$

Force ✓ ① $= 3000$ N ✓ ①   **(2)**

TEACHER'S COMMENTS

1) a) i) and **ii)** The first two questions are straightforward, recalling and applying simple ideas in a familiar situation. Two marks are awarded.

b) i) and **ii)** The student has handled the mathematical parts of the question correctly.

iii) The student almost certainly knew which direction the force was acting in (forwards) but loses the mark because 'horizontally' has two possibilities – forwards and backwards. This is an easy slip to make, and the student might have noticed the mistake if they had time to check through their answers.

Question 8

Two students want to find the density of clay.

They each have a sample of clay.

a) State the equation linking density, mass and volume. .... **(1)**

The students suggest different methods to find the volume of their sample of clay.

b) The first student shapes his sample of clay into a regular cube shape.

Then he measures the length of the sides.

He finds the volume by doing a calculation with his measurements.

  i) How should the student choose his equipment to make his measurement of
    volume as precise as possible? .... **(2)**

  ii) Describe a feature of this method that may lead to inaccurate results. .... **(1)**

c) The second student decides to find the volume of her sample of clay using a
measuring cylinder. Describe how she should do this. .... **(4)**

d) Describe how the students can use an electronic balance to find the mass of their
samples of clay. .... **(1)**

  i) If the electronic balance is incorrectly calibrated, how will this affect their
    measurements? .... **(1)**

  ii) How could the students check the calibration of the electronic balance? .... **(2)**

(Total 12 marks)

Most things in the world are either a solid, a liquid or a gas. These are the three main states of matter. Substances can change from a solid to a liquid in a process called melting, and from liquid to gas in a process called evaporation. Gases change to liquids by condensation and liquids change to solids in solidification.

You are probably most familiar with these changes for water. It is possible for the states to exist at the same time: for example, there is a temperature at which ice, water and steam are all present. This is called the triple point of water and is used to define the kelvin scale of temperature, which you will meet later in this section.

STARTING POINTS

1. Describe how particles are arranged in: a) a solid; b) a liquid; and c) a gas.

2. What happens to the particles when a solid melts?

3. Explain what happens when a solid dissolves in a liquid.

4. Are evaporation and boiling the same thing? Give a reason for your answer.

5. What happens to the speed of gas molecules as temperature increases?

CONTENTS

a) Simple kinetic molecular model of matter

b) Thermal properties

c) Transfer of thermal energy

d) Exam-style questions

2
Thermal physics

△ Water exists as a solid, a liquid and a gas in the world around us.

Simple kinetic molecular model of matter

△ Fig. 2.1 Water in all three states of matter.

INTRODUCTION

Almost all matter can be classified as a solid, a liquid or a gas. These are called the three states of matter.

The fourth state of matter is called 'plasma'. It only exists at high temperatures seldom seen on Earth, so we won't consider it further here, even though most of the matter in the Universe and most stars are made of plasma.

KNOWLEDGE CHECK

✓ Know what happens when you heat a solid, liquid or gas.
✓ Know what happens when you cool down a solid, liquid or gas.
✓ Know that matter is made of tiny particles called atoms.
✓ Know how to define and calculate pressure.
✓ Know some everyday properties of gases – for example that they expand when heated and they exert a pressure on container walls.

LEARNING OBJECTIVES

✓ State the distinguishing properties of solids, liquids and gases.
✓ Be able to describe qualitatively the molecular structure of solids, liquids and gases.
✓ Be able to interpret the temperature of a gas in terms of the motion of its molecules.
✓ Be able to describe qualitatively the pressure of a gas in terms of the motion of its molecules.
✓ Be able to describe qualitatively the effect of a change of temperature on the pressure of a gas at constant volume.
✓ Show an understanding of the random motion of particles in a suspension as evidence for the kinetic molecular model of matter.
✓ Be able to describe this motion (sometimes known as Brownian motion) in terms of random molecular bombardment.
✓ EXTENDED Relate the properties of solids, liquids and gases to the forces and distances between molecules and to the motion of the molecules.
✓ EXTENDED Show an appreciation that massive particles may be moved by light, fast-moving molecules.
✓ Be able to describe evaporation in terms of the escape of more-energetic molecules from the surface of a liquid.
✓ Relate evaporation to consequent cooling of the liquid.
✓ EXTENDED Demonstrate an understanding of how temperature, surface area and draught over a surface influence evaporation.

✓ Relate the change in volume of a gas to change in pressure applied to the gas at constant temperature.

✓ EXTENDED Recall and use the equation pV = constant at constant temperature.

STATES OF MATTER

The three states of matter each have different properties:

- A solid has a fixed volume and shape, is not easily compressed (squashed) and does not flow easily.
- A liquid assumes the shape of the part of the container that it occupies, usually occupying the lowest level, is not easily compressed and flows easily.
- A gas assumes the shape and volume of its container, occupying the whole volume, can be compressed and flows easily.

MOLECULAR MODEL

In this topic, these properties of matter are explained in terms of the molecular structure of the three states.

◁ Fig. 2.2 The main body of this rocket is filled with liquid oxygen and liquid hydrogen, which have to be kept at extremely low temperatures to prevent them from heating up and turning back into gas. If the fuel were made colder it would turn into a solid.

△ Fig. 2.3 The molten iron can be poured into a mould before it cools down and turns back into a solid.

We now know that all materials are made of tiny particles called **atoms** that can attract each other. The atoms in a solid are locked together by the forces between them. However, even in a solid, the particles are not completely still. They vibrate constantly about their fixed positions. When the material is heated, it is given more internal energy, and the particles vibrate faster and further.

When the temperature is increased more, the vibrations of the particles increase to the point at which the forces are no longer strong enough to hold the structure together in the rigid order of a solid. The forces can no longer prevent the atoms moving around, but they do prevent them from flying apart from each other. This is what makes a liquid. The volume of the liquid is the volume occupied by the particles from which it is made.

When the temperature is increased even more, then the particles do fly apart. They now form a gas. The particles fly around at high speed – several hundred kilometres per hour. If they are in a container, they travel all over it, bouncing off the walls. The volume of a gas is not fixed; it just depends on the size of the container that the gas is put into. We use the **kinetic molecular model** to explain the behaviour of solids, liquids and gases. Table 2.1 summarises this model.

	Solid	Liquid	Gas
Arrangement of particles	Regular pattern, closely packed together, particles held in place	Irregular, closely packed together, particles able to move past each other	Irregular, widely spaced, particles able to move freely
Diagram			
Motion of particles	Vibrate in place within the structure	'Slide' over each other in a random motion	Random motion, faster movement than the other states

△ Table 2.1 The kinetic molecular model of matter.

The kinetic molecular model uses this idea that all materials are made up of atoms that behave rather like tiny balls. When the model is used to try to explain the behaviour of gases it is often called the **kinetic theory of gases**.

EXTENDED

The arrangement of atoms can be used to explain the properties of solids, liquids and gases that you met earlier.

Solids:

- retain a fixed shape and volume because the particles are locked into place in the lattice
- are not easily compressed because there is little free space between the particles
- do not flow easily because the particles cannot move/slide past one another.

Liquids:

- assume the shape of the part of the container that they occupy because the particles can move/slide past one another
- are not easily compressed because there is little free space between the particles
- flow easily because the particles can move/slide past one another.

Gases:

- assume the shape and volume of their container because the particles move past one another continuously
- are compressible because there is lots of free space between the particles
- flow easily because the particles can move past one another.

END OF EXTENDED

QUESTIONS

1. What happens to the motion of atoms as the temperature increases?

2. Explain why it is easier to compress a gas than a liquid.

3. Describe the arrangement of particles in: a) a solid; b) a liquid; c) a gas.

4. What does the volume of a gas depend on?

What are molecules?

In Table 2.1, you can see that the particles in the liquid and the gas consist of single atoms. There are materials like this – elements such as helium and neon. In most materials, though, the particles that move around in the liquid or the gaseous state are groups of atoms called **molecules**. A water molecule is H_2O and a nitrogen molecule is N_2. This means that the particles moving around in liquid or gaseous water each consist of two hydrogen atoms and one oxygen atom. In liquid nitrogen or in nitrogen gas, the particles each consist of two nitrogen atoms.

Taking the idea of particles one step further, you can start to apply your knowledge of forces and motion to the molecules of a gas. This step is building up a theory – the kinetic theory of gases – to see if the predictions that come from our ideas match what happens when we experiment with gases.

△ Fig. 2.4 This balloon rises because the gas inside it is less dense than the surrounding area.

It is quite a simple theory to begin with. We only look at gases where the particles are generally separated from each other and the maths is not too difficult. However, the ideas have proved to be remarkably successful in describing the behaviour of materials.

The kinetic theory of gases build ups a set of ideas from the basic idea that a gas is made of many tiny particles called molecules. These ideas give a picture of what happens inside a gas (Table 2.2).

Observed feature of a gas	Related ideas from the kinetic theory
Gases have a mass that can be measured	The total mass of a gas is the sum of the masses of the individual molecules.
Gases have a temperature that can be measured	The individual molecules are always moving. The faster they move (the more kinetic energy they have), the higher the temperature of the gas.
Gases have a pressure that can be measured	When the molecules hit the walls of the container they exert a force on it. It is this force, divided by the surface area of the container, that we observe when measuring pressure.
Gases have a volume that can be measured	Although the volume of each molecule is only tiny, they are always moving about and spread out throughout the container.
Temperature has an absolute zero	As the temperature falls, the speed of the molecules (and their kinetic energy) becomes less. At absolute zero the molecules would have stopped moving.

△ Table 2.2 What happens inside a gas.

These ideas help to explain Boyle's law.

Boyle's law states that when the temperature of the gas stays constant, the volume of the gas is inversely proportional to the pressure. The link to kinetic theory is as follows. The temperature stays constant, so the average speed of the molecules stays constant. If the volume of the gas is reduced by half, then the molecules make the same number of collisions with half the surface area of wall, so the pressure (= force/area) must be doubled. This is **inverse proportionality.**

Gases only follow Boyle's law if the mass of the gas remains constant (that is, no particles move in or out of the system) and the gases are ideal, that is they do not liquefy or solidify.

QUESTIONS

1. How does the kinetic theory explain the measurable volume of a gas?

2. A fixed mass of gas is at a constant temperature. What happens to the volume when you increase the pressure?

3. What conditions must be met for gases to follow Boyle's law

Brownian motion

Evidence for the molecular model of matter comes from observations such as **Brownian motion**. When viewed under a microscope, small particles (such as pollen grains or fine smoke particles) can be seen moving in a random way. The explanation is that the particles are constantly being hit by even smaller particles, which are too small to see (such as water molecules or air molecules).

EXTENDED Massive particles may be moved by light, fast-moving particles.

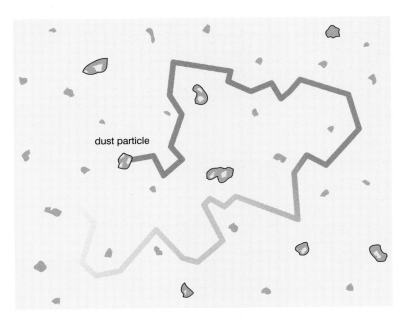

△ Fig. 2.5 Brownian motion as seen in dust particles.

Molecules in a gas

The molecular model says that the pressure on the walls of a container is caused by the collisions made by the speeding gas molecules. You can feel this pressure if you try to hold a bicycle pump in the pushed-in position while blocking the air outlet with your finger as shown in Fig. 2.6. (If the pump is broken and allows the air to escape, this does not work.)

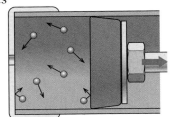

△ Fig. 2.6 The molecules of the gas are colliding with the piston and trying to push it out.

In Fig. 2.6 the piston is not moving. However, there is a force trying to push it out. It is clear that if the molecules travel faster then they will hit the piston in the pump more often and harder. The pressure on the piston and on the walls will go up. This is exactly what will happen when the air gets hotter.

Note that the molecules will also hit each other as well as the walls of the container. At normal pressures they travel a lot less than 1 mm between collisions. This does not affect the way that the model works.

◁ Fig. 2.7 The inner tube from a tyre has been pumped up with air to use as a toboggan. It is the pressure caused by the movement of the air molecules that keeps it inflated. Because the temperature is low, the inner tube will need a lot of air to provide a high enough pressure. On a hot day this tube could burst.

QUESTIONS

1. What is Brownian motion?

2. How does the kinetic theory explain Brownian motion?

3. How does the model explain pressure on the walls of a container?

4. Why does the pressure in a pump increase when the molecules move faster?

EVAPORATION

When particles break away from the surface of a liquid and form a **vapour**, this is known as **evaporation**. The more energetic molecules of the liquid escape from the surface as shown in Fig. 2.8. This reduces the average energy of the molecules remaining in the liquid, and so the temperature of the liquid falls.

Therefore, evaporation causes cooling. The evaporation of sweat helps to keep your body cool in hot weather. The cooling in a refrigerator is also due to evaporation of a special liquid inside the freezing compartment at the top of the refrigerator. The vapour is collected and compressed back into liquid inside the condenser behind the refrigerator. The liquid is circulated by a pump and recycled.

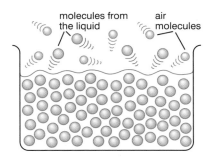

△ Fig. 2.8 Evaporation.

The rate of evaporation is increased at higher temperatures. It is also increased by a strong flow of air across the surface of the liquid, as in this way the evaporating molecules are carried away quickly. A certain amount of water will also evaporate more quickly when you increase its surface area. Tea or coffee in a shallow, wide cup cools down much more quickly than in a tall, narrow mug because the large surface area of the cup allows more evaporation.

Imagine you are a particle that has experienced evaporation. Write a letter to your friend describing the experience. Your letter should answer the following questions.

1. What change of state did you go through?

2. How close to your neighbours were you in your original state?

3. What was given to you to make you change state?

4. How did you change state?

QUESTIONS

1. What factors increase the rate of evaporation?

2. Why does tea in a narrow mug cool down more slowly than tea in a wide mug?

PRESSURE CHANGES

Pressure and volume

When the piston of a bicycle pump is pushed in with the air outlet blocked, then the more you push it in, the harder and harder it gets to push it further. This is because the pressure in the container goes up.

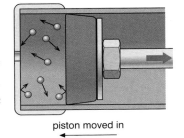

piston moved in

△ Fig. 2.9 The pressure increases when the volume is reduced.

The molecular model says that there is the same number of molecules in the container travelling at the same speed. However, because the molecules are now packed in more densely, there will be more collisions with the walls (and with the piston) per second. When the volume is halved, then the number of collisions per second with the walls and with the piston will double, and the pressure on the piston will double. This law is often called Boyle's law. It only applies when the temperature of the air does not change.

A fixed amount of gas in a sealed container at constant temperature obeys the following equation:

pressure × volume = constant

$$pV = \text{constant}$$

Where: p = pressure in Pa (or N/m²)

V = volume in m³

Pascals and newtons per square metre are the same thing. When using this equation, you can use whichever units you like so long as you continue to use the same ones.

The constant will be a constant for a particular sample of gas in a particular container. So, in an experiment (or an exam question) you can write that the initial values of pressure and volume multiplied together, $p_1 \times V_1$ are constant.

The final values of pressure and volume multiplied together, $p_2 \times V_2$, are also constant.

This is the same constant in both cases. So:

$p_1 V_1 = \text{constant} = p_2 V_2$

or

$p_1 V_1 = p_2 V_2$

This equation, representing Boyle's law, only applies if the temperature stays constant.

WORKED EXAMPLE

A bicycle pump contains 400 cm³ of air at atmospheric pressure. The air is compressed slowly. What is the pressure when the volume of the air is compressed to 125 cm³? What would happen to the pressure if the air were compressed quickly? (Remember that atmospheric pressure = 100 kPa.)

Write down equation: $\qquad\qquad\qquad p_1 V_1 = p_2 V_2$

Substitute values into the equation: $100 \times 400 = p_2 \times 125$

$$p_2 \times 125 = 40\,000$$

Rearrange the equation to find p_2: $p_2 = 40\,000 / 125$

Work out the answer and write down the unit: $p_2 = 320$ kPa

If the air were compressed quickly, it would also heat up to a higher temperature. This would mean that the final pressure will be greater than 320 kPa. Because the temperature had changed, $p_1 V_1 = p_2 V_2$ could not then be used.

END OF EXTENDED

QUESTIONS

1. Describe the link between the pressure of a gas and its volume at constant temperature (this is Boyle's law).

2. What factors must remain constant for the law to apply?

3. EXTENDED An aerosol has a volume of 150 cm³. It contains gas at a pressure of 350 kPa. When the temperature stays constant, what will be the volume of gas if it is allowed to expand at a pressure of 101 kPa?

ABSOLUTE ZERO AND THE KELVIN SCALE OF TEMPERATURE

As a gas is cooled down, its molecules have less energy and move round more slowly. If you kept cooling the gas down, it would eventually reach a temperature so low that all movement of the molecules would have stopped. This temperature is the lowest that can be reached. It is known as **absolute zero**, and it has been shown to be at a temperature of −273 °C. There can be no lower temperature, as clearly the molecules cannot do less than not move!

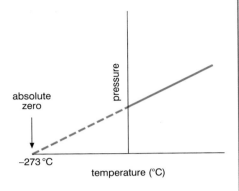

△ Fig. 2.10 Absolute zero is the lowest possible temperature.

Because there is an absolute zero, a system of measuring temperature has been set up in which the temperature at absolute zero is given the number 0. All other temperatures are then higher than this. The steps are the same size as in the Celsius scale: you have to go up 273 degrees to reach the melting point of ice, and another 100 degrees to reach the boiling point of water. This scale is known as the kelvin scale of temperature.

Table 2.3 shows how the two temperature scales work.

Scale	Absolute zero	Melting point of ice	Boiling point of water	Melting point of gold
Celsius (°C)	−273	0	100	1064
kelvin (K)	0	273	373	1337

△ Table 2.3 The Celsius and kelvin scales compared.

- To convert a temperature in degrees Celsius to kelvin, you add 273.

- To convert a temperature in kelvin to degrees Celsius, you subtract 273.

Note that the unit for the Celsius scale is always called 'degree Celsius' and written as °C, though you will sometimes see 'deg C'. The unit for the kelvin scale is kelvin and is always written as K.

SIMPLE KINETIC MOLECULAR MODEL OF MATTER

End of topic checklist

Key terms

absolute zero, Boyle's law, Brownian motion, Charles' law, evaporation, kelvin scale, kinetic molecular model, kinetic theory of gases, pressure law, vapour

During your study of this topic you should have learned:

○ About the distinguishing properties of solids, liquids and gases.

○ About the molecular structure of solids, liquids and gases.

○ **EXTENDED** How the motion of particles and the forces and distances between them relate to their properties.

○ How temperature affects the way gases behave.

○ How pressure affects the way gases behave.

○ About the effect of a change in temperature on the pressure of a gas at constant volume.

○ That the random motion of particles in a suspension gives evidence for the kinetic molecular model of matter.

○ About Brownian motion in terms of random molecular bombardment.

○ That massive particles may be moved by light, fast-moving molecules.

○ How evaporation can be described in terms of escape of more-energetic molecules from the surface of a liquid.

○ How evaporation is related to the consequent cooling of a liquid.

○ **EXTENDED** That evaporation is affected by temperature, surface area and draught over a surface.

○ How a change in the volume of a gas is related to a change in pressure applied to the gas at constant temperature.

○ **EXTENDED** To use the equation pV = constant at constant temperature.

End of topic questions

Note: The marks awarded for these questions indicate the level of detail required in the answers. In the examination, the number of marks awarded to questions like these may be different.

1. Give an example of a material for each state of matter that demonstrates the properties of that state. **(3 marks)**

2. Use ideas about particles to explain why:

   a) solids keep their shape, but liquids and gases don't **(3 marks)**

   b) solids and liquids have a fixed volume, but gases fill their container. **(3 marks)**

3. How does kinetic theory explain the existence of absolute zero? **(3 marks)**

4. Use the kinetic molecular model to explain the following observations in detail:

   a) It is possible to keep a bottle of drink cold by standing it in a bowl and covering it with a wet cloth. **(3 marks)**

   b) EXTENDED The drink gets even colder when you place the bowl in a strong draught. **(3 marks)**

5. How is the speed of a gas molecule linked to the temperature of the gas? **(2 marks)**

6. How does the kinetic theory explain the fact that gases exert a pressure on their container? **(2 marks)**

7. EXTENDED A student blows up a balloon. At room temperature, 20 °C, she measures the volume of the balloon as 1500 cm^3. Then she puts the balloon in a freezer where the temperature is −13 °C. Assuming the pressure stays constant, work out the new volume of the balloon. **(3 marks)**

8. EXTENDED A sample of gas is sealed in a 20 cm^3 metal container at a pressure of 1×10^5 Pa. Calculate the new pressure of the gas when the metal container is slowly crushed to a volume of 5 cm^3 with the same temperature. **(3 marks)**

End of topic questions continued

9. **EXTENDED** The volume of a cylinder is 0.05 m³. 1.4 m³ of air at atmospheric pressure (1×10^5 Pa) is pumped into the tyre. What is the pressure in the cylinder? Assume that the temperature remains constant.

   (3 marks)

10. **EXTENDED** A gas cylinder contains gas at a pressure of 1.5×10^6 Pa. What volume of gas would be released from the cylinder at a pressure of 1×10^5 Pa? (Hint: remember that some of the gas will remain in the cylinder.) Assume the temperature does not change.

    (3 marks)

11. **EXTENDED** The correct pressure in a tyre should be 2.4×10^5 Pa. A driver has checked the pressure and it is 1.5×10^5 Pa. What volume of air at atmospheric pressure (1×10^5 Pa) should the driver pump into the tyre to increase it to the correct pressure? The volume of the tyre is 0.013 m³.

    (4 marks)

12. **EXTENDED** A cylinder with a volume of 0.17 m³ containing 20 kg of compressed air is stored at a temperature of 7 °C. The pressure of the gas in the cylinder is 950 kPa. The compressed air is used in a process in which the air at a temperature of 7 °C has to be supplied from the cylinder at a pressure of 150 kPa and at a rate of 1000 cm³ per minute.

    a) What volume would the gas occupy at a pressure of 150 kPa at 7 °C?   **(3 marks)**

    b) What volume of air can one cylinder supply to the process?   **(1 mark)**

    c) For what length of time can one cylinder supply the process?   **(3 marks)**

Thermal properties

INTRODUCTION

Some things expand when they are heated. In this topic you will find out why. You will also find out how thermometers work, and learn what happens at the molecular level when there is a change of state.

You will also find out how the expansion of different materials can be used to measure temperature.

△ Fig. 2.11 This expansion joint on a bridge stops the bridge from buckling when it expands in hot weather.

KNOWLEDGE CHECK

✓ Know the kinetic model for the states of matter.
✓ Know the equation energy $= mc\Delta T$
✓ Know thermal capacity $= mc$

LEARNING OBJECTIVES

✓ Be able to describe qualitatively the thermal expansion of solids, liquids and gases.
✓ **EXTENDED** Show an appreciation of the relative order of magnitude of the expansion of solids, liquids and gases.
✓ Be able to identify and explain some of the everyday applications and consequences of thermal expansion.
✓ Be able to describe qualitatively the effect of a change of temperature on the volume of a gas at constant pressure.
✓ Appreciate how a physical property that varies with temperature may be used for the measurement of temperature, and state examples of such properties.
✓ **EXTENDED** Demonstrate understanding of sensitivity, range and linearity.
✓ Recognise the need for and identify fixed points.
✓ Be able to describe the structure and action of liquid-in-glass thermometers.
✓ **EXTENDED** Be able to describe the structure of a thermocouple and show understanding of its use for measuring high temperatures and those that vary rapidly.
✓ Relate a rise in temperature of a body to an increase in internal energy.
✓ **EXTENDED** Be able to describe an experiment to measure the specific heat capacity of a substance.
✓ Show an understanding of the term 'thermal capacity'.
✓ Be able to describe melting and boiling in terms of energy input without a change in temperature.
✓ **EXTENDED** Distinguish between boiling and evaporation.
✓ State the meaning of melting and boiling point.

✓ Be able to describe condensation and solidification.
✓ **EXTENDED** Be able to use the terms 'latent heat of vaporisation' and 'latent heat of fusion' and give a molecular interpretation of latent heat.
✓ **EXTENDED** Be able to describe an experiment to measure specific latent heat for steam and for ice.

THERMAL EXPANSION OF SOLIDS, LIQUIDS AND GASES

With only two or three exceptions, all materials (solids, liquids and gases) expand as they become warmer. In the case of solids, the atoms vibrate more as the temperature goes up. So, even though they stay joined together, they move slightly further apart, and the solid expands a little in all directions.

The effect is small but not trivial. A metre rule that is heated from 0 °C to 100 °C (from the freezing point of water to its boiling point) will increase in length by 1–2 mm depending on what material it is made of. Some plastics do not make good metre rules as they get up to 10 mm longer when heated.

On a hot day, a 1000 km railway track can possibly become more than 300 m longer. In the case of a track that has joints, there is a gap of a few millimetres every 20 m, to allow the rails to expand. Modern long welded tracks have no expansion gaps of this type, although as can be seen from the photo in Fig. 2.12 the track has to be held extremely firmly to stop it moving. This track is on a curve, so it will try to bend sideways to the left when it gets hot.

Liquids expand for the same reason. The atoms vibrate as they move around, and get slightly further apart. This means that the volume of liquids increase as the temperature increases.

It is very difficult to restrict the thermal expansion of solids and liquids, as very large forces will be created in the material if it is not allowed to expand. So, for example, a large bridge is always built with expansion joints to allow it to get longer on a hot day (Fig. 2.13).

Δ Fig. 2.12 This track has to be held very firmly to stop it from bending sideways when it gets hot.

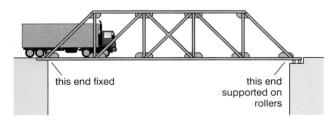

Δ Fig. 2.13 Expansion joints on a bridge.

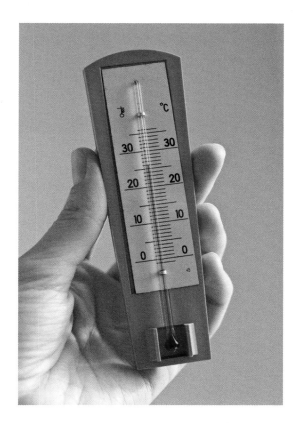

◁ Fig. 2.14 This thermometer has a bulb of coloured alcohol at the base, attached to a very narrow tube that is half full of alcohol (ethanol). As the alcohol expands and contracts with change in temperature, the length of the column of alcohol goes up and down. The top of the tube is sealed off to prevent the alcohol from evaporating.

However, the effect of expanding metal can also be useful. Metals expand at different rates as their temperatures rise. So when strips of two metals are bound closely together, and are warmed, they bend as one metal expands more than the other. **Bimetallic strips** like this can be used to control the temperature in a heating system such as an electric iron.

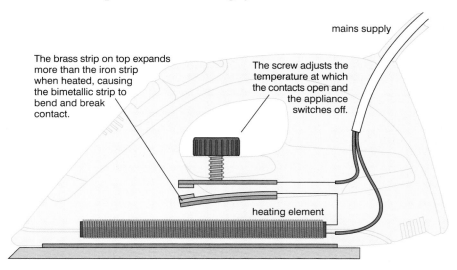

The brass strip on top expands more than the iron strip when heated, causing the bimetallic strip to bend and break contact.

The screw adjusts the temperature at which the contacts open and the appliance switches off.

mains supply

heating element

△ Fig. 2.15 The temperature control mechanism in an electric iron.

Like other liquids, water contracts as its temperature falls and its density increases. Unlike other liquids, when its temperature falls below 4 °C, water begins to expand again, and becomes less dense. This is called the anomalous expansion of water.

The density falls even further as it freezes, because the water molecules form an open crystal structure in the solid state. So ice is less dense than water, while almost all other materials are more dense in the solid state than as a liquid.

REMEMBER

The properties of water are very strange. Not only does it require a great deal of heat to change its temperature, it is also unique in that it expands as it freezes. This makes ice less dense than liquid water, so ice floats on water (as the *Titanic* found out). This has been vital to evolution – life can survive at the bottom of ponds, where in very cold weather the water stays liquid, even when the surface has frozen.

Gases behave completely differently. Firstly, there is no need to allow the gas to expand if it gets hotter; if you put it in a sealed container, then you can just allow the pressure to increase instead.

EXTENDED

Secondly, if a gas is allowed to expand, then it will increase in volume much more than solids or liquids do as it gets hotter. Between 0 °C and 100 °C it will expand by a third, so 300 cm³ of gas will become 400 cm³.

END OF EXTENDED

In Fig. 2.16 the piston compresses the gas with a constant force so that the pressure of the gas is constant. You know from the molecular model that the piston is supported by the collisions of the molecules with the underside of the piston. If the temperature of the gas increases, the pressure starts to increase because the molecules travel faster, and they hit the piston harder. The piston starts to move up. It stops moving up when the pressure has dropped to the original value.

gas at low temperature

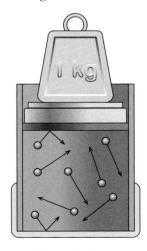
gas at high temperature

Δ Fig. 2.16 The piston compresses the gas. As the gas is heated, the pressure increases and the piston moves up until the pressure returns to the original value.

The result is that the gas has been heated and its volume allowed to increase at constant pressure. Note that initially the pressure was caused by many molecules hitting the piston at moderate speeds. After the gas has heated up and expanded, the same pressure is now caused by the same number of molecules hitting the piston less frequently (because they are more spread out), but the molecules are moving faster. Each molecular collision produces a greater change of momentum and a bigger force.

EXTENDED Gases expand more than liquids, which expand more than solids.

QUESTIONS

1. Why do bimetallic strips bend?

2. Explain why a solid expands when it is heated.

3. What is the anomalous expansion of water?

4. How does the behaviour of gases differ from that of solids and liquids?

MEASUREMENT OF TEMPERATURE

Many everyday applications require you to be able to measure temperature accurately. In this part of the topic we will consider some ways of doing this.

Temperature can be measured using any suitable physical property that changes with temperature. Common examples in use include:

• volume of a liquid – mercury-in-glass or alcohol-in-glass thermometer
• length of a solid – bimetallic strip in a thermostat.

Many other properties are also used:

• the pressure of a fixed volume of gas
• the electrical resistance of a platinum wire
• the electromotive force (e.m.f.) generated by a thermocouple, etc.

All thermometers need calibrating before they are first used. In the case of a liquid-in-glass thermometer, this means that a scale must be fixed to it in the right place. To do this, two fixed points are needed. This type of thermometer has a bulb of the liquid (such as mercury or coloured alcohol) at the base attached to a very narrow tube that is half-full of the liquid. As the liquid expands and contracts with change in temperature, the length of the column of liquid goes up and down. The top of the tube is sealed off (Fig. 2.17).

The Celsius scale is used in science, although other scales are used elsewhere. The two fixed points used by the Celsius scale,

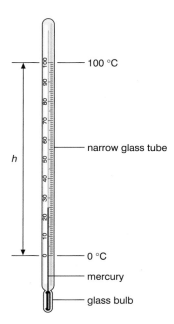

△ Fig. 2.17 A mercury-in-glass thermometer.

as originally defined, are the melting point of ice, defined as 0 °C, and the boiling point of water at standard atmospheric pressure, defined as 100 °C. (At lower pressures water boils at a lower temperature.)

To calibrate the mercury-in-glass thermometer at these two fixed points, the thermometer is immersed first in a funnel containing melting ice, and the 0 °C point is marked. It is then immersed in the steam from a boiling kettle and the 100 °C point is marked. Finally, the distance between the marks (distance h in Fig. 2.17) is divided into 100 equal distances, each corresponding to 1 degree Celsius. The scale can be extended beyond 100 °C to measure higher temperatures, and below 0 °C to measure negative temperatures.

Sensitivity, range and linearity

To measure temperature, you need a thermometer using a property that varies in a regular way over a suitable range of temperatures.

Sensitivity

A thermometer is **sensitive** when it gives a large response to a small change in temperature. This gives you a better chance of detecting a small temperature change.

Range

Different thermometers can read different ranges of temperatures. Mercury freezes at −39 °C, so would be of no use in the Antarctic. There you would need to use alcohol, which doesn't freeze until it gets down to −114 °C. Likewise, a thermometer filled with alcohol would be no use for measuring temperatures in an oven, as the alcohol would boil when the temperature reached 78 °C.

Linearity

When a thermometer is calibrated it is common to mark the freezing point (0 °C) and the boiling point (100 °C) and to divide the region between them into 100 equal parts. This assumes that the property used for measuring changes by the same amount for every unit of temperature change. This property means that the thermometer has **linearity**.

Accuracy

An **accurate** thermometer gives correct values of temperature. Students sometimes get confused between the terms 'sensitive' and 'accurate'. However, a sensitive thermometer is not necessarily an accurate one. A sensitive thermometer is one that can detect small changes in temperature, but if the scale has been incorrectly marked, or if the measuring property varies in a noticeably non-linear manner, then the readings from this sensitive thermometer will not be accurate. Try to avoid using the word *accurate* in places where you mean *sensitive*.

The thermocouple

The **thermocouple** is an electrical thermometer that is the most common type used in industry. As it is electrical it can be read on a remote dial. It can measure temperatures of over 1000 °C and it is cheap to make. This makes it ideal for measuring the temperature of the inner parts of a jet engine, which are hard to get at, and for measuring the temperature of molten steel.

Another major advantage of the thermocouple is that it can be made very small, which means that it responds very quickly to a change in temperature; it can be made to respond in less than 1 second.

The thermocouple is based on the fact that any two metals in contact generate a tiny voltage (actually a tiny e.m.f.; see section 4). In order to measure this voltage with a voltmeter, the two metals need to form a circuit, which, means that there must be two junctions (see Fig. 2.18). When the junctions are at the same temperature there will be no voltage, because the two voltages will cancel out; but when the junctions are at different temperatures, the difference between the two voltages can be measured with a voltmeter. One junction is placed at the point where the temperature is to be measured. The other junction is kept at room temperature, or for accurate work it is placed in a beaker of melting ice to take it to 0 °C.

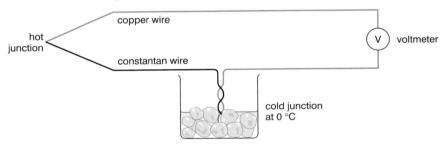

△ Fig. 2.18 A thermocouple.

Tables of data are available to show what voltage corresponds to what temperature.

In practice, many different metals are used in thermocouples, but the two metals often chosen are copper and an alloy called constantan. The junctions are made by twisting the wires tightly together.

An oil refinery such as the one in figure 2.19 uses hundreds of thermocouples to measure the temperature at critical points and send the information to display panels and computers in the central control room.

△ Fig. 2.19 Hundreds of thermocouples are used at an oil refinery to monitor and control the temperature at different points.

1. Give examples of suitable properties that can be used to measure temperature.

2. What fixed points are used for calibration on the Celsius scale?

3. EXTENDED What does it mean when we say a thermometer is sensitive?

4. EXTENDED Describe how a thermocouple works.

THERMAL CAPACITY

You make things hotter by transferring energy to them. When you heat up soup on a cooker ring, heat flows from the hot ring to the cold saucepan and then to the soup. You can also make things hot by rubbing or shaking them (see Fig. 2.20). For example, rubbing your hands together helps to warm them up on a cold day. The kinetic energy of the movement is transferred to internal energy in your hands. A rise in temperature of an object shows that its internal energy has increased.

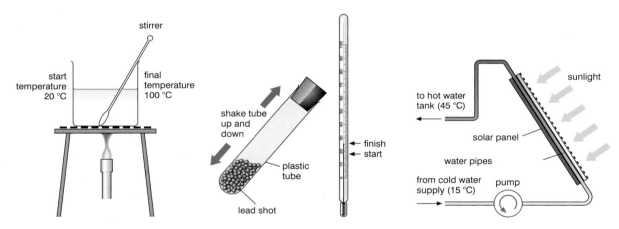

Δ Fig. 2.20 Different methods of transferring energy to things to make them hotter.

The larger the amount of material, the more energy you need to heat it up. All materials are made up of tiny particles. The larger the mass of the material, the more particles there are to share the added heat energy, so the smaller the temperature rise. Some materials are harder to heat up than others. Here you will find out how to measure how much energy is needed to heat different materials by different amounts.

A large object, made of a material that takes a large amount of energy to heat up, will be able to store a great quantity of internal energy. This object has a high **thermal capacity**. The thermal capacity of an object can be very important. The low thermal capacity of a thermocouple means it can respond very quickly to changes in temperature. On the other hand, the high thermal capacity of the world's oceans allows countries near the sea to avoid suffering from extremes of temperature, as the oceans release large amounts of heat when the land is cooler than the sea, and absorb it when the land is hotter.

A traditional mud house like the one in Fig. 2.21 has very thick walls and is ideally suited to hot countries. The high thermal capacity of the walls causes the house to warm up slowly during the day and to cool down slowly at night.

△ Fig. 2.21 A mud house has a high thermal capacity, making it suitable for a hot climate.

Specific heat capacity

The amount of energy (in joules) needed to raise the temperature of 1 kg of a material by 1 °C is called the **specific heat capacity** (see Table 2.4):

$$\text{specific heat capacity (J/kg °C)} = \frac{\text{energy used (J)}}{\text{mass (kg)}} \times \text{temperature change (°C)}$$

Material	Specific heat capacity/J/kg °C
Pure water	4200
Coal ash	900
Copper	390
Aluminium	910
Brick	800
Pyrex glass	780
Stainless steel	510
Concrete	3350
Magnetite (Fe_3O_4)	940

△ Table 2.4 The specific heat capacity of different materials.

Measuring specific heat capacity

To measure the specific heat capacity of a solid material, drill two holes into a block of the material – one for a thermometer and one for an electrical heater (Fig. 2.22).

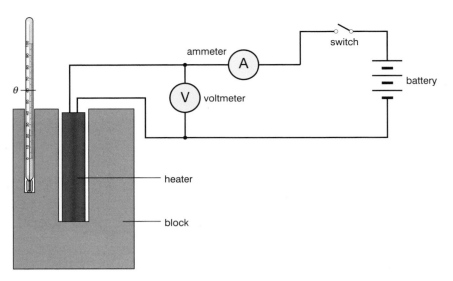

△ Fig. 2.22 Measuring the specific heat capacity of a solid material.

The electrical heater is connected to a low-voltage power supply or a battery. Two meters are needed: an ammeter to measure the electrical current in the heater and a voltmeter to measure the potential difference across the heater. As an alternative, a joulemeter can be fitted in place of the ammeter (in which case the voltmeter is not needed).

The heater should have a start and stop switch, and you need an accurate thermometer to measure the temperature of the block. To make the experiment more accurate, the surface of the block can be covered with thermal insulation such as expanded polystyrene to prevent heat loss.

The temperature of the block should be read at regular intervals, perhaps every 10 seconds. The heater should then be switched on for long enough to get a reasonable temperature rise.

A graph of results should look something like Fig 2.23:

You will note that the maximum temperature is reached many seconds after the heater is switched off. This is because it takes time for the heat energy to spread through the block. From the graph, the maximum temperature change $(\theta_2-\theta_1)$ can be measured.

In this graph, the block was still cooling down slowly when the experiment was started. It would have been better to wait for the temperature to become steady before starting.

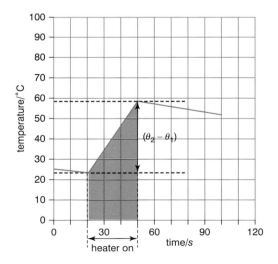

△ Fig. 2.23 Graph of results.

Some of the physics here is covered in more detail in section 4 on electricity.

What about cooling down?

When the energy is being *transferred away* from an object – that is, it is *cooling down* – the formula is used in exactly the same way. This time, instead of calculating the energy transferred to the object, the answer refers to the energy transferred away from it.

END OF EXTENDED

QUESTIONS

1. How do you make things hotter? Explain your answer in terms of energy.

2. What does a rise in temperature tell you about the internal energy of an object?

3. What is meant by the *thermal capacity* of an object?

4. Why is a traditional mud house ideally suited to hot countries?

MELTING AND BOILING

We experience melting and boiling many times in everyday life. This part explores what happens at the molecular level when materials melt and boil.

The **melting point** of a substance is the temperature at which it changes from a solid to a liquid. **Solidification** is when a substance changes from a liquid to a solid. The **boiling point** of a substance is the temperature at which it changes from a liquid to a gas. **Condensation** is when a substance changes from a gas to a liquid.

EXTENDED

Latent heat

The extra energy stored by water at 0 °C, as opposed to ice at 0 °C, is the **latent heat of fusion** (symbol L) of the water. It is measured in joules. ('Fusion' is another word for melting.)

The heat required to melt a *unit mass* of solid and turn it into liquid is known as the **specific latent heat of fusion** of that solid (symbol l), and is measured in J/kg or J/g.

When you heat a liquid or a solid and raise its temperature without boiling it or melting it, the extra heat energy that you put in is transferred as more vibrations (in a solid) or more movement (in a liquid), as we have already discussed.

However, while the solid is melting, the extra heat energy is used to weaken the bonds between the molecules and move the atoms slightly further apart against the attraction of the bonds. This energy is stored as potential energy, as in a stretched spring. So the internal energy of a liquid or a gas, consists of some energy that is kinetic and some that is potential.

The term **latent heat of vaporisation** is used to describe the energy that is needed to change the state from liquid to gas at the boiling point of the liquid.

THERMAL PROPERTIES

143

The latent heat of vaporisation is the additional potential energy carried by the gas, stored in the broken bonds between the molecules. This extra energy is carried by the steam, and is what makes steam so dangerous.

The heat required to turn a *unit mass* of liquid into gas is known as the **specific latent heat of vaporisation** (symbol l), and is measured in J/kg or J/g.

Developing Investigative Skills

Students set up this experiment to investigate latent heat fusion. Before using the apparatus shown in Fig. 2.24 you must take a number of practical precautions both for safety and to make the experiment more accurate.

Why must you secure the beaker of water?

Why must you wrap lagging around the beaker? no lagging shown - ?

Why might you need to stir the water when the ice is nearly melted?

Why must you connect a power supply to the heater with an on/off switch and with either a joulemeter, or both a voltmeter and an ammeter?

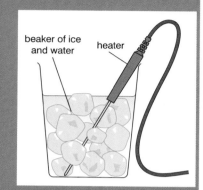

△ Fig. 2.24 Apparatus for the investigation.

Using and organising techniques, apparatus and materials

❶ Weigh the beaker without the heater, and then assemble the apparatus.

❷ Take some ice and check that it is at 0 °C by noting that the outside of the ice is starting to melt.

❸ Dry the ice on a cloth or tissues and put a suitable amount into the beaker.

❹ Switch on the heater and start a stopwatch. Note the readings on the meters.

❺ When the ice is almost melted, start stirring the water gently.

❻ Measure the time taken for the ice to melt.

❼ Weigh the beaker plus the water.

WORKED EXAMPLE

A group of students carried out the experiment. Their results were as follows:

Mass of beaker   = 100 g

Mass of beaker + water   = 237 g

Mass of water	$= 237 - 100$
	$= 137$ g
	$= 0.137$ kg

The initial mass of ice was also 0.137 kg.

| Time for ice to melt | $= 5$ min 20 s |
| | $= 320$ s |

Energy, E, put into the ice $= V \times I \times t$

Where:

E = change in internal energy in joules

V = potential difference in volts

I = electrical current in amps

t = time in seconds

Substitute the values:

$V = 24$ V

$I = 6$ A

$t = 320$ s

$E = 24 \times 6 \times 320$

Work out the answer and write down the unit:

$E = 46\,080$ J

Specific latent heat of fusion $l = \dfrac{E}{m}$

Where:

E = change in internal energy in joules

m = mass in kg

Substitute the values:

$l = \dfrac{46\,080}{0.137}$

Work out the answer and write down the unit:

$l = 336\,350$ J/kg

$= 336.35$ kJ/kg

This idealised experiment gives approximately the value that is generally accepted. If you try the same experiment you are likely to get a different value, as it is all too easy to get a large error due to heat loss from the beaker. In addition, the ice absorbs heat energy from the surroundings and there are other factors that are hard to eliminate.

To measure the specific latent heat of vaporisation of water

1. Use the same apparatus as in the previous experiment. Put sufficient water in the beaker and weigh the beaker plus water.
2. Put the heater into the beaker and switch it on. Check the readings on the meters.
3. When the water boils, start the stopwatch and let the water boil for a few minutes.
4. Let the beaker cool to a safe temper ature and weigh it again.

WORKED EXAMPLE

A group of students carried out the experiment. Their results were as follows:

Mass of beaker + water before the experiment	= 237 g
Mass of beaker + water after the experiment	= 218 g
Mass of water boiled off	= 237 − 218
	= 19 g
	= 0.019 kg
Water boiled for 5 minutes	= 300 s

Energy, E, put into the boiling water $= V \times I \times t$

Where:

E = change in internal energy in joules

V = potential difference in volts

I = electrical current in amps

t = time in seconds

Substitute the values: $E = 24 \times 6 \times 300$

Work out the answer and write down the unit: $E = 43\,200$ J

Specific latent heat of evaporation $I = \dfrac{E}{m}$

Where:

$$E = \text{change in internal energy in joules}$$

$$m = \text{mass in kg}$$

Substitute the values:

$$I = \frac{43\,200}{0.019}$$

Work out the answer and write down the unit:

$$I = 2\,273\,684 \text{ J/kg}$$

$$I = 2273 \text{ kJ/kg}$$

END OF EXTENDED

Water is strange

Water has a surprisingly high specific heat capacity. This means that a lot of energy has to be transferred to change the temperature of water significantly. This is important in several ways:

- Water makes an excellent **coolant** for machines such as car engines. It can remove a lot of heat energy from the machine without boiling.
- The temperature of the seas and oceans remains fairly steady, as huge energy transfers are needed to significantly change the temperature of that much water. This helps keep the planet at a fairly even temperature, which is good for living things.

Note: A lot of confusion is caused by the different uses of the word 'steam'. In science, the word should be used to mean the invisible vapour that water turns into when it boils. This vapour is at 100 °C and is extremely dangerous to human skin due to the energy that it contains. As soon as steam cools a little, it turns into the white clouds that we see when a kettle boils. These white clouds are made of small droplets of water, and are much safer than true steam. (It is true that in casual conversation we all call these clouds 'steam', but they are not steam in the scientific meaning.)

△ Fig. 2.25 In this photograph you can see that the steam coming out of the chimney is almost invisible. As the steam travels up, its temperature drops and it turns into clouds of water droplets.

The words 'evaporation' and 'boiling' also cause confusion. When a liquid evaporates it loses molecules from its surface. This will occur in an open container of water at any temperature. For example, water from a hot drink left in a cup will eventually evaporate. The molecules of water in the cup will have a range of energies, and even at room temperature the molecules with the highest energies will leave the surface.

A liquid **boils** when its temperature reaches boiling point. At this temperature the molecules have enough energy to leave the liquid in large quantities, even those inside the liquid. These molecules collect to form large bubbles of vapour and cause the liquid to bubble violently.

Many solids evaporate slowly, which is why you can smell dry food – coffee beans, for example. Some people even claim to be able to smell a sheet of zinc metal, even though the evaporation rate is incredibly low.

QUESTIONS

1. In terms of energy and temperature, what happens when a substance boils?

2. At boiling point, what happens to the molecules of a liquid?

3. What happens when a liquid evaporates?

BOILING POINT

Why can't you make a good cup of tea at the top of a high mountain? This is a question often used by physics teachers to check your understanding of ideas about particles. The answer is that to make a good cup of tea you need your water to be boiling at 100 °C and at the top of a high mountain the water will boil at a lower temperature than that. For example, water will boil at about 69 °C at the top of Mount Everest. To see why, we need to look a little more closely at boiling.

In a liquid, the particles are not held in fixed positions like they are in a solid, but they are still closely packed. Intermolecular forces give a liquid a fixed volume but not a fixed shape and a liquid will take the shape of the container it is in. Raising the temperature of the liquid by heating it increases the average kinetic energy of the particles. When this energy becomes great enough, a particle will be able to break apart from the liquid and escape, becoming part of a vapour.

How much energy does this require? It depends on two things – the strength of the forces within the liquid and also the pressure of the gases surrounding it. The forces within the liquid will remain constant wherever the liquid is, but why should the outside pressure make a difference?

If you think about it, when water boils and the particles escape, they are not really escaping into a completely empty space. The air is full of particles and these collide with the escaping water particles, often knocking them back towards the liquid. So for some water to boil, the particles have to have enough energy to break apart from each other *and then* push their way through the air particles. At higher altitudes (at the top of a high mountain for example) there is less air pressure and so the water particles can push through more easily. This means that the water particles do not need to have as much energy overall – and less energy per particle means a lower temperature.

So what if you removed the air altogether, what would happen in space? Your blood is mostly water – would it boil at body temperature if the outside pressure was reduced to almost zero?

Well, no. Even if there is a vacuum outside the body, your blood is kept under pressure by the body itself. You would 'swell up' a bit, but you could survive exposure to space – at least for a short time. However, to maintain your body in safe conditions you would need a suit to keep you closer to the air pressure you experience all the time. That is why astronauts wear full pressure suits in space and not just an oxygen mask to help them breathe.

End of topic checklist

Key terms

bimetallic strip, latent heat of fusion, latent heat of vaporisation, specific heat capacity, specific latent heat of fusion, specific latent heat of vaporisation, thermal capacity, thermocouple

During your study of this topic you should have learned:

◯ How to describe the thermal expansion of solids, liquids and gases.

◯ **EXTENDED** About the relative order of magnitude of the expansion of solids, liquids and gases.

◯ About some of the everyday applications and consequences of thermal expansion.

◯ About the effect of a change of temperature on the volume of a gas at constant pressure.

◯ How a physical property that varies with temperature may be used for the measurement of temperature, with examples of such properties.

◯ **EXTENDED** About sensitivity, range and linearity.

◯ About the need for fixed points and how to identify them.

◯ How to describe the structure and action of liquid-in-glass thermometers.

◯ **EXTENDED** About the structure of a thermocouple and its use for measuring high temperatures and those that vary rapidly.

◯ About the relationship between a rise in temperature of a body and an increase in internal energy.

◯ **EXTENDED** About an experiment to measure the specific heat capacity of a substance.

◯ The term 'thermal capacity'.

◯ How to describe melting and boiling in terms of energy input without a change in temperature.

◯ **EXTENDED** How to distinguish between boiling and evaporation.

◯ The meaning of melting point and boiling point.

◯ How to describe condensation and solidification.

◯ **EXTENDED** How to use the terms 'latent heat of vaporisation' and 'latent heat of fusion' and give a molecular interpretation of latent heat.

◯ **EXTENDED** How to describe an experiment to measure specific latent heats for steam and for ice.

End of topic questions

Note: The marks awarded for these questions indicate the level of detail required in the answers. In the examination, the number of marks awarded to questions like these may be different.

1. Explain the following observations:

a) A steel ruler is often marked 'Use at 20 °C'. **(2 marks)**

b) When you pour boiling water into a drinking glass, the glass may crack. **(2 marks)**

c) When you pour a very cold drink into a drinking glass, the outside of the glass will become wet. **(2 marks)**

d) When you leave frozen food in a freezer for several weeks without covering it, the outside surface of the food will suffer from what is called 'freezer burn' and will look dry and unpleasant. **(2 marks)**

2. EXTENDED A bimetallic strip consists of a thin strip of aluminium, 100 mm × 10 mm, attached to a thin strip of stainless steel of the same size.

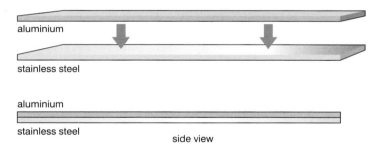

aluminium

stainless steel

aluminium

stainless steel
side view

The two strips are joined together face to face, to give a thicker strip that is still 100 mm × 10 mm. They are joined together at 20 °C using epoxy glue.

a) The strip is fixed to a block of metal at one end. What happens to the other end at each change of temperature if the temperature goes to 100 °C, then to −10 °C, and finally back to 20 °C? (Note that aluminium expands more than stainless steel when equal lengths are exposed to the same change in temperature.) **(3 marks)**

b) Explain how this strip could be used as a thermometer. **(2 marks)**

c) Design an electrical circuit that will use the bimetallic strip to switch on a warning light if the temperature of the bimetallic strip drops below room temperature and approaches the freezing point of water. (Such a device is known as a 'frost stat' and is used to prevent damage from freezing.) **(3 marks)**

d) Explain what would happen if the warning light heated the bimetallic strip. **(2 marks)**

3. What happens to the temperature of a material when it absorbs energy? **(1 mark)**

End of topic questions continued

4. EXTENDED 100 g of glass is heated until its temperature rises from 19 °C to 33 °C. How much energy has it absorbed? The specific heat capacity of glass is 840 J/kg °C. **(2 marks)**

5. EXTENDED 250 g of the brick inside a storage heater (specific heat capacity = 910 J/kg °C) absorbs 5000 joules of energy. By how much will its temperature rise? **(2 marks)**

6. EXTENDED A student measures the specific latent heat of fusion of ice in the following way. She knows that the specific heat capacity of water is 4.2 J/g °C.

She takes a polystyrene beaker of negligible mass, and puts 400 g of warm water into it. She stirs the water gently and measures its temperature with a thermocouple connected to a temperature display. The water temperature is 50 °C.

She then takes some wet ice that is at 0 °C, dries it on a tissue, drops it gently into the beaker and stirs until the ice has melted. The temperature is now 32 °C.

She checks the final weight of the beaker and finds that it is 460 g.

a) **i)** What was the temperature difference between the start and finish of the experiment? **(1 mark)**

   ii) How many joules of heat did the warmed water give out as it cooled? **(2 marks)**

The energy given out, E, $= m \times c \times \Delta t$, where m is the mass of water in grams, c is the specific heat capacity in J/g °C and Δt is the temperature drop in °C.

b) How many grams of ice did she add? **(2 marks)**

c) After the ice had melted, it consisted of cold water at 0 °C.

   i) By how many degrees did this then heat up during the experiment? **(2 marks)**

   ii) How many joules of heat did this cold water take in as it heated up? **(2 marks)**

d) How many joules of heat that were given out by the warmed water are still unaccounted for? **(2 marks)**

e) If all of these joules of heat were used to melt the ice, what answer does she get for the specific latent heat of the ice in J/g? **(2 marks)**

Transfer of thermal energy

INTRODUCTION

Energy will always try to flow from areas at high temperatures to areas at low temperatures. This is called **thermal transfer**.

Thermal energy can be transferred by conduction, convection and radiation.

In this topic we shall consider all three methods of heat transfer.

△ Fig. 2.26 These paragliders stay in the air longer by using of convection currents in the atmosphere to take them higher.

KNOWLEDGE CHECK

✓ Know and be able to explain the molecular structure of solids, liquids and gases.
✓ Know what is meant by energy.
✓ Know that internal energy (heat) can be transferred from one place to another.

LEARNING OBJECTIVES

✓ Be able to describe experiments to demonstrate the properties of good and bad conductors of heat.
✓ **EXTENDED** Be able to give a simple molecular account of heat transfer in solids.
✓ Be able to relate convection in fluids to density changes and describe experiments to illustrate convection.
✓ Be able to identify infra-red radiation as part of the electromagnetic spectrum.
✓ **EXTENDED** Be able to describe experiments to show the properties of good and bad emitters and good and bad absorbers of infra-red radiation.
✓ Be able to identify and explain some of the everyday applications and consequences of conduction, convection and radiation.

CONDUCTION

Materials that allow thermal energy to transfer through them quickly are called **thermal conductors**. Those that do not are called **thermal insulators**.

If someone talks about an 'insulator', you will have to work out from the context if it refers to a thermal insulator or to an electrical insulator. If the context is energy, then it is could be a thermal insulator. If the context is electricity, it is likely to be an electrical insulator.

If one end of a conductor is heated, the atoms that make up its structure start to vibrate more vigorously. As the atoms in a solid are linked together by chemical bonds, the increased vibrations can be passed on to other atoms. The energy of movement (kinetic energy) passes through the whole material.

Metals are particularly good thermal conductors because they contain freely moving electrons that transfer energy very rapidly.

As the electrons travel through the piece of metal, they take the thermal energy with them. This is in addition to the thermal energy that is transferred by vibrations of the atoms making up the structure of the metal. Fig. 2.27 shows conduction in a solid. Particles in the hot part of a solid (top) vibrate further and faster than particles in the cold part (bottom). The vibrations are passed on through the bonds from particle to particle. It is the movement of the free electrons that makes metals act as good thermal conductors.

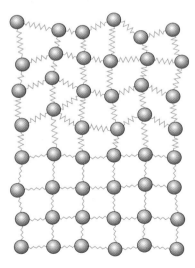

△ Fig. 2.27 Conduction in a solid.

Conduction cannot occur when there are no particles present, so a vacuum is a perfect insulator. Gases and liquids are poor heat conductors because their particles are so far apart.

Conduction can be demonstrated using the equipment shown in Fig. 2.28.

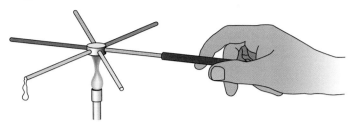

◁ Fig. 2.28 In this experiment to show conduction, the rods are made of different metals, so the heat conducts along them at different rates. The better the conductor, the quicker the wax at the end of the rod melts.

Another way to demonstrate the properties of good and bad conductors of thermal energy is to wrap a piece of paper around a bar made of wood on one side and copper on the other side. The bar is then held just above a Bunsen flame. The paper only chars on the wood side of the bar, as copper is a good thermal conductor so heat travels away from the paper on the copper side. Wood is a thermal insulator so doesn't conduct the heat away.

Another example is the fact that metal handlebars of a bike always feel colder than the plastic grips – heat is conducted away from your hands by the metal but not by the plastic.

QUESTIONS

1. Why are metals particularly good conductors?

2. Why is outer space a perfect insulator?

3. How is heat energy transferred in a thermal conductor?

4. Describe an experiment to demonstrate conduction.

5. EXTENDED Devise an experiment to find out whether or not the rate of energy transfer varies along a strip of copper. Explain how you could tell if any change is linear.

CONVECTION

Convection is the main method of thermal transfer in fluids.

Convection occurs in liquids and gases because these materials flow (they are fluids). The particles in a fluid move all the time. When a fluid is heated, energy is transferred to the particles, causing them to move faster and further apart. This makes the heated fluid less dense than the unheated fluid. The less dense, warmer fluid rises above the more dense, colder fluid, causing the fluid to circulate as shown in Fig. 2.29. This **convection current** is how the thermal energy is transferred.

◁ Fig. 2.29 Potassium manganate(VII) crystals in water demonstrate convection currents. The warmer water expands, becomes less dense and rises, making a trail as some of the dissolved potassium permanganate is carried along as well. Colder water sinks and replaces the warmer water that has risen.

If a fluid's movement is restricted, energy cannot be transferred. That is why many insulators, such as ceiling tiles, contain trapped air pockets. Wall cavities in some houses are filled with fibre to prevent air from circulating and transferring thermal energy by convection.

QUESTIONS

1. Why does convection only occur in liquids and gases?

2. Explain why warm air rises.

3. How could you demonstrate convection in a laboratory?

4. Describe how cavity-wall insulation in houses reduces heat loss by convection.

RADIATION

Radiation, unlike conduction and convection, *does not need particles* at all. Radiation can travel through a vacuum. This is clearly shown by the radiation that arrives at the Earth from the Sun. Radiated heat energy is carried mainly by **infra-red radiation**, which is part of the **electromagnetic spectrum**. Infra-red radiation is similar to light, but has a longer wavelength.

All objects take in and give out infra-red radiation all the time. Hot objects radiate more infra-red than cold objects. The amount of radiation given out or absorbed by an object depends on its temperature and on its surface. Figure 2.30 shows a **thermogram**. Thermograms give a visual representation of the amount of infra-red radiation that is given out by an object at any particular moment.

-10 - +55 E=0.00 Trefl=20   °C

<️ Fig. 2.30 Thermogram of a house.

Type of surface	As an emitter of radiation	As an absorber of radiation	Examples
Dull black	Good	Good	Emitter: cooling fins on the back of a refrigerator are dull black to radiate away more energy. Absorber: the surface of a black bitumen road gets far hotter on a sunny day than the surface of a white concrete one.
Bright shiny	Poor	Poor	Emitter: marathon runners, at the end of a race, wrap themselves in shiny blankets to prevent them from cooling down too quickly by radiation (and convection). Absorber: fuel storage tanks are sprayed with shiny silver or white paint to reflect radiation from the Sun.

△ Table 2.5 Comparison of different surfaces as emitters or absorbers of infra-red radiation

radiometer

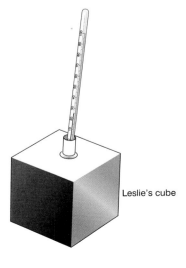

Leslie's cube

<️ Fig. 2.31 A Leslie's cube. The meter measures the amount of radiation that is emitted by each surface.

To show the properties of good and bad emitters of infra-red radiation, you can use a Leslie's cube (Fig. 2.31.), which is filled with boiling water. Its sides have different surfaces – shiny, dull, dark, light – to shown how they emit thermal radiation at different rates. Because all sides of the cube are heated by the same water inside the cube, any differences in the way they radiate energy can only be due to the differences in their surfaces.

To show how different surfaces absorb radiation, you can use boiling tubes covered with foil or with a matt black surface heated by radiation from an infra-red (IR) bulb and measure the temperature rise in each case.

END OF EXTENDED

QUESTIONS

1. How does radiation differ from conduction and convection?

2. Which is the better emitter of infra-red radiation: a hot object or a cold object?

3. State two factors that affect the amount of thermal radiation emitted by an object.

4. EXTENDED Which side of a Leslie's cube will emit thermal radiation at the greatest rate?

CONSEQUENCES OF ENERGY TRANSFER

This part of the topic considers some everyday consequences of energy transfer.

Radiators

Radiators are used to heat homes in countries that have cool winters. A radiator does radiate some heat, and if you stand near a hot radiator your hands can feel the infra-red radiation being emitted. However, this is only around one quarter of the heat being released by the radiator. *Three quarters* of the heat is taken away by the hot air that rises from the radiator. Colder air from the room flows in to replace this hot air, and a convection current is formed as shown in Fig. 2.32. So a 'radiator' is mainly a convection heater.

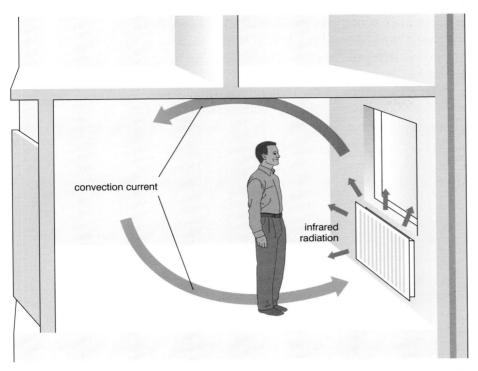

△ Fig. 2.32 A side view of a room with a hot-water radiator underneath the window. You will see from this that the convection current is far more efficient at heating the top of the room than it is at heating the person standing in front of the radiator.

Vacuum flask

Another example of thermal transfers in everyday life is a vacuum flask (Fig. 2.33). A vacuum flask will keep a hot drink hot or a cold drink cold for hours by almost completely eliminating the flow of heat out or in.

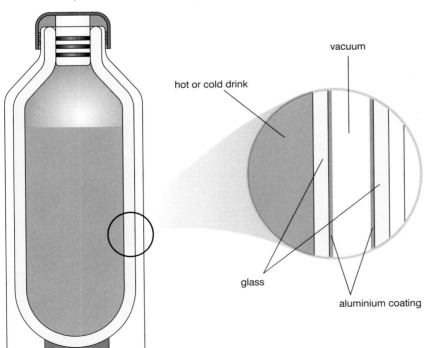

△ Fig. 2.33 A vacuum flask.

Conduction is almost entirely eliminated by making sure that any heat flowing out must travel along the glass of the neck of the flask. The path is a long one, the glass is thin, and glass is a very poor conductor of heat. Energy cannot be lost by conduction across the vacuum space between the two walls of the glass flask. The bung in the top of the flask must also be a very poor conductor of heat – cork or expanded polystyrene are good materials to use.

Convection is eliminated because the space between the inner wall and the outer wall of the flask is evacuated so that there is no air to form convection currents.

When the contents are hot, radiation is greatly reduced because the inner walls of the flask are coated with pure aluminium. Because the aluminium is in a vacuum, it stays extremely shiny forever, so the wall in contact with the hot liquid emits very little infra-red radiation.

When the contents are cold, the shiny outer surface of the aluminium-coated glass reflects almost all the infra-red radiation falling on it, so hardly any is absorbed.

QUESTIONS

1. What is the main method of heat transfer in a radiator?

2. Which part of a room is heated most efficiently by a radiator?

3. For a vacuum flask, describe which features reduce the energy transfer by:

   a) conduction
   b) convection
   c) radiation.

4. Explain why a vacuum flask is good at keeping hot drinks hot *and* cold drinks cold.

End of topic questions

Note: The marks awarded for these questions indicate the level of detail required in the answers. In the examination, the number of marks awarded to questions like these may be different.

1. Why are several thin layers of clothing more likely to reduce thermal transfer than one thick layer of clothing? **(3 marks)**

2. The diagram shows a cross-section of a steel radiator positioned in a room next to a wall.

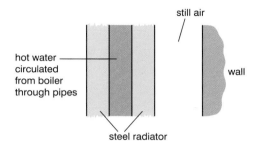

still air

hot water circulated from boiler through pipes

wall

steel radiator

   Describe how energy from the hot water reaches the wall behind the radiator.
   (6 marks)

3. Suggest a colour for a fire fighter's uniform. Explain your choice.
   (3 marks)

4. Discuss how you might design a solar cooker to heat water using infra-red radiation from the Sun. **(3 marks)**

5. Explain why seawater absorbs infra-red radiation faster than snow and ice.
   (4 marks)

6. Imagine you are a local councillor. You are deciding whether or not to give grants for installing home insulation. Discuss all the factors you would consider and what other information you would need before making a decision. **(6 marks)**

7. Explain why solids transfer energy mainly by conduction. **(3 marks)**

8. Describe how a convection heater warms a room. **(4 marks)**

9. Using conduction in your answer, suggest why serving dishes are usually made from glass or china. **(3 marks)**

10. Which factors affect the rate at which an object transfers energy?
    (3 marks)

Exam-style questions

Note: The questions, sample answers and marks in this section have been written by the authors as a guide only. The marks awarded for these questions indicate the level of detail required in the answers. In the examination, the number of marks awarded to questions like these may be different.

Sample student answers

Question 1

This question is about particles.

a) Brownian motion is often used as evidence supporting the particle model of matter.

  i) What is Brownian motion?

     Atoms in a gas moving about ✗   **(2)**

  ii) How does the explanation of Brownian motion support the particle model of matter?

     The particles move about very fast ✗ ✗ ✗   **(3)**

b) The photo shows bubbles rising in water.

TEACHER'S COMMENTS

1) a) i) This student obviously does not remember what Brownian motion is, so they are guessing. Brownian motion is the random motion of pollen grains on the surface of the water. It is also the random motion of smoke particles in air.

  ii) As this part of the question asks for an explanation of the observation described in the first part, the student loses quite a lot of marks all in one go.

The small particles are constantly being hit by even smaller particles, which are too small to see.

When you are preparing for exams, make sure you cover every little point in the syllabus – remember that is the document the examiners work with. Your teachers will use it as well, but that is not an excuse for you to ignore it!

b) i) These parts of the question are handled well and score full marks.

ii) The student made a good use of the relevant equations to make their argument. This is a powerful way to answer questions of this type and can save a lot of descriptive writing.

The bubbles increase in volume as they move towards the surface of the water.

i) Explain why the bubbles rise to the surface.

The bubbles are less dense than the water ✓ ① *.so the forces on them are unbalanced and they float upwards* ✓ ①. **(2)**

ii) Explain why the volume of the bubbles increases as they rise.

The pressure = depth x density xg, ✓ ① *so the pressure gets less as the bubbles move upwards.* ✓ ① *Also, pressure x volume is constant, so if the pressure decreases then the volume increases.* ✓ ① *So as the pressure on the bubbles decreases their volume will increase and the bubbles will get bigger.* ✓ ① **(4)**

(Total 11 marks)

$\frac{6}{11}$

Question 2

A student investigates the effect of insulation on cooling.

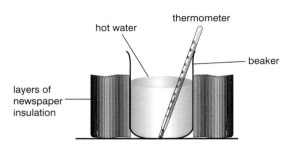

The student puts some hot water into a beaker and measures the temperature drop in 20 minutes.

He repeats the experiment using layers of paper as insulation.

His results are shown in the table.

Number of layers of insulation	Temperature drop in 20 minutes/°C
0	21
5	20
10	18
15	17
20	18

a) Draw a graph of these results. .... (5)

b) The student concludes that the graph shows that thicker insulation reduces heat loss.

   Is this a correct conclusion form this data?

   Explain your answer. .... (2)

(Total 7 marks)

Question 3

Two experiments are carried out to investigate energy transfer in water.

In experiment 1, cold water is gently heated at the top of a glass boiling tube. A block of ice trapped at the bottom remains solid even when the water at the top begins to boil.

In experiment 2, cold water is gently heated at the bottom of the tube. Ice at the top of the tube melts before the water boils.

a) What is the process by which thermal (heat) energy travels through the glass?

.... (1)

b) i) What is the principal process in Experiment 2 which takes the energy from the water at the bottom to the ice at the top? .... (1)

ii) Describe how the process in b) i) occurs. .... (2)

c) Suggest two reasons why the ice in Experiment 1 does not melt, even when the water at the top begins to boil. .... (2)

(Total 6 marks)

What is the connection between the waves you see on water and light? Light is a wave that behaves in a similar way to water waves. Sound is another type of wave, as you will learn later in this section. Studying the behaviour of waves will help you to understand many of your everyday experiences, ranging from how you see objects to how you hear sounds.

You should already know that energy can be transferred as sound and light. White light is made up of a range of different colours and that light can be reflected and refracted. You should also know how the frequency and amplitude of a sound wave are related to the pitch and loudness of the sound.

STARTING POINTS

1. Explain why a red object looks red.

2. Describe the pitch and loudness of the sound you hear when the sound wave has a large amplitude and the frequency is low.

3. Explain the meaning of the words translucent, transparent and opaque.

4. How could you demonstrate the difference between a light wave and a sound wave using: a) a rope; b) a spring; c) water? (If you cannot use one or more of these to demonstrate the difference, explain why.)

5. How does light travel through space?

6. Draw a diagram to show how light is reflected by a plane mirror.

CONTENTS

a) General wave properties

b) Light

c) Sound

d) Exam-style questions

3
Properties of waves

△ Light is a wave and has many properties in common with a wave in the sea.

General wave properties

△ Fig. 3.1 This photo shows many examples of waves in action.

INTRODUCTION

The behaviour of waves affects us every second of our lives. Waves are reaching us constantly: sound waves, light waves, infra-red (heat), television and mobile-phone microwave signals, and radio waves, the list goes on. The study of is one of the central subjects of physics.

The woman in Fig. 3.1 is surrounded by waves: she can feel the heat waves from the Sun coming in through the windows; she can hear the sound waves of her friend on the phone; the phone uses microwaves; and she can see around her with light waves.

KNOWLEDGE CHECK

✔ Know some simple examples of wave motion.
✔ Be able to measure lengths and times.
✔ Be familiar with everyday examples of reflection.

LEARNING OBJECTIVES

✔ Be able to describe what is meant by wave motion as illustrated by vibration in ropes and springs and by experiments using water waves.
✔ Be able to use the term 'wavefront'.
✔ Be able to give the meaning of speed, frequency, wavelength and amplitude.
✔ Be able to distinguish between transverse and longitudinal waves and give suitable examples.
✔ Be able to describe the use of water waves to show reflection, refraction and diffraction.
✔ EXTENDED Be able to recall and use the equation $v = f\lambda$.
✔ EXTENDED Be able to interpret reflection, refraction and diffraction using wave theory.

LONGITUDINAL AND TRANSVERSE WAVES

Wave motion can be illustrated by vibrations in ropes and springs. Fig. 3.2 shows two types of wave motion illustrated by a spring.

In a **longitudinal wave**, the vibrations are in the direction of travel of the wave. This type of wave can be shown by pushing and pulling a spring. The spring stretches in places and squashes in others. The stretching produces regions of **rarefaction**, where the coils spread out, whilst the squashing produces regions of **compression**. Sound is an example of a longitudinal wave.

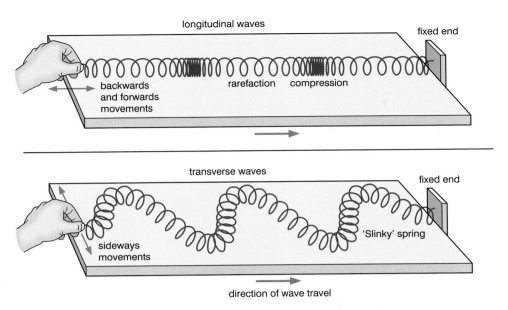

△ Fig. 3.2 Longitudinal and transverse waves are made by vibrations. Both types of wave have a repeating shape or pattern.

In a **transverse wave**, the vibrations are at right angles to the direction of travel of the wave. Light, radio and other **electromagnetic waves** are transverse waves.

In the examples in Fig. 3.2 the waves are very narrow, and are confined to the spring or the string that they are travelling down. Most waves are not confined in this way. Clearly a single wave on the sea, for example, can be hundreds of metres wide as it moves along.

Longitudinal and transverse waves are made by vibrations. Both types of wave have a repeating shape or pattern.

Amplitude, frequency, wavelength and period

Waves have a wavelength, frequency, amplitude and time period.

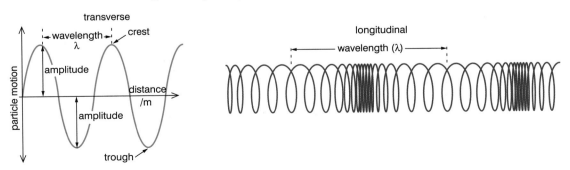

△ Fig. 3.3 The wavelength and amplitude of a transverse wave and the wavelength of a longitudinal wave.

Take care with graphs or diagrams like the one in Fig. 3.3. Make sure you notice if it is 'distance' or 'time' along the x-axis. Some labels only apply to one type of graph.

- The **wavelength** is the distance between two adjacent peaks or, if you prefer, the distance between two adjacent troughs of the wave. In the case of longitudinal waves, it is the distance between two consecutive points of maximum compression, or the distance between two consecutive points of minimum compression.
- The **frequency** is the number of complete waves that go past each second (measured in Hz).
- The time period is the time taken for each complete cycle of the wave motion.
- The **amplitude** is the maximum particle displacement of the medium's vibration from the undisturbed position. In transverse waves, this is half the crest-to-trough height.
- The **speed** of the wave is the distance the wave travels in 1 s. The speed depends on the substance or **medium** the wave is passing through.

The largest ocean wave measured accurately had a wavelength of 340 m, a frequency of 0.067 Hz (that is to say one peak every 15 s), and a speed of 23 m/s. The amplitude of the wave was 17 m, so the ship that was measuring the wave was going 17 m above the level of a smooth sea and then 17 m below. (The wave went down 34 m from crest to trough.)

Water waves are often used to demonstrate the properties of waves because the **wavefront** of a water wave is easy to see. A wavefront is the moving line that joins all the points on the crest of a wave.

Waves transfer energy and information

A wave carries energy and can also carry information. You can feel the energy in infra-red waves from the Sun as they strike your hands; you can see the energy contained in the ocean waves from a typhoon as they reach the coast after travelling hundreds of miles. And you can see the information contained in the light reaching your eyes from this page, or from a movie screen.

Note that in none of these cases has any object or matter travelled by vibrations from the source of the waves to the destination. Instead the wave is passed on from point to point along the route taken by the wave. One good example is a piece of wood in the sea. It is shaken up and down, and to and fro, by a wave, but after the wave has passed it ends up where it started.

Surfers can travel by catching a wave and 'riding' it, but they are outside the wave, not part of it.

QUESTIONS

1. Describe how the vibrations travel in:

    a) a longitudinal wave

    b) a transverse wave.

2. What is: **a)** the wavelength, **b)** the frequency, **c)** the amplitude of a wave?

3. How far does a wave with speed 5 m/s travel in 3 s?

4. What do all waves transfer?

EXTENDED

Relationship between speed, frequency and wavelength

The speed of a wave in a given medium is constant. When you change the wavelength, the frequency *must* change as well. If you imagine that some waves are going past you on a spring or on a rope, then they will be going at a constant speed. When the waves get closer together, then more waves must go past you each second, and that means that the frequency has gone up. The speed, frequency and wavelength of a wave are related by the equation:

wave speed = frequency × wavelength

$$v = f \times \lambda$$

Where: v = wave speed, usually measured in metres/second (m/s)

f = frequency, measured in cycles per second or hertz (Hz)

λ = wavelength, usually measured in metres (m)

END OF EXTENDED

WORKED EXAMPLES

1. A loudspeaker makes sound waves with a frequency of 300 Hz. The waves have a wavelength of 1.13 m. Calculate the speed of the waves.

Write down the formula: $v = f \times \lambda$

Substitute the values for f and λ: $v = 300 \times 1.13$

Work out the answer and write down the unit: $v = 339$ m/s

2. A radio station broadcasts on a wavelength of 250 m. The speed of the radio waves is 3×10^8 m/s. Calculate the frequency.

Write down the formula with f as the subject: $f = \dfrac{v}{\lambda}$

Substitute the values for v and λ: $f = \dfrac{3 \times 10^8}{250}$

Work out the answer and write down the unit: $f = 1\,200\,000$ Hz or 1200 kHz

Using water waves to show reflection, refraction and diffraction

A ripple tank can be used to show reflection, refraction and diffraction (Fig. 3.4).

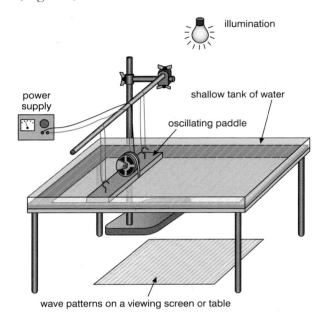

illumination

power supply

shallow tank of water

oscillating paddle

wave patterns on a viewing screen or table

◁ Fig. 3.4 A ripple tank.

To show **reflection**, you put a plane surface in the tank some distance from the paddle. To show **refraction**, you put a thin glass sheet in the water to change the depth of the water in a given region. To show **diffraction**, you put a plane surface with a gap approximately the same width as the wavelength of the water waves.

Fig. 3.5 shows how water waves can be used to explain reflection (see Reflection of light) at a plane surface. Waves hit a barrier at an angle of incidence, i. The waves bounce off with the angle of incidence, i, equal to the angle of reflection, r. The reflected wave is the same shape as the incident wave.

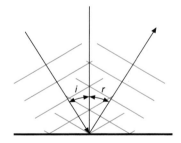

△ Fig. 3.5 Reflection at a plane surface.

When a wave moves from one medium into another, it will either speed up or slow down. For example, a wave going along a rope will speed up if the rope becomes thinner. (This is why you can 'crack' a whip.) And sound waves going from cold air to hotter air will speed up. When a wave slows down, the wavefronts crowd together – the *wavelength gets smaller*.

Fig. 3.6 shows this happening as a wave moves from deep water to shallow water. The wave slows down as it travels across the boundary to a more dense medium. The frequency of the wave

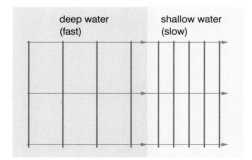

deep water (fast)   shallow water (slow)

△ Fig. 3.6 When waves slow down, their wavelength gets shorter.

does not change as it crosses the boundary, so if the speed decreases and the frequency stays the same, the wavelength must also decrease. When a wave speeds up, the wavefronts spread out – the *wavelength gets larger*. If the speed increases but the frequency stays the same, then the wavelength must also increase. Note that in both cases the same number of waves will pass you per second; the wavelength may have changed, but the frequency has not.

When waves slow down, their wavelength gets shorter. When a wave enters a new medium at an angle then the wavefronts also change direction. This is known as refraction (see Refraction of light in the following topic). The amount that the wave is bent by depends on the change in speed. Water waves are slower in shallower water than in deep water, so water waves will refract when the depth changes as shown in Fig. 3.7.

Wavefronts change shape when they pass the edge of an obstacle or go through a gap (Fig. 3.8). This process is known as diffraction. Diffraction is strongest and most noticeable when the width of the gap is similar in size to the wavelength of the waves.

Diffraction is a problem in communications when radio and television signals are transmitted through the air. Diffraction of the wavefront means that not all the energy transmitted with the wavefront reaches the receiving dishes.

Short-wavelength signals, such as those used by television and mobile phones, diffract very little, with the result that you start to get poor reception when you cannot see the transmitter, and tall buildings will cast shadows that will make it difficult to get reception. To reduce this problem, mobile phone companies use many transmitters in cities, automatically switching your phone to the transmitter with the best path to your phone.

Satellite television has the great advantage that your receiving dish can look up in the sky at the satellite and get a direct view of it.

EXTENDED The equation $v = f\lambda$ applies in both media. The diagrams show how reflection, refraction and diffraction can be interpreted using wave theory.

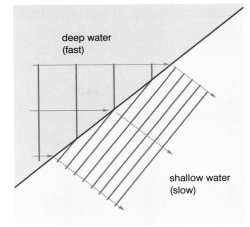

△ Fig. 3.7 If waves cross into a new medium at an angle, their wavelength and direction change.

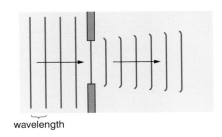

wavelength

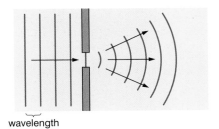

wavelength

△ Fig. 3.8 Diffraction of a wave.

High-frequency notes from a CD track have wavelengths of around 10–20 cm. For these to diffract efficiently and spread out as they leave the opening of the loudspeaker, a speaker with a smaller diameter is used. For lower-frequency notes, which have larger wavelengths, a speaker with a larger diameter is used in order to generate enough volume.

▷ Fig. 3.9 A loudspeaker with a tweeter for the higher frequencies (top) and a woofer for the lower frequencies (bottom).

QUESTIONS

1. Explain why wavefronts get closer together when a wave slows down.

2. A wave changes direction as it moves from one medium to another. What affects the amount of change and direction?

3. If diffraction is noticeable, what must be true about the width of the gap and the wavelength of the wave?

End of topic checklist

Key terms

amplitude, compression, diffraction, electromagnetic wave, frequency, longitudinal wave, medium, reflection, rarefaction, refraction, speed, transverse wave, wavefront, wavelength

During your study of this topic you should have learned:

○ What is meant by *wave motion*, as illustrated by vibration in ropes and springs and by experiments using water waves.

○ How to use the term *wavefront*.

○ The meaning of *speed*, *frequency*, *wavelength* and *amplitude*.

○ The difference between transverse and longitudinal waves, with suitable examples.

○ About the use of water waves to show: reflection at a plane surface; refraction due to a change of speed; diffraction produced by wide and narrow gaps.

○ EXTENDED To use the equation $v = f\lambda$.

○ EXTENDED To interpret reflection, refraction and diffraction using wave theory.

End of topic questions

Note: The marks awarded for these questions indicate the level of detail required in the answers. In the examination, the number of marks awarded to questions like these may be different.

1. A sound wave is displayed using a cathode ray oscilloscope. It has a simple, smooth repeating pattern.

   a) Draw a trace of what is seen on the screen and label it to indicate:
   the crest of the wave, the wavelength of the wave and the amplitude of the wave. **(6 marks)**

   b) The frequency of the wave is 512 Hz. How many waves are produced each second? **(2 marks)**

2. EXTENDED Radio waves of frequency 900 MHz are used to send information to and from a portable phone. The speed of the waves is 3×10^8 m/s. Calculate the wavelength of the waves.
   (1 MHz = 1 000 000 Hz, 3×10^8 = 300 000 000.) **(2 marks)**

3. EXTENDED a) Calculate the wavelength of waves of speed 3×10^8 m/s with frequency of 400 MHz. **(2 marks)**

   b) For the waves in part a) to diffract, about how wide should the opening be? **(2 marks)**

4. EXTENDED What is the frequency of waves of speed 3×10^8 m/s and wavelength 0.1 m? **(2 marks)**

5. EXTENDED What is the speed of a wave of 20 Hz with a wavelength of 4 m? **(2 marks)**

6. EXTENDED Copy the table and calculate the missing quantities.

Speed/ms^{-1}	Frequency/Hz	Wavelength/m	Period/s
	10	2	
20	5		
		6	0.2
340		34	
160	8		
		12	0.004

(12 marks)

7. What are the most likely explanations of the following effects? Give careful explanations.

   a) The captain of an ocean-going ship is proceeding slowly into waves coming towards the ship. She suddenly notices that the waves change in two ways about 200 m ahead of where the ship is. They get further apart and change direction quite noticeably. **(3 marks)**

   b) You find that you can listen to radio stations in all of the rooms in your home, but you cannot get a mobile phone signal in certain rooms even when you open the windows. **(3 marks)**

Light

INTRODUCTION

Visible light is just part of the electromagnetic spectrum, but without it your life would be very different. Close your eyes for a moment and imagine a world of darkness. What would you miss the most? There are different processes involved in seeing the world around us, including reflection and refraction. You may already know that, as light enters your eyes, it is refracted by the lens in your eye and brought to a focus on your retina.

△ Fig. 3.10 A music concert uses both light and sound.

KNOWLEDGE CHECK

✓ Know how to describe waves using keywords such as wavelength, amplitude and frequency.
✓ Know the difference between longitudinal and transverse waves.
✓ EXTENDED Be able to describe the processes of reflection, refraction and diffraction in terms of wavefronts.

LEARNING OBJECTIVES

✓ Be able to describe the formation of an optical image by a plane mirror, and give its characteristics.
✓ Be able to use the law angle of incidence = angle of reflection.
✓ EXTENDED Be able to perform simple constructions, measurements and calculations.
✓ Be able to describe an experimental demonstration of the refraction of light.
✓ Be able to use the terminology for the angle of incidence i and angle or refraction r and describe the passage of light through parallel-sided transparent material.
✓ Be able to give the meaning of critical angle.
✓ Be able to describe internal and total internal reflection.
✓ EXTENDED Be able to recall and use the definition of refractive index n in terms of speed.
✓ EXTENDED Be able to recall and use the equation $\sin i/\sin r = n$.
✓ EXTENDED Be able to describe the action of optical fibres, particularly in medicine and communications technology.
✓ Be able to describe the action of a thin converging lens on a beam of light.
✓ Be able to use the terms 'principal focus' and 'focal length'.
✓ Be able to draw ray diagrams to illustrate the formation of a real image by a single lens.
✓ EXTENDED Be able to draw ray diagrams to illustrate the formation of a virtual image by a single lens.
✓ EXTENDED Be able to use and describe the use of a single lens as a magnifying glass.

- ✓ Be able to give a qualitative account of the dispersion of light as shown by the action of light on a glass prism.
- ✓ Be able to describe the main features of the electromagnetic spectrum and state that all e.m. waves travel with the same high speed in a vacuum.
- ✓ Be able to describe the role of electromagnetic waves in: radio and television communications; satellite television and telephones; electrical appliances, remote controllers for TVs and intruder alarms; medicine and security.
- ✓ Be able to demonstrate an awareness of safety issues regarding the use of microwaves and X-rays.
- ✓ **EXTENDED** Be able to state the appropriate value of the speed of electromagnetic waves.
- ✓ **EXTENDED** Be able to use the term 'monochromatic'.

SCIENCE IN CONTEXT **HOW SUNGLASSES WORK**

A good pair of sunglasses changes incoming light, making it more comfortable for your eyes to deal with. Light intensity, or brightness, is measured in lumens. Human eyes can cope with intensities of up to around 3500 lumens. However, on a sunny day light intensities may be more than 6000 lumens on a large stretch of road. When the brightness of direct or reflected light gets to around 4000 lumens, your eyes have difficulty absorbing the light and you

△ Fig. 3.11 Sunglasses help to filter out glare, protecting our eyes.

see these brighter areas as flashes of white light, which is called glare. At this intensity, your eyes try to reduce the discomfort by squinting.

Light is a transverse wave. It has both a vertical and horizontal component, and it is possible for only one of these components to travel through a particular medium when that medium is a polarising medium and only lets one component through. So, as a light wave approaches your eye, it could contain both the horizontal and vertical components, it could be vertically **polarised** or it could be horizontally polarised.

Light from the Sun, or a light bulb, radiates in all directions. When light waves hit a surface, the reflected waves (which reach your eyes) are polarised to match the surface. Most of the glare that causes you to wear sunglasses comes from horizontal surfaces, such as water or roads. A surface that reflects a lot of light, like a lake, will produce a lot of horizontally polarised light. Polarised lenses in sunglasses are fixed so that only vertically polarised light can reach your eyes. So the glare from the lake (or other horizontal surface) will not reach your eyes and cause discomfort.

REFLECTION OF LIGHT

Perhaps the most familiar types of wave in everyday life (along with water waves) is light. Light does not need a medium to travel through as it is an electromagnetic wave (see the electromagnetic spectrum in the following topic).

Light waves have all of the properties of waves. You have already learned about their speed and wavelength. In addition, they are **transverse** waves.

Like all other waves, light can be reflected, refracted and diffracted. Reflection and refraction are easy to demonstrate with a mirror and a glass of water. The effects caused by diffraction of light waves are very hard to see. The effects are small because the wavelength of light is so short.

Reflection of light and ray diagrams

When you look in a plane mirror you see an **image** of yourself (Fig. 3.12). The image is said to be **laterally inverted** because when you raise your right hand your image raises what you would call its left hand. The image is formed as far behind the mirror as you are in front of it and is the same size as you. The image cannot be projected onto a screen. It is known as a **virtual image**.

△ Fig. 3.12 As you look at the face of the girl and her image in the mirror, you can see that every part of her face is directly opposite its image in the mirror, and that each part is the same distance away from the mirror as its image.

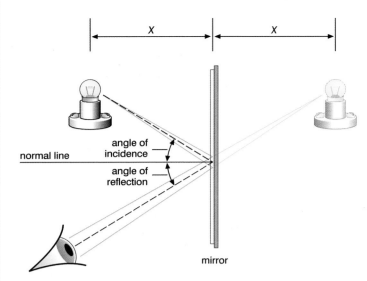

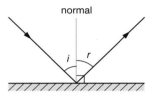

Fig. 3.13 Rays of light travel outwards from the lamp in all directions. Here just two rays are drawn to show how light goes from the lamp to the observer's eye. After the rays have reflected from the mirror, they travel along lines that *look* as if they started from the image. The eye is tricked into thinking that the light really did start from the image.

A ray of light is a line drawn to show the path that the light waves take. We need to study what happens when an incident light ray (a light ray that is going to fall on a surface) hits a mirror and is reflected off. Light rays are reflected from mirrors in such a way that

angle of incidence (i) **= angle of reflection** (r)

The angles are measured to an imaginary line at 90° to the surface of the mirror. This line is called **the normal**.

△ Fig. 3.14 The angles of incidence and reflection are the same when a mirror reflects light.

EXTENDED

When you are given the position of the object, then you can construct a diagram to show the position of the image. The diagrams in Fig. 3.15 show you how. Notice that in each case the angle of incidence (angle between normal and blue ray) is the same as the angle of reflection (angle between normal and red ray).

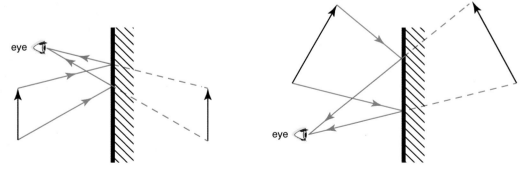

△ Fig. 3.15 Calculating the position of an image. The blue rays are the incident rays and the red rays are the reflected rays.

END OF EXTENDED

In a plane mirror the image is always the same size as the object. Examples of plane mirrors include household 'dressing' mirrors, security mirrors for checking under vehicles, and periscopes.

An image formed by a plane mirror, such as the one in Fig. 3.12, is:

- virtual
- laterally inverted
- the same size as the object
- the same distance behind the mirror as the object is in front of the mirror.

Note that the image is never formed on the surface of the mirror. This is a mistake which is often made by candidates in examinations.

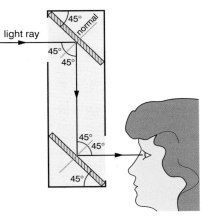

▷ Fig. 3.16 A periscope uses reflection to allow you to see above your normal line of vision – or even round corners.

Developing Investigative Skills

A student wants to find the position of an image in a plane mirror. To do this she sets up a plane mirror with an object pin placed vertically a few centimetres in front of it (Fig. 3.17). To find the image, the student looks into the mirror at an angle a little further along the mirror. She can see the image of the object pin in the mirror and she places two 'sighting pins' in line with the image in the mirror. The student repeats this process from a slightly different angle, again putting in two sighting pins.

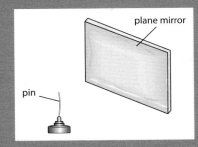

△ Fig. 3.17 The apparatus needed for the investigation.

Using and organising techniques, apparatus and materials

❶ How can the student use the positions of these sighting pins to find the position of the image?

❷ How can the student use the positions of the sighting pins to show that the angle of incidence is equal to the angle of reflection for light reflecting off the mirror?

Observing, measuring and recording

❸ Draw a plan view diagram to show this experiment. Include the object pin, sighting pins and position of the image.

❹ On your diagram, check that the image is as far behind the mirror as the object is in front. Check also that the line joining the object and image cuts through the mirror at 90°.

Handling experimental observations and data

❺ Apart from checking the measurements as in your diagram, how could the student check that she has marked the position of the image correctly?

❻ Would this method for finding the image work with a curved mirror? Explain your answer.

REFRACTION OF LIGHT

The view through some windows is deliberately obscure – the image that you see is distorted. This is because the glass has a different thickness in different places. Rays of light passing through the window are bent to a different extent. Plain windows in old houses can give slightly distorted images because it used to be much harder to make large, flat panes of glass.

The bending of light is the phenomenon known as refraction, which we shall study in this part of the topic.

Light waves *slow down* when they travel from air into glass. When they are at an angle to the glass, light rays bend *towards* the normal as they enter the glass. When the light rays travel out of the glass into the air, their speed increases and they bend *away* from the normal. When the block of glass has parallel sides, the light resumes its original direction after passing through. This is why a sheet of window glass has so little effect on the view beyond. However, the view is shifted slightly sideways when you look through the glass at an angle.

Fig. 3.18 shows how you can demonstrate the refraction of light through a glass block.

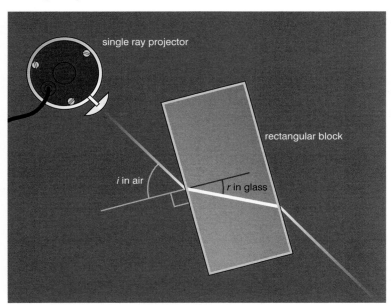

single ray projector

rectangular block

i in air

r in glass

△ Fig. 3.18 Refraction of light.

The angle of incidence, *i*, is the angle between the incident light ray and the normal to the surface. The angle of refraction, *r*, is the angle between the refracted light ray and the normal to the surface inside the material.

(Note that people tend to use the letter *r* both for the angle of reflection and the angle of refraction. It should be clear from the context whether they are talking about reflection or refraction.)

QUESTIONS

1. Refraction of light at the surface of a pond can make the pond look shallower than it really is. Explain why.

2. Sound waves can be refracted when they travel through balloons filled with different gases. How would the motion of a sound wave be changed if it travelled through a balloon filled with carbon dioxide?

EXTENDED

Refractive index

The **refractive index** of a material indicates how much the material changes the direction of the light. It is calculated using the following formula:

refractive index $n = \dfrac{\sin i}{\sin r}$

Where:
i = angle of incidence
r = angle of refraction

The refractive index of a vacuum is 1 and the refractive index of air is fractionally higher, but we will take it as 1. Other common refractive indices are water 1.3; window glass 1.5; sapphire 1.75; diamond 2.4.

The refractive index n can also be defined as:

$$n = \frac{\text{speed of light in vacuum (or air)}}{\text{speed of light in the material}}$$

WORKED EXAMPLES

1. When the speed of light in a vacuum is 300 000 000 m/s. What is the speed of light in glass with a refractive index of 1.5?

Write down the formula: $n = \dfrac{\text{speed of light in vacuum (or air)}}{\text{speed of light in the material}}$

Rearrange the formula: $\text{speed in material} = \dfrac{\text{speed in vacuum}}{n}$

Substitute the values: $\text{speed in material} = \dfrac{300\ 000\ 000}{1.5}$

Work out the answer and write down the unit:
$\text{speed in material} = 200\ 000\ 000$ m/s
$= 2 \times 10^8$ m/s

2. A light ray approaches a block of plastic at an angle of incidence of 60°. When the refractive index of the plastic is 1.4. What is the angle of refraction?

Write down the formula: $n = \dfrac{\sin i}{\sin r}$

When $i = 60°$, $\sin i = 0.866$

Rearrange the formula: $\sin r = \dfrac{\sin i}{n}$

Substitute the values: $\sin r = \dfrac{0.866}{1.4}$

Work out the answer: $\sin r = 0.619$

From a calculator, when $\sin r = 0.619$, then $r = 38.2°$
The angle of refraction is 38.2°.

QUESTIONS

1. EXTENDED The refractive index of a particular glass is 1.5 and the angle of incidence is 50°. What is the angle of refraction?

2. EXTENDED The angle of refraction for a ray of light in a block of plastic with refractive index 1.4 is 25°. What was the angle of incidence?

3. EXTENDED The angle of incidence of a ray of light on a material is 55°. The angle of refraction in the material is 35°. What is the refractive index of the material?

4. EXTENDED Light travels faster than anything else known to science, but it travels at different speeds in different materials. The refractive index of the material light passes through determines at what speed it travels. Here is a table of refractive indices.

Material/substance	Refractive index
Air	1.003
Water	1.333
Glass	1.52
Diamond	2.417

a) Does light travel faster or more slowly in water than it does in air?

b) In which of these materials do you think light will travel slowest? Give a reason for your answer.

c) Calculate the speed of light in each of the materials in the table and confirm (or otherwise) your prediction from part b).

Developing Investigative Skills

A student wants to find the refractive index of a rectangular block of glass. He draws around the block and marks the position of a ray of light that travels through the block. With the block removed, the student can draw in a normal line and then measure the angle of incidence and the angle of refraction. The student repeats this process for different angles of incidence. His measurements are shown in the table.

△ Fig. 3.19 Ray of light being refracted by a glass block.

Angle of incidence/°	Angle of refraction/°
10	6.5
20	13
30	20
40	25
50	32
60	35

Observing, measuring and recording

❶ Draw a diagram to show the measurements the student needs to make.

❷ How should the student mark the normal line during the experiment?

Handling experimental observations and data

❸ What was the independent variable in this investigation? What was the dependent variable?

❹ State the equation linking refractive index, sin i and sin r.

❺ Draw a graph of sin i (y-axis) against sin r (x-axis).

❻ Use your graph to find a value for the refractive index of the block.

Planning and evaluating investigations

❼ Describe two possible reasons why the measurements may not be completely accurate.

❽ What difference would it make to the results if light of a different colour was used in the experiment?

Total internal reflection and the critical angle

When rays of light pass from a *dense medium* to a *less dense medium* they bend *away* from the normal.

As the angle of incidence increases, an angle is reached at which the emerging light rays would travel along the surface (the angle of refraction = 90°). The angle of incidence at which the angle of refraction becomes equal to 90° is known as the **critical angle** for the material. At greater angles of incidence, the rays are entirely reflected back inside the medium. This process is known as **total internal reflection**. In Fig. 3.20 the angle is 2 or 3 degrees less than the critical angle, and light is just managing to escape from the glass.

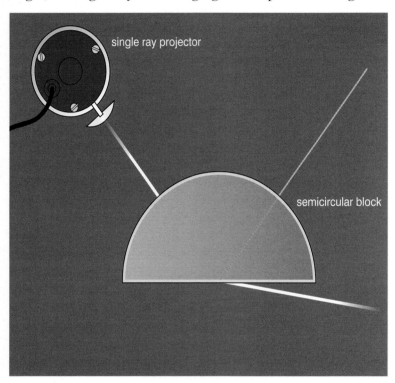

single ray projector

semicircular block

Δ Fig. 3.20 The angle of incidence is just less than the critical angle here.

Total internal reflection is used in fibre optic cables. A fibre optic cable can be made of a single glass fibre. The light continues along the fibre by being constantly internally reflected. Light does not escape from the fibre because it always hits the internal surface at an angle greater than the critical angle and is internally reflected.

Telephone and TV communications systems rely increasingly on fibre optics instead of the more traditional copper cables. Fibre optic cables do not use electricity – the signals are carried by infra-red rays. The signals are very clear because they do not suffer from electrical interference. Other advantages are that the fibre optic cables are cheaper than copper cables and can carry thousands of different signals down the same fibre at the same time.

light beam

Δ Fig. 3.21 Fibre optic cable.

Bundles of several thousand optical fibres are used in medical endoscopes for internal examination of the body. The bundle carries an image from one end of the bundle to the other, each fibre carrying one tiny part (one pixel) of the image.

END OF EXTENDED

QUESTIONS

1. What is the critical angle?

2. What is the critical angle for a material of refractive index 1.4?

3. What is the refractive index for a material that has a critical angle of 51°?

SCIENCE IN CONTEXT OPTICAL FIBRES

Optical fibres transfer data in signals consisting of pulses of light following each other rapidly. The bandwidth of the fibre is the maximum number of pulses per second that can be transferred along the fibre and still be recognised as separate pulses at the receiving end. There is a limit to this bandwidth due to a process called pulse spreading. This is where the signal, originally a rectangular pulse, becomes weaker and spreads over a longer time interval as it travels along the fibre.

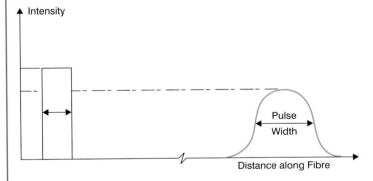

△ Fig. 3.22 Signal transmitted down an optical fibre.

Some signal may be lost from the sides of the fibre, and the fibre material absorbs some of the intensity. Spreading may cause pulses to become merged, meaning that the precise data transfer required for digital signals is not delivered with perfect accuracy.

The spreading of the pulse is due to two *dispersion* effects. First, chromatic dispersion happens because the refractive index of the fibre is different for different frequencies (colours) of light. This effect causes light to be 'split' into colours in a prism or in raindrops, producing a rainbow. This means that the different frequencies of light will travel at different speeds in the fibre and lead to slightly different arrival times at the far end – the pulse will have 'spread'.

Secondly, when the width of the fibre is larger than the wavelength of the light there will be alternative paths (called 'modes') along the fibre.

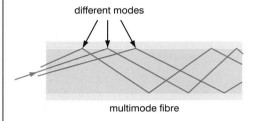

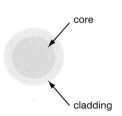

△ Fig. 3.23 Different modes in an optical fibre.

Each path is a slightly different length so, again, the pulse arrives spread over a longer time. This multi-mode dispersion can be reduced by using a graded-index material for the fibre core. Here, the refractive index of the core material reduces gradually from the centre to the edge.

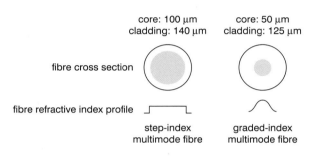

△ Fig. 3.24 Multimode fibres.

The result of this is that the light travels more quickly towards the edge of the fibre, compensating for the extra distance it has to travel. The refraction occurs gradually as the light moves towards the edge of the fibre, so the light is always bent back towards the centre path and total internal reflection does not happen.

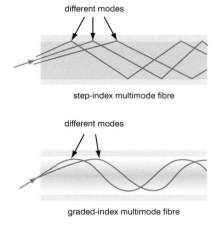

△ Fig. 3.25 Reflection in the two types of optical fibre.

THIN CONVERGING LENS

Convex (converging, positive) lenses cause parallel rays of light to **converge** (Fig. 3.26). The light rays are bent by refraction, as described earlier in this topic in 'Refraction of light', except that the amount of refraction increases from the middle of the lens (where there is no refraction) to a maximum at the outer edge of the lens. The point where the parallel light rays arriving along the axis of the lens all cross over is known as the **principal focus**, *F*, and the **focal length**, *f*, is the most important feature of the lens. Note that there are two principal foci. (The word 'foci' is the plural of 'focus'.) The foci are each side of the lens, at the same distance away from it.

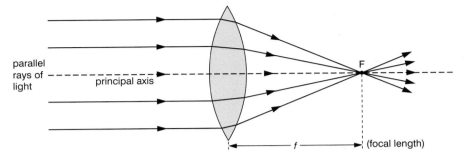

△ Fig. 3.26 Rays through a convex lens converge to a focus.

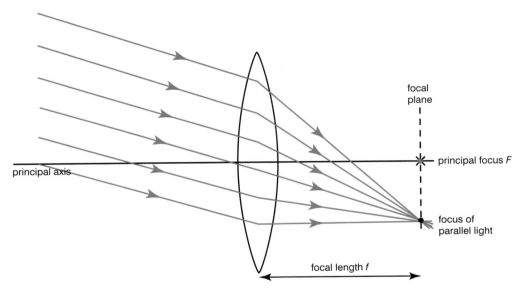

△ Fig. 3.27 Incoming rays converge to a point in the focal plane.

The principal axis is the line through the middle of the lens and at right angles to it. The principal foci lie on this line.

Converging lenses are used to form images by magnifying glasses, cameras, telescopes, binoculars, microscopes, film projectors and spectacles for long-sighted people.

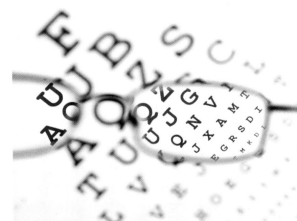

▷ Fig. 3.28 What type of lenses do these spectacles have?

You can check your spectacles to see if they act as a weak magnifying glass, or if they make things seem smaller. If they magnify, then you are long-sighted and you see distant things more clearly. If they do the opposite, then you are short-sighted and see close-up things more clearly. Long sight is corrected with a converging lens. Short sight uses a different lens that diverges light and is not covered in this course.

When the object is further from the lens than the focal length, the converging lens forms a **real image**. For example, a cinema projector makes a real image on the screen of the film inside the projector, and a camera makes a real image of the object being photographed on the film or the digital sensor inside. In the first case the image is bigger than the object; in the second case it is smaller.

To find the position of an image

To find the position of the image of an object formed by a converging lens, you can draw a **ray diagram**. There are three standard rays that you can use to do this. A standard ray is one whose complete path you know. In ray diagrams, you need any two of the standard rays to find the position and size of the image. In addition, it is a wise precaution to draw the third ray to check the accuracy with which you drew the first two.

For convenience, ray diagrams are usually drawn with the bottom of the object on the principal axis. This means that the bottom of the image is also on the principal axis, and you need only locate the top of the image. Figs. 3.29, 3.30 and 3.31 show the standard rays.

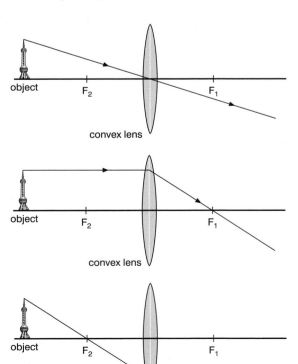

◁ Fig. 3.29 A ray from the top of the object, straight through the centre of the lens.

◁ Fig. 3.30 A ray from the top of the object, parallel to the principal axis until it reaches the lens, and then down through the principal focus F_1 on the far side of the lens.

◁ Fig. 3.31 A ray from the top of the object through the principal focus F_2 on the near side of the lens, down to the lens and then parallel to the axis.

You can use a suitable combination of these three rays to locate images. Three examples are given here.

Here the image is real, inverted, smaller than the object and closer to the lens than the distance of the object from the lens. A real image is one through which the rays actually pass, and which could be picked up on a suitable screen. Examples of the formation of this type of image are in the eye and in a camera.

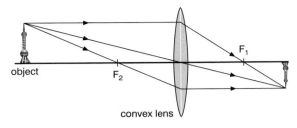

△ Fig. 3.32 The object is a long way from the lens (more than twice the focal length).

Here the image is real, inverted, larger than the object and further from the lens than the distance of the object from the lens. Examples of the formation of this type of image are in a film projector and in a photographic enlarger.

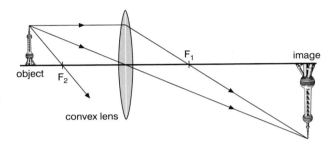

△ Fig. 3.33 The object is closer to the lens (between ×1 and ×2 the focal length)

Here the image is virtual, upright, larger than the object and further away from the lens than the distance of the object from the lens. A virtual image is one through which the rays do not actually pass, but from which they appear to come. Such an image cannot be picked up on a screen. An example where this type of image is formed is in the magnifying glass.

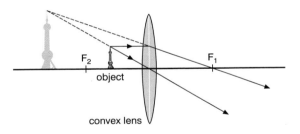

△ Fig. 3.34 The object is closer to the lens than the focal length.

Fig. 3.35 shows how the eye sees the image through a magnifying glass.

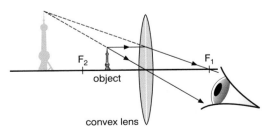

△ Fig. 3.35 Looking at an image through a magnifying glass. Note that to see the image, you have to look through the lens.

The image in all these cases is never on the lens itself. This is a mistake that students often make in examinations.

Let's find the position of the image in Fig. 3.36. As you can see in Fig. 3.37, we use the two rays to find where the image would be. It is clear that one of the rays cannot really be followed by light because the lens is too small. The lines are some of the real light rays that go through the lens, but these rays cannot be used to find the position of the image. We use two rays to find where the image would be, as shown in Fig. 3.37.

Note that these special rays are 'construction lines'. You may find that if the lens has a smaller diameter, the upper ray could miss the lens completely. This does not matter, simply pretend that the lens has a large enough diameter and work out where the image is. That is where all of the real rays will go. The image will not move just because the real lens has a smaller diameter.

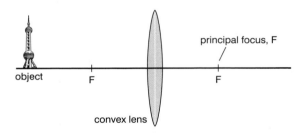

△ Fig. 3.36 Using rays to find the position of an image.

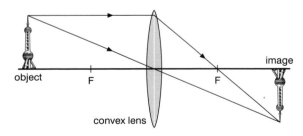

△ Fig. 3.37 The camera forms a small inverted image of the object in front of it on the digital sensor or the film at the back.

DISPERSION OF LIGHT

When white light is passed through a triangular **prism** (a glass or plastic block), it is split into a spectrum of different colours (see Fig. 3.38).

This is called **dispersion**. The refractive index of the glass or plastic is slightly different for each colour of light, so each colour is refracted by a different amount. The light rays are bent or refracted twice: once as they enter the prism, and again in the same direction as they leave it. The dispersion increases each time, which is why the colours are separated so much. Red is always bent least and violet is bent most.

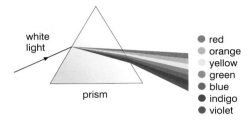

△ Fig. 3.38 Dispersion of light by a prism.

THE ELECTROMAGNETIC SPECTRUM

The electromagnetic spectrum is a 'family' of waves. Electromagnetic waves all travel at the same high speed in a vacuum. This high speed explains why you can have a phone call between China and New Zealand with a delay of only 0.1 s before you hear the reply from the person at the other end. It takes the infra-red signal this long to travel there and back through an optical fibre.

△ Fig. 3.39 These satellite dishes are receiving high-energy radio waves, which are part of the electromagnetic spectrum.

EXTENDED

The speed of light is 300 000 000 m/s. This can be written more conveniently as 3×10^8 m/s.

END OF EXTENDED

However, for astronomical distances the delays quickly become longer. Even when Mars is at its nearest to Earth, it takes 10 minutes to send a message to a robot on the surface and receive a reply. Getting a reply from the nearest star would take 8½ years.

Note that all electromagnetic waves can travel through a vacuum, which is why we can see the light and feel the heat coming from the Sun. Other waves, such as sound waves, cannot travel through a vacuum.

Order of the electromagnetic spectrum

White light is a mixture of different colours and can be split by a prism into the **visible spectrum**. All the different colours of light travel at the same speed in a vacuum, but they have different frequencies and wavelengths. Red light has a wavelength almost twice as long as that of violet light. When the colours enter glass or perspex, they all slow down, but by different amounts, because their wavelengths are slightly different. The different colours are therefore refracted through different angles. Violet is refracted the most, red the least. Fig. 3.40 shows the refraction of white light through a triangular prism, which splits it into the spectrum of visible light: red, orange, yellow, green, blue, indigo, violet (you can remember this as *ROYGBIV*).

△ Fig. 3.40 A prism splits white light into the colourful spectrum of visible light.

The visible spectrum is only a small part of the full electromagnetic spectrum. The electromagnetic spectrum has waves of wavelength of the order of 10^4 m right down to wavelengths of the order of 10^{-12} m. Visible light has wavelengths ranging between 10^{-6} and 10^{-7} m. All electromagnetic waves travel at the same speed in a vacuum, which is 3×10^8 m/s. This means that the different wavelengths must have different frequencies, and that the longest wavelengths have the lowest frequencies. Fig. 3.41 shows the full electromagnetic spectrum.

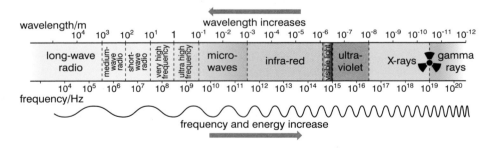

△ Fig. 3.41 The electromagnetic spectrum.

REMEMBER

The energy associated with an electromagnetic wave depends on its frequency. The waves with the higher frequencies are potentially the more hazardous ones, because they carry most energy.

The visible light region of the spectrum contains the colours ranged from red, through orange, yellow, green and blue to violet. Infra-red lies next to red, and ultraviolet is next to violet.

Light of one wavelength, that is to say of just one colour, is known as **monochromatic** light.

QUESTIONS

1. Describe how white light can be split into a spectrum by a prism.

2. What is the speed of electromagnetic waves in free space?

3. Which has greater frequency, microwaves or X-rays?

4. Put these electromagnetic radiations into order of increasing wavelength.

microwaves   gamma rays   infra-red
visible light   ultraviolet

Uses and hazards of electromagnetic radiation

From Fig. 3.41 you will have seen that there are different types of electromagnetic radiation. Some of these types of radiation can have harmful effects on the human body when exposure to them is excessive.

Gamma rays, which as you see in Fig. 3.41 are the electromagnetic waves with the shortest wavelength, and therefore the greatest frequency and energy, are produced by radioactive nuclei. They carry more energy than X-rays and can cause cancer or mutation in body cells. Gamma rays are frequently used in radiotherapy to kill cancer cells.

Radioactive substances that emit gamma rays are used as **tracers**. A tracer is something that can be used to track the flow of a substance, and is often used to track substances in biological systems. For example, if scientists want to know where in a plant the phosphorus goes, they can feed the plant a radioactive isotope of phosphorus and then measure the radioactivity that is given off by different parts of the plant.

X-rays, which have the next highest energy radiation after gamma on the electromagnetic spectrum, are produced when high-energy electrons are fired at a metal target. Bones absorb more X-rays than other body tissue. When a person is placed between an X-ray source and a photographic plate, the bones appear to be white on the developed photographic plate compared with the rest of the body. X-rays have high energy, as shown in Fig. 3.42, and can damage or destroy body cells. They may also cause cancer. An X-ray could save your life, but it is not free from danger. A doctor will only arrange for an X-ray when it is clear that the benefits to you are far greater than the tiny risk that it will make you ill.

However, X-rays are also used to treat cancer. X-rays are targeted at the tumour with the aim of destroying the tumour cells while leaving healthy cells surrounding the tumour untouched.

X-rays are also used to screen baggage at airports and other places. It works in the same way as a medical X-ray. Different materials absorb different amounts of X-rays.

X-ray scanners can also be used to scan bodies and much larger objects. They can even be used to scan trucks and shipping containers to see if there are any things such as weapons or people hidden in the truck or container.

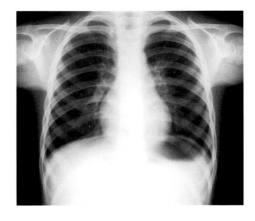

△ Fig. 3.42 An X-ray of the lungs.

Ultraviolet radiation (UV) is the component of the Sun's rays that gives you a suntan. UV is also created in fluorescent light tubes after exciting the atoms in a mercury vapour. The UV radiation is then absorbed by the coating on the inside of the fluorescent tube and re-emitted as visible light. Fluorescent tubes are more efficient than light bulbs because they do not emit heat energy, so more energy is available to produce light. Ultraviolet can also damage the surface cells of the body, which can lead to skin cancer. It can also damage the eyes, leading to blindness.

All objects give out **infra-red radiation** (IR). The hotter the object is, the more radiation it gives out. Thermograms are photographs taken to show the infra-red radiation given out from objects. Infra-red radiation grills and cooks our food in an ordinary oven and is used in remote controls to operate televisions and videos. Excessive exposure to infra-red, such as when you get close to a very hot object, can burn skin and other body tissue.

Microwaves are high-frequency **radio waves**. They are used in **radar** to find the position of aircraft and ships. Metal objects reflect the microwaves back to the transmitter, enabling the distance between the object and the transmitter to be calculated. Microwaves are also used for cooking. Water particles in food absorb the energy carried by microwaves. They vibrate more, making the food much hotter. Microwaves penetrate several centimetres into the food and so speed up the cooking process. Because of their ability to penetrate several centimetres, which is useful when cooking food, microwaves can heat body tissue internally, so care must be taken to ensure they cannot escape from a microwave oven.

REMEMBER

Infra-red radiation is absorbed by the surface of the food, then the energy is spread through the rest of the food by conduction. In contrast, microwaves penetrate a few centimetres into the food and then the energy is transferred throughout the food by conduction.

Radio waves have the longest wavelengths and lowest frequencies.

- **UHF (ultra-high frequency)** waves are used to transmit television programmes to homes.
- **VHF** (very high frequency) waves are used to transmit local radio programmes.
- **Medium** and **long** radio waves are used to transmit over longer distances because their wavelengths allow them to diffract around obstacles such as buildings and hills.
- Communication satellites above the Earth receive signals carried by high-frequency (**short-wave**) radio waves. These signals are amplified and re-transmitted to other parts of the world.

SCIENCE IN CONTEXT

PROTECTION FROM ULTRAVIOLET RAYS

In 2007, scientists at the University of Virginia published a study about how cells protect themselves (or fail to protect themselves) from damage to the DNA caused by ultraviolet rays. The study showed that there is a simple switch mechanism inside cells, which is triggered by exposure to ultraviolet and helps cells to survive and even thrive after exposure to ultraviolet rays.

After DNA damage caused by exposure to ultraviolet rays, cells normally stop moving and responding to stimuli until they are repaired. If the repair work is not carried out properly, the result can be cancer, as the damaged cell keeps dividing.

QUESTIONS

1. Gamma rays and X-rays are both used in medical contexts. Describe how each is produced.

2. How is UV created in fluorescent tubes?

3. What is a thermogram?

4. How do microwaves cook food?

△ Fig. 3.43 Radar uses pulses of very short radio waves and is used in ships for navigation.

1. Imagine that you are the communications manager in a company that markets radar for installation on yachts. Produce a web page for your internet site explaining to prospective customers:

- how radar works
- the properties of the radio waves.

Provide illustrations for the site, informing prospective buyers of the advantages of using radar.

2. There are many different departments in a hospital, for example:

- eye clinic
- X-ray
- nuclear radiation
- thermography
- physiotherapy.

Produce a table detailing the following:

- the name of the electromagnetic wave used in each department
- the wavelength of the wave used
- the application of the wave, detailing the specific medical use for the wave
- health and safety precautions that should be taken, where appropriate.

End of topic checklist

Key terms

angle of incidence, angle of reflection, converging lens, convex lens, critical angle, dispersion, focal length, gamma ray, horizontally polarised, image, infra-red, laterally inverted, long-range radio wave, medium-range radio wave, microwave, monochromatic light, polarised light, positive lens, principal focus, prism, radar, radio wave, ray diagram, real image, refractive index, the normal, total internal reflection, tracer, ultra-high frequency (UHF), ultraviolet light, vertically polarised, very high frequency (VHF), virtual image, visible spectrum, X-ray

During your study of this topic you should have learned:

○ How to describe the formation of an optical image by a plane mirror and give its characteristics.

○ About the law angle of incidence = angle of reflection.

○ EXTENDED How to perform simple constructions, measurements and calculations.

○ About an experimental demonstration of the refraction of light.

○ About the angle of incidence i and the angle of refraction r and about the passage of light through parallel-sided transparent material.

○ The meaning of critical angle.

○ About internal and total internal reflection.

○ EXTENDED The definition of refractive index n in terms of speed.

○ EXTENDED How to use the equation $\sin i/\sin r = n$.

○ EXTENDED How to describe the action of optical fibres, particularly in medicine and communications technology.

○ How to describe the action of a thin converging lens on a beam of light.

○ The terms 'principal focus' and 'focal length'.

○ How to draw ray diagrams to illustrate the formation of a real image by a single lens.

○ EXTENDED How to draw ray diagrams to illustrate the formation of a virtual image by a single lens.

○ EXTENDED How to use and describe the use of a single lens as a magnifying glass.

End of topic checklist continued

○ About dispersion of light, as shown by the action on light of a glass prism.

○ About the main features of the electromagnetic spectrum and that all e.m. waves travel with the same high speed in a vacuum.

○ EXTENDED About the approximate value of the speed of electromagnetic waves.

○ EXTENDED How to use the term 'monochromatic'.

○ About the role of electromagnetic waves in:

- radio and television communications (radio waves)
- satellite television and telephones (microwaves)
- electrical appliances, remote controllers for televisions and intruder alarms (infra-red)
- medicine and security (X-rays).

○ About safety issues regarding the use of microwaves and X-rays.

End of topic questions

Note: The marks awarded for these questions indicate the level of detail required in the answers. In the examination, the number of marks awarded to questions like these may be different.

1. Write down all four characteristics that describe the image formed by a plane mirror. Use the correct scientific language. **(4 marks)**

2. a) Rays of light can be reflected and refracted. State one difference between reflection and refraction. **(1 mark)**

b) The diagram shows a glass block and two rays of light.

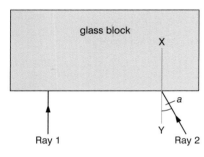

    i) Copy the diagram and complete the paths of the two rays as they pass into and then out of the glass block. **(2 marks)**

    ii) What name is given to the angle marked a? **(1 mark)**

    iii) What name is given to the line marked XY? **(1 mark)**

3. The diagram shows light entering a prism. Total internal reflection takes place at the inner surfaces of the prism.

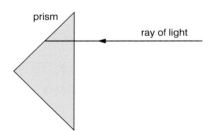

a) Copy the diagram and complete the path of the ray. **(1 mark)**

b) Suggest one use for a prism like this. **(1 mark)**

c) Copy and complete the table about total internal reflection by glass. Use T for total internal reflection or R for refraction.

Angle of incidence at the second face/°	Total internal reflection (T) or refraction (R)
36	
42 (critical angle)	
46	

(3 marks)

4. EXTENDED A student traces the path of a red light beam through a rectangular block of plastic, and finds that the angle of incidence is 50° and the angle of refraction is 21.7°.

    a) What is the refractive index of the block? **(3 marks)**

    b) What will be the critical angle for this material? **(3 marks)**

5. An object is 2 cm tall and placed 2 cm from a convex lens that has a focal length of 4 cm. Draw the ray diagram. Complete the rays backwards as dotted lines to draw the image. **(3 marks)**

6. What is meant by a 'virtual' image? **(1 mark)**

7. Where must you place the object so that a convex lens gives an image with a magnification of more than 1? **(2 marks)**

8. Explain why dispersion occurs. **(6 marks)**

9. EXTENDED Which has the higher refractive index in a prism: red or violet light? **(2 marks)**

10. Here is a list of types of wave:

gamma, infra-red, microwaves, radio, ultraviolet, visible, X-rays

Choose from the list the type of wave that best fits each of these descriptions:

    a) Stimulates the sensitive cells at the back of the eye. **(1 mark)**

    b) Necessary for a suntan. **(1 mark)**

    c) Used for rapid cooking in an oven. **(1 mark)**

    d) Used to take a photograph of the bones in a broken arm. **(1 mark)**

    e) Emitted by a TV remote control unit. **(1 mark)**

11. Gamma rays are part of the electromagnetic spectrum. Gamma rays are useful to us but can also be very dangerous.

    a) Explain how the properties of gamma rays make them useful to us. **(3 marks)**

    b) Explain why gamma rays can cause damage to people. **(3 marks)**

    c) Give one difference between microwaves and gamma rays. **(1 mark)**

    d) Microwaves travel at 300 000 000 m/s. What speed do gamma rays travel at? **(2 marks)**

12. a) Write down the parts of the electromagnetic spectrum in order of increasing wavelength. **(4 marks)**

    b) How would your list in part **a)** be different if you wrote it in order of increasing frequency? **(1 mark)**

13. Copy and complete the table describing waves of the electromagnetic spectrum.

Wave type	Source of wave	Use	Property
Radio	Radio transmitter and aerial		
X-rays	X-ray tubes	Security at airports	
	Lamps, sun, flames		Can be dispersed into seven colours
Ultraviolet	Mercury vapour lamps	Security markings	
		Thermal imaging	Can cause burns
Gamma	Radioactive substances		Very penetrating
Sound		Hearing	
	Magnetron	Heating food quickly	

(13 marks)

14. Why do microwave ovens take less time to cook food than normal ovens?

(3 marks)

15. a) Copy the electromagnetic spectrum shown and complete it by filling in the gaps.

Radio waves		Infra-red	Light		X-rays	

(3 marks)

b) Which waves have the longest wavelength? **(1 mark)**

c) Which type of wave carries the greatest energy? **(1 mark)**

d) What do all of the waves in the electromagnetic spectrum have in common? **(2 marks)**

e) What part of the spectrum is detected by: **i)** the eyes; **ii)** the skin? **(2 marks)**

16. Refraction and total internal reflection lead to the 'heat haze' that you can see over hot surfaces, particularly roads in the summer. Use ideas about how heat affects the density of air to explain how this happens. **(6 marks)**

17. Optical fibres are very narrow. By thinking about the different paths the light could take in an optical fibre, explain why optical fibres must not be too wide. **(6 marks)**

Sound

△ Fig. 3.44 Sound is caused by vibrations which can be seen by the motion recorded in this photo of active speakers.

INTRODUCTION

You communicate with other people using sound. Think about the importance of sound in your life. If there were no sounds, which sounds would you miss most?

Sound is a form of wave, like light. However, light is a transverse wave and sound is a longitudinal wave. Some of the properties of sound are the same as light, but some of them are different. In this section you are going to find out how these sound waves operate.

KNOWLEDGE CHECK

✓ Know how to describe waves using keywords such as wavelength, amplitude and frequency.
✓ Know the difference between longitudinal and transverse waves
✓ Be able to describe the processes of reflection, refraction and diffraction.

LEARNING OBJECTIVES

✓ Be able to describe the production of sound by vibrating sources.
✓ Be able to describe the longitudinal nature of sound waves.
✓ Be able to state the approximate range of audible frequencies.
✓ Be able to show an understanding that a medium is needed to transmit sound waves.
✓ Be able to describe an experiment to determine the speed of sound in air.
✓ Be able to relate the loudness and pitch of sound waves to amplitude and frequency.
✓ Be able to describe how the reflection of sound may produce an echo.
✓ EXTENDED Be able to describe compression and rarefaction.

✓ EXTENDED Be able to state the order of magnitude of the speed of sound in air, liquids and solids.

WHAT IS SOUND?

Sound is caused by vibrations – of the front of a violin or a cello, or of the column of air inside a trumpet. In the case of a loudspeaker it is particularly clear that the cone of the loudspeaker moves in and out and changes the pressure in the air in front of it. The sound travels as longitudinal waves.

The compressions (where vibrations are closer together on the wave) and rarefactions (where vibrations are further apart on the wave) of sound waves result in small differences in air pressure (see Fig. 3.2 in General wave properties)

Like other longitudinal waves, sound waves can be reflected, refracted or diffracted. Sound waves travel faster through liquids than through air. The speed of sound in air is 340 m/s. The speed of sound in water is 1484 m/s. Sound travels fastest through solids (in iron it travels at 5120 m/s. This is because particles are linked most strongly in solids. Note, however, that sound must have a medium through which to travel. Unlike electromagnetic waves, sound will not travel through a vacuum.

Δ Fig. 3.45 This orchestra is creating a single longitudinal wave of very complicated shape. In ways that we barely understand, our brains can pick out the sounds of all the individual instruments that are playing together.

Sounds humans can hear

The human ear can detect sounds with pitches in the range 20 Hz to 20 000 Hz. Sound with frequencies above this range is known as **ultrasound**. Ultrasound is used by bats for navigation. It can also be used to build up images of organs within the body, since different tissues reflect ultrasound waves in different ways. By combining the various reflections, an image is generated. A well-known example of the use of ultrasound scanning is for checking the development of a fetus during pregnancy.

Measuring the speed of sound in air

The simplest method to measure the speed of sound in air uses two microphones and a fast recording device such as a digital storage oscilloscope.

1. A sound source and the two microphones are arranged in a straight line, with the sound source beyond the first microphone.

2. The distance between the microphones (x), called microphone basis, is measured.

3. The time of arrival between the signals (delay) reaching the different microphones (t) is measured.

4. Then speed of sound = x / t

SCIENCE IN CONTEXT **DAMAGING EARS**

The ear is far more easily damaged than most people realise. You should always take care, both with the volume of sound and the length of time that your ear is exposed to it. The damage is cumulative, so is not noticed at first. Many older rock musicians have serious hearing problems, and many of the younger ones now wear earplugs to prevent their own performances from damaging their hearing.

Earplugs worn by rock musicians are designed to reduce the range of audio frequencies equally, so that the wearer hears the upper and lower frequencies at the same relative levels as they would without the earplugs. (If this were not the case, then the bass guitarist, for example, may feel that he or she was not playing loudly enough to balance the vocalist, simply because the lower frequencies were reduced in level too much in relation to the higher vocal frequencies.)

This type of earplug usually has a tiny diaphragm to reduce low frequencies (100 to 50 Hz), and absorbent or damping material to reduce high frequencies (5 to 2 kHz). They are quite expensive and are intended to be used again and again. They reduce noise levels by about 20 **decibels** (dB) but are not intended to protect the wearer from noise levels above 105 dB (Fig. 3.46).

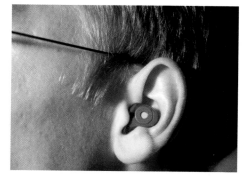

△ Fig. 3.46 A musician's earplug.

QUESTIONS

1. What type of wave are sound waves?

2. What happens to the air as a result of compressions and rarefactions in a sound wave?

3. What is the frequency range for human hearing?

4. What is ultrasound?

5. Describe a simple method for measuring the speed of sound in air.

Using an oscilloscope and microphone to display sound waves

Sound waves can be represented on an **oscilloscope** by using a microphone and a loudspeaker as shown in Fig. 3.47. This produces a voltage/time graph for the sound wave on the screen of the oscilloscope. From the voltage/time graph, you can find the frequency of the sound wave, since you will know the time taken for one cycle of the wave (which is the frequency).

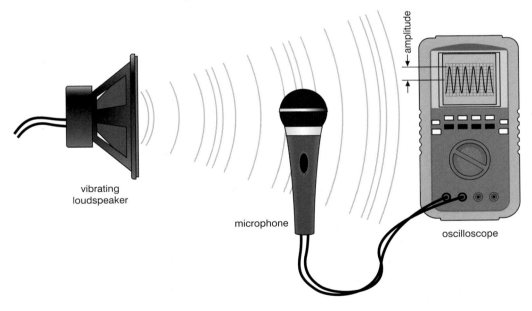

vibrating
loudspeaker

microphone

oscilloscope

amplitude

△ Fig. 3.47 Displaying sound waves on an oscilloscope screen.

Pitch, frequency, amplitude and loudness

Sounds with a high **pitch** have a high frequency. Examples of high-pitch sounds include birdsong and all the sounds that you hear from someone else's personal stereo when they have set the volume too high. Low-pitch sounds have a low frequency. Examples of low-pitch sounds include the horn of a large ship and a bass guitar.

Loud sounds have large amplitude, whereas quiet sounds have small amplitude. The loudness of sounds can be compared using decibels. Typical sound wave patterns are shown in Fig. 3.48.

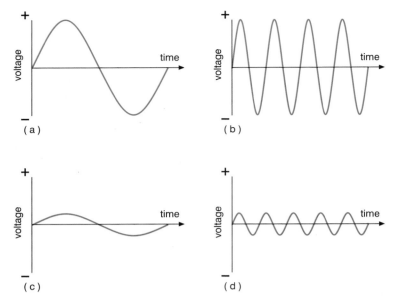

△ Fig. 3.48 Wave sound patterns: (a) A loud sound of low frequency; (b) A loud sound of high frequency; (c) A quiet sound of low frequency; (d) A quiet sound of high frequency.

WORKED EXAMPLE

Using this displacement/time graph for a sound wave, calculate the amplitude of the waveform.

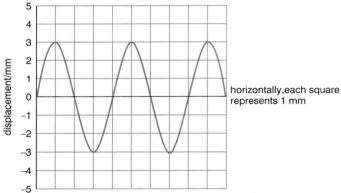

horizontally, each square represents 1 mm

◁ Fig. 3.49 Displacement/time graph for a sound wave.

The amplitude is the maximum displacement from the mean position, so can be read straight from the graph.

Amplitude = 3 mm.

Echoes

Hard surfaces reflect sound waves. An **echo** is a sound that has been reflected before you hear it. For an echo to be clearly heard, the obstacle needs to be large compared with the wavelength of the sound. So, you will hear an echo when you make a loud noise when you are several hundred metres from a brick wall or a cliff, for example. You will not hear an echo when you are several hundred metres from a pole stuck in the ground. There will still be an echo, even when you are much closer to the wall, but because sound travels very quickly, the echo will return in such a short time that you will probably not be able to distinguish it from the sound that caused it.

Measuring the speed of sound by an echo method

The following worked example illustrates how echoes may be used to measure the speed of sound.

WORKED EXAMPLE

Two students stand side by side at a distance of 480 m from the school wall. Student A has two flat pieces of wood, which make a loud sound when clapped together. Student B has a stopwatch.

As student A claps the boards together, student B starts the stopwatch. When student B hears the echo, he stops the stopwatch. The time recorded on the stopwatch is 2.9 s.

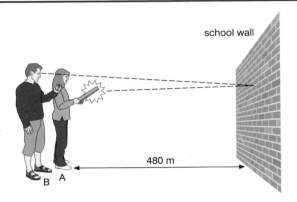

school wall

480 m

B A

△ Fig. 3.50 Two students carrying out investigations into the speed of sound.

Calculate the speed of sound.

Write down the formula:	speed of sound	= distance travelled / time taken
Work out the distance:	distance to wall and back	= 2 × 480
		= 960 m

Record the time the sound took to travel there and back:

	time	= 2.9 s
Substitute in the formula:	speed of sound	= 960 / 2.9
		= 331 m/s

See if you can think of some things that might be done to improve the accuracy of this experiment.

Developing Investigative Skills

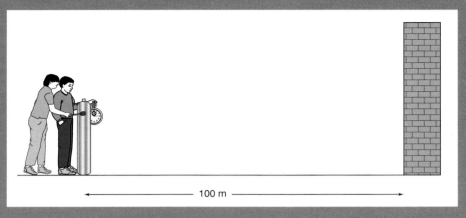

△ Fig. 3.51 Two students measuring the speed of sound.

Two students are finding the speed of sound. They stand 100 m from a large wall. The first student strikes a piece of metal with a hammer. The sound this makes reflects back from the wall and the student hears an echo. The student hits the metal again in time with the echo and continues to do so, tapping out a steady rhythm.

The second student is in charge of timing. He knows that in between each sound that the first student makes the sound travels 200 m (to the wall and back again). By timing the interval for a number of strikes, the second student can record the data he needs.

Observing, measuring and recording

❶ Explain whether the students should repeat their measurements for this experiment.

❷ The students stand 100 m away from the wall that provides the echo. Explain why this is a suitable distance to use.

❸ The students measure a time of 2.3 s from striking the metal to striking the metal at the fourth following echo. Calculate the speed of sound given by this measurement.

❹ A better way to find the speed of sound would be through the use of a graph. Describe how the students could collect suitable data and how a graph could be used to find the speed of sound.

❺ Explain why using a graph to find the speed of sound would improve the accuracy of the experiment.

Handling experimental observations and data

❻ What effect will reaction time have on the measurements made?

❼ Suggest how the timing in this experiment could be improved.

End of topic checklist

Key terms

decibel, echo, oscilloscope, pitch, ultrasound

During your study of this topic you should have learned:

○ How sound waves are produced by vibrating sources.

○ About the longitudinal nature of sound waves.

○ About the approximate range of audible frequencies.

○ That a medium is needed to transmit sound waves.

○ About an experiment to determine the speed of sound in air.

○ That loudness and pitch of sound waves are related to amplitude and frequency.

○ How to describe how the reflection of sound may produce an echo.

○ EXTENDED About compression and rarefaction.

○ EXTENDED About the order of magnitude of the speed of sound in air, liquids and solids.

End of topic questions

Note: The marks awarded for these questions indicate the level of detail required in the answers. In the examination, the number of marks awarded to questions like these may be different.

1. a) i) What causes a sound? **(2 marks)**

    ii) Explain how sound travels through the air. **(2 marks)**

  b) Astronauts in space cannot talk directly to each other – they have to speak to each other by radio. Explain why this is so. **(3 marks)**

2. Ayesha and Salma are doing an experiment to measure the speed of sound. They stand 150 m apart.

  Ayesha starts the stopwatch when she sees Salma make a sound and she stops it when she hears the sound herself. She measures the time as 0.44 s. Calculate the speed of sound in air from this data. **(3 marks)**

3. **EXTENDED** The speed of sound is approximately 340 m/s.

  a) Calculate the wavelength of the musical note middle C, which has a frequency of 256 Hz. **(3 marks)**

  b) A student hears two echoes when she claps her hands. One echo is 0.5 s after the clap, and one echo is 1.0 s after the clap. She decides that the two echoes are from two buildings in front of her. How far apart are the buildings? **(3 marks)**

4. Draw an oscilloscope trace representing each of the following sounds.

  a) low-frequency quiet sound **(1 mark)**

  b) high-frequency loud sound **(1 mark)**

  c) high-frequency quiet sound **(1 mark)**

  d) low-frequency loud sound. **(1 mark)**

5. A polystyrene ball is suspended so it is touching the prongs of a vibrating tuning fork. The ball kicks away from the tuning fork and then moves back to it.

  a) Explain the behaviour of the ball by:

    i) describing how the prongs of the tuning fork move **(2 marks)**

    ii) describing how a sound wave is created by the tuning fork **(2 marks)**

    iii) making a drawing of the sound wave, labelling the key features. **(2 marks)**

  b) Explain what you would see if the tips of the tuning fork were dipped into a beaker of water. **(3 marks)**

Note: The questions, sample answers and marks in this section have been written by the authors as a guide only. The marks awarded for these questions indicate the level of detail required in the answers. In the examination, the number of marks awarded to questions like these may be different.

Sample student answers

Question 1

The table shows some of the regions of the electromagnetic spectrum.

Gamma	X-rays	A	Visible	Infra-red	B	Radio

a) i) Complete the chart be writing the names of the missing regions (A and B) of the spectrum.

A: UV ✗ (1)

B: microwaves ✓ ① (1)

ii) The table lists the spectrum in what order?

A. increasing amplitude

B. increasing density

C. increasing frequency

D. increasing wavelength

D ✓ ① (1)

b) i) Describe one situation in which X-rays are useful.

in a hospital ✗ (1)

ii) Explain why X-rays are useful in the example you have given.

X-rays can show broken bones because they will pass through the skin and flesh. ✓ ① (1)

but there will be a shadow where the bones are. ✓ ① (1)

c) i) Describe one situation in which X-rays can be harmful.

When they get into your body. ✗ (1)

TEACHER'S COMMENTS

a) i) The question clearly asks for the name of the missing regions. Writing 'UV' is not a name, nor even a recognised standard symbol, so it loses a mark. The student must take care to read the question carefully and answer it in the way it is asked.

ii) The student should know the different ways to describe the order of the spectrum. Here the answer is given in terms of increasing wavelength, but they should also be able to describe the sequence in order of frequency and possibly in order of energy.

b) i) Stating 'in a hospital' is too vague to be a 'situation' as the question asks.

ii) Clearly, the candidate was aware of the correct situation – imaging – so should have written this in their answer.

c) i) Again, the student has not described a situation, so cannot gain the first mark.

Exam-style questions continued

ii) Describe how X-rays can be harmful and how the risks can be reduced.

They can damage body cells ✓ ① **(1)**

and cause some cells to become cancer cells. ✗ **(1)**

d) A remote control for a television uses infra-red signals.

The human body detects infra-red radiation as heat.

Explain why the infra-red signal from a television remote control does not make your skin feel hot.

The signal from the remote is not strong enough to make you feel hot. ✗

There is not enough energy to burn you. ✓ ① **(2)**

(Total 11 marks)

ii) The student has two valid points, but there is only one mark available. The second was for describing how the risks can be reduced and the candidate has failed to give any response to this. Always read the question carefully and answer each point required.

d) 'Not strong enough' is too vague. The correct term 'amplitude' is required here. The second part of the answer correctly links to energy and the candidate might have thought a little further about this, possibly then getting the link from 'strong' to 'amplitude'.

This part of the question tests basic definitions and these should be learned thoroughly.

Question 2

The diagram shows some waves on the surface of water in a ripple tank.

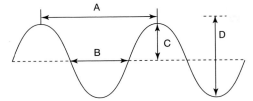

a) **i)** Which letter represents the wavelength of the wave? (1)

ii) Which letter represents the amplitude of the waves? (1)

The waves in the water are transverse waves.

b) **i)** Give another example of a transverse wave. (1)

ii) Describe the difference between transverse waves and longitudinal waves. (2)

c) A student makes some observation about the waves in the ripple tank.

number of waves passing by in 6 seconds – 10

distance between wave crests – 5 cm

i) State the equation linking wave speed, frequency and wavelength. (1)

ii) Calculate the wave speed of these waves in m/s. (2)

(Total 8 marks)

Question 3

a) Describe an experiment to find the refractive index of glass, using a glass block.
You should include:

the equipment needed

a diagram of how the equipment will be used

what measurements should be made

how the measurements will be used to find the refractive index. (6)

b) Use ideas about reflection and refraction to explain how information can be sent along optical fibres.

You may use diagrams to help your explanation. (5)

(Total 11 marks)

You will probably have experienced magnetism in simple toys and in bar magnets. The magnetic field around a bar magnet, when plotted, looks very similar to the one around the Earth. However, it is the existence of electromagnetism that really makes a difference to your life.

Without electromagnetism, the generation of electricity would not happen in the way that it does. Without electromagnetism, the high voltages transmitted down power lines could not be transformed into the lower voltages that you need in your home. Electricity is something that many people use every day – for lighting, heating, cooking and to power many different items of equipment. However, it can be dangerous.

You will already have explored different models to explain the flow of current and the transfer of electrical energy, and you will have evaluated these models. You will also have investigated current and voltage in circuits and drawn conclusions from data. You should be able to explain, using data and a simple model, the differences between series and parallel circuits.

STARTING POINTS

1. How can electromagnets be made stronger?

2. Describe some similarities and differences between magnets and electromagnets.

3. Describe the form of the electromagnetic field around the Earth.

4. What is the difference between a magnetically 'hard' and a magnetically 'soft' material?

5. How could you investigate the magnetic field pattern for: a) a permanent bar magnet; b) the field between two bar magnets?

6. What is an electric circuit?

7. What is a solenoid?

CONTENTS

a) Simple phenomena of magnetism

b) Electrical quantities

c) Electric circuits

d) Dangers of electricity

e) Electromagnetic effects

f) Cathode-ray oscilloscopes

g) Exam-style questions

4

Electricity and magnetism

△ Electricity is an essential part of our lives - we rely on it to operate many devices.

Simple phenomena of magnetism

△ Fig. 4.1 A compass on a boat.

INTRODUCTION

The property of magnetism has been known for many centuries. Ancient travellers used naturally magnetic rocks such as lodestone to guide their journeys. Lodestone, which is magnetic, points towards the north when suspended. The development of the compass made it possible to make long sea voyages of discovery, whereas previously ships had stayed within sight of land. There is evidence that some animals, such as birds, can sense the magnetic field of the Earth and that they have their own 'in-built compass', which may help navigation during long migrations.

The magnetic field of the Earth has a wider importance. It acts as a shield, protecting the surface of the Earth from many charged particles emitted from the Sun. A study of magnetism helps us to understand our Earth better and will be crucial when we start to learn about electromagnetism later in this section.

KNOWLEDGE CHECK

✓ Know that the ends of a bar magnet are called poles and that is where the magnetism is strongest.
✓ Know that only some materials are magnetic.
✓ Know that the Earth has a magnetic field, which is how compasses are able to point to the North.

LEARNING OBJECTIVES

✓ State the properties of magnets.
✓ Give an account of induced magnetism.
✓ Distinguish between ferrous and non-ferrous materials.
✓ Describe methods of magnetisation and of demagnetisation.
✓ Describe an experiment to identify the pattern of field lines around a bar magnet.
✓ Distinguish between the magnetic properties of iron and steel.
✓ Distinguish between the design and use of permanent magnets and electromagnets.

MAGNETS REPEL AND ATTRACT

When a permanent magnet is suspended and allowed to swing, it will line up approximately north–south. Because of this, the two ends of a magnet (which are the most strongly magnetic parts) are called the north pole and the south pole, often labelled N and S. (Strictly speaking, they are called the north-seeking pole and the south-seeking pole.)

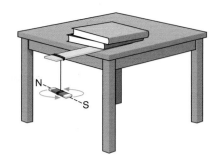

△ Fig. 4.2 A bar magnet aligns itself with the Earth's magnetic field when it is suspended.

When two north poles from different magnets are brought together, there will be a **repulsion** between them. This also happens when two south poles are used. However, when a north pole and a south pole are brought together, there will be an **attraction**. Magnets will also attract magnetic substances such as iron, nickel and cobalt.

QUESTIONS

1. What happens when a north-seeking pole of a magnet is brought close to a south-seeking pole of another magnet?

2. What happens when two like poles are brought close to each other?

3. What happens when a bar magnet is suspended freely?

Magnetically hard and soft materials

Several elements are magnetic, the most important of which are iron, cobalt and nickel. Scientists have developed **alloys** and ceramics made from combinations of elements to get the exact properties that they want. Some of these materials are **magnetically hard** (such as steel, which is an alloy of iron and other elements such as carbon or tungsten). This means that they stay magnetic once they have been magnetised.

When we refer to a 'magnet', we mean **a permanent magnet** that is made of magnetically hard materials. Permanent magnets are used in situations where magnetism is always needed, such as magnetic strips.

Other materials are **magnetically soft** (such as pure iron), which means that they do not stay magnetic – this is particularly useful in some electromagnetic devices such as the electromagnet and the relay. In these cases, magnetism is only needed under particular circumstances, such as when a switch is closed.

Alloys are made by melting different metallic elements (iron, aluminium, copper, tungsten, etc.) together. The resulting alloy is known as a **ferrous** alloy if it contains significant iron, and as a **non-ferrous** alloy if it does not. For example nickel and brass (copper + zinc) are non-ferrous.

In the past all magnetic materials were ferrous, but this is no longer true. The strongest magnets may not contain any iron at all – for example, samarium–cobalt (SmCo), often used in headphones.

Note also that iron is magnetically soft but steel is magnetically hard.

'Magnetically hard' and 'magnetically soft' materials do not refer to their physical hardness, or 'feel', but to their magnetic behaviour. You may have seen rubberised magnetic strips used on notice boards. These strips are permanent magnets, but they feel physically soft. Headphones like the ones shown in Fig. 4.3 also contain magnets.

◁ Fig. 4.3 The headphones worn by this radio announcer contain samarium–cobalt (SmCo) magnets.

QUESTIONS

1. Describe the difference between magnetically hard and magnetically soft materials.

2. Explain the meaning of the terms *alloy* and *ferrous*.

3. What do we mean when we use the term *magnet*?

4. Where are magnetically soft materials particularly useful?

Magnetic induction

When a soft magnetic material is brought near to a magnet it will be attracted. It has had magnetism **induced** in it; it has become **magnetised**. When the magnet is taken away, the material loses its magnetism again. The magnet will continue to attract the soft magnetic material even when the material is turned round. This is the opposite behaviour to two magnets, as two magnets will repel each other in certain orientations. This simple method enables you to work out whether you are holding two magnets or one magnet and one piece of soft magnetic material.

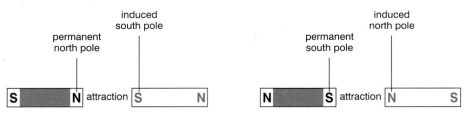

△ Fig. 4.4 The pole of a permanent magnet always induces the opposite pole in an unmagnetised piece of magnetic material.

1. Describe what happens when a soft magnet is brought near to a permanent magnet.

2. If a soft magnet is brought near to a permanent north pole, what pole is induced in the end of the soft magnet nearest the north pole?

3. To see if a piece of metal is a magnet, you should check to see if it repels a known magnet. Explain why attracting a known magnet is not sufficient.

4. In which orientations will two magnets repel each other?

Methods of magnetisation

Permanent magnets are usually magnetised by putting them into a coil of wire and passing a large direct current of electricity through the coil for a moment. Very high currents are used, and special equipment must be used to make the method safe.

A steel bar can be magnetised by stroking it with a strong magnet.

With some modern alloys, the magnetic field is applied to the molten alloy at very high temperature, and then the alloy is allowed to solidify while remaining in the magnetic field.

Steel can be magnetised to a certain degree by placing the bar north–south and hammering it. Ships become magnetised in this way during manufacture, as the hammering during construction allows the Earth's field to magnetise them slightly.

Methods of demagnetisation

The only method of demagnetisation that is guaranteed to work is to heat the magnet. All magnets have a temperature (called the Curie temperature) at which they lose their magnetism. This temperature ranges from less than 100 °C to over 500 °C. When the magnet is cooled down, some of the magnetism may return.

Many magnets can be demagnetised by placing them in a coil of wire connected to an alternating electric current (a.c.) source. The current is switched on and the object is slowly taken out of the coil. In this way the object is magnetised in the opposite direction each time the current reverses, but as it is removed from the coil the amount of magnetisation is reduced each time.

Hammering or dropping a powerful magnet may cause the loss of some of its magnetisation.

Magnetic field lines

Magnets have a **magnetic field** around them – a region of space where their magnetism affects other objects. We describe the magnetic field using **magnetic field lines**. These lines show the path that a free north pole would take: that is, heading away from a north pole and ending up at a south pole. The more concentrated the field lines are, the stronger the magnetic effect.

Identifying the pattern of field lines around a bar magnet

To show field lines, you can place a bar magnet under a thin sheet of plastic, and sprinkle iron filings on to the top of the plastic. The iron filings will arrange themselves into strings of filings along the field lines (Fig. 4.5).

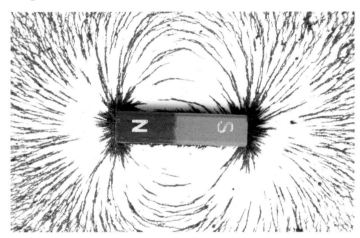

◁ Fig. 4.5 The iron filings show the field lines around a bar magnet.

It is also possible to follow the path of the field lines by placing a small compass (known as a plotting compass) on the plastic in place of the iron filings. When you move the compass in the direction that its north pole is pointing it will follow a field line.

QUESTIONS

1. What is a magnetic field?

2. What do magnetic field lines show?

3. Describe two methods to show magnetic field lines for a bar magnet.

Magnetic field patterns

The idea of field lines was first developed by the 19th-century scientist Michael Faraday, the inventor of the electric motor. You can see in Fig. 4.6 that where the magnets are repelling each other, the field lines do not go from one magnet to the other. Where the magnets are attracting each other, lines do cross from one to the other. This fact will help you to draw the lines more easily. You can investigate the field patterns using the techniques described in the previous section.

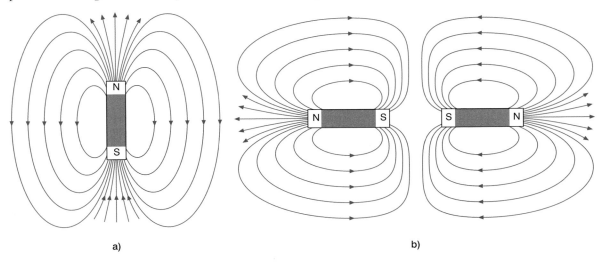

a)

b)

△ Fig. 4.6 a) The magnetic field pattern of a bar magnet; b) The magnetic field pattern between two repelling bar magnets.

Charging an electroscope by induction

Stage 1

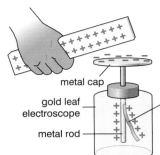

cloth

acetate bar

When you rub an acetate bar with a cloth, electrons from the acetate get rubbed on to the cloth, so the acetate becomes positively charged.

Stage 2

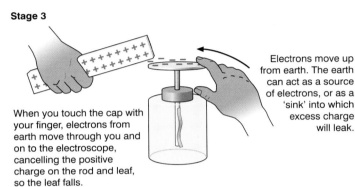

metal cap

gold leaf electroscope

metal rod

The positively charged bar attracts negatively charged electrons in the metal, so the cap becomes negative. The rod and leaf become positive, and repel each other, so the leaf rises. Giving something a charge like this, without actually touching it, is called **induction**. The bar has induced a charge in the electroscope.

piece of fine gold leaf

Remember: the bar does not repel the protons. The protons are trapped within the nucleus of each atom. Only electrons are free to move.

Stage 3

When you touch the cap with your finger, electrons from earth move through you and on to the electroscope, cancelling the positive charge on the rod and leaf, so the leaf falls.

Electrons move up from earth. The earth can act as a source of electrons, or as a 'sink' into which excess charge will leak.

Stage 4

When the bar and your finger are removed, the negative charge on the cap spreads down. The rod and leaf are both negative, so they repel, and the leaf rises again.

△ Fig. 4.21 Charging an electroscope by induction.

Testing charge

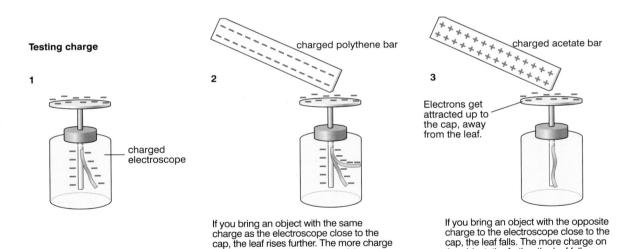

1

charged electroscope

2

charged polythene bar

If you bring an object with the same charge as the electroscope close to the cap, the leaf rises further. The more charge on the object, the further the leaf rises.

3

charged acetate bar

Electrons get attracted up to the cap, away from the leaf.

If you bring an object with the opposite charge to the electroscope close to the cap, the leaf falls. The more charge on the object, the further the leaf falls.

△ Fig. 4.22 You can use an electroscope to test if an object is positively or negatively charged.

END OF EXTENDED

Developing Investigative Skills

A student is trying to design an experiment to measure how electrostatically charged a plastic rod is. She knows that a charged rod will deflect a stream of water from a tap.

Her plan is to bring a charged rod up to the stream of water and then measure the angle of deflection of the water. She expects that the bigger the angle of deflection is, the greater the charge on the rod will be. She expects to be able to devise a relative scale for how charged different rods are.

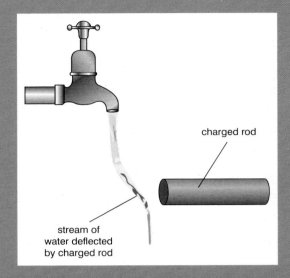

△ Fig. 4.23 Water being deflected by a charged rod.

The student hopes to extend her experiment to show which type of charge is on a charged rod – she expects that if a negatively charged rod attracts the water stream, then a positively charged rod will repel it. However, she does not know that a stream of water is neutral: that is, it has no overall charge of its own.

Using and organising techniques, apparatus and materials

❶ How could the student measure the angle of deflection of a stream of water from a tap? Draw a diagram of the arrangement.

❷ The student will need to know that the flow from the tap is constant – describe how she could check this.

❸ What is the independent variable in this investigation? What is the dependent variable?

Observing, measuring and recording

❹ The student hopes to 'devise a relative scale for how charged different rods are'. What does 'relative' mean in this sentence?

Handling experimental observations and data

❺ The student plans to 'bring a charged rod up to the stream of water'. Explain why this part of her plan needs further improvement.

❻ Water is electrically neutral. Use ideas about charged particles to explain why the student is wrong about using a water stream to tell the difference between positive and negative rods.

HAZARDS OF ELECTROSTATICS

The sudden discharge of electricity caused by friction between two insulators can cause shocks in everyday situations – for example:

- combing your hair
- pulling clothes over your head
- ironing synthetic fabrics
- getting out of a car.

You may have noticed that you can get a nasty spark from your finger if you touch a metal object after rubbing your feet on a nylon carpet. This is similar to the effect you can sometimes feel if you touch a metal door handle. It is for this reason that workers who make sensitive electronic devices connect themselves to ground using devices such as antistatic wrist straps (Fig. 4.24), which link to a grounding point (a point that is connected to 0 V) so that any static charge can discharge safely via the wrist strap and not damage the equipment before starting work. Also, to protect against sparks of this type, aircraft are connected to the ground by a special wire before refuelling starts.

△ Fig. 4.24 An antistatic wrist strap in use.

Lightning is a spectacular example of electrostatics in action. Scientists believe that the electrical charge is generated by induction when ice particles in clouds collide. One bolt of lightning carries about 5 C of electrical charge. Lightning conductors on buildings usually prevent lightning strikes by discharging the cloud above, but if a strike still occurs the charge should be carried safely to ground.

△ Fig. 4.25 Lightning.

CURRENT

When there is no current in a conductor, the free electrons move randomly between atoms, with no overall movement. When you connect it in an electrical circuit with a power source like a **battery**, there is a current in the conductor. Now the electrons drift in one direction, while still moving in a random way as well. The drift speed is very slow, often only a few millimetres each second. There can only be a current in a conductor when it is connected in a complete circuit. When the circuit is broken, the current stops.

The size of an electric current depends on the number of electrons that are moving and how fast they are moving. However, instead of measuring the actual number of electrons we use the total charge carried by the electrons round the circuit each second. So current is a flow of charge.

Electric current is measured in **amperes**, or **amps** (A).

EXTENDED

When there is a current of 1 A in a wire, then one coulomb of charge is passing any point on the circuit each second. (1 A = 1 C/s.)

This coulomb is the same one that we referred to earlier on. The coulomb of charge is vastly safer when it is made of electrons flowing along a conducting wire because it is then closely surrounded by positive charges, and there are no large electric fields.

END OF EXTENDED

You use an **ammeter** to measure current in an electrical circuit. When the current is very small, you might use a milliammeter, which measures current in milliamps (1 mA = 0.001 A). Even smaller currents are measured with a **microammeter**.

When you want to measure the current in a particular component, such as a lamp or motor, the ammeter must be connected in series with the component. In a series circuit, the current is the same at all points so it does not matter where the ammeter is put. This is not the case with a parallel circuit (see topic on Electric circuits for more about series and parallel circuits).

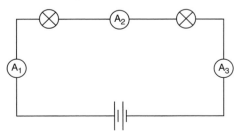

◁ Fig. 4.26 In this series circuit, the current will be the same throughout the circuit so $A_1 = A_2 = A_3$.

EXTENDED

The electric current is the amount of charge flowing every second (the number of coulombs per second):

$$I = Q / t$$

Where: I = current in amperes (A)

    Q = charge in coulombs (C)

    t = time in seconds (s)

Scientists now know that electric current in the wires of a circuit is really a *flow of electrons* around the circuit from negative to positive. Unfortunately, early scientists guessed the direction of flow incorrectly. Consequently all diagrams were drawn showing the current flowing from positive to negative. This way of showing the current has not been changed, so the **conventional current** that everyone uses gives the direction in which positive charges would flow (Fig. 4.28).

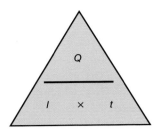

△ Fig. 4.27 Equation triangle for charge, current and time.

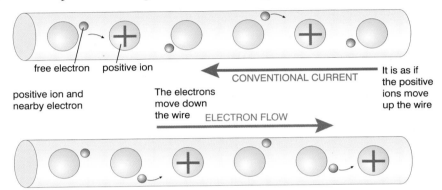

△ Fig. 4.28 Conventional current is drawn in the opposite direction to the electron flow.

QUESTIONS

1. EXTENDED Calculate the flow of charge in the following.

   a) current 3 A for 5 s

   b) current 2 A for 10 s

   c) current 4 A for 23 s

   d) current 1.5 A for 0.5 min.

2. EXTENDED A charge of 120 C flows for 4 minutes. What is the current?

3. EXTENDED A charge of 60 C produces a current of 0.5 A. How long does this take?

END OF EXTENDED

ELECTROMOTIVE FORCE

The battery in an electrical circuit can be thought of as pushing electrical charge around the circuit to make a current. It also transfers energy to the electrical charge. The **electromotive force** (e.m.f.) of the battery, measured in volts, measures how much 'push' it can provide and how much energy it can transfer to the charge.

The electromotive force is therefore defined in terms of how much energy the source supplies to drive charge around a complete circuit.

POTENTIAL DIFFERENCE

The electrons moving around a circuit have some kinetic energy, which can be referred to as electrical energy. As electrons pass through the battery, or other power supply, they are given potential energy, and as they move around a circuit, they transfer energy to the various components in the circuit. For example, when the electrons move through a lamp they transfer some of their energy to the lamp.

The amount of energy that a unit of charge (a coulomb) transfers between one point and another (the number of joules per coulomb) is called the **potential difference** (p.d.). Potential difference is measured in **volts**, so it is often referred to as **voltage** (Fig. 4.29).

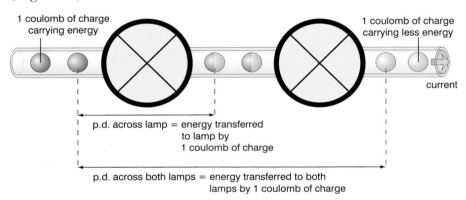

1 coulomb of charge carrying energy

1 coulomb of charge carrying less energy

current

p.d. across lamp = energy transferred to lamp by 1 coulomb of charge

p.d. across both lamps = energy transferred to both lamps by 1 coulomb of charge

◁ Fig. 4.29 Potential difference (p.d.) is the difference in energy of one coulomb of charge between two parts of a circuit.

Potential difference is measured between two points in a circuit. It is like an electrical pressure difference and measures the energy transferred per unit of charge flowing.

Measuring electricity

Potential difference is measured using a **voltmeter**. When you want to measure the p.d. across a component then the voltmeter must be connected in parallel across that component. Testing with a voltmeter does not interfere with the circuit provided the voltmeter has a high resistance.

A voltmeter can be used to show how the potential difference varies in different parts of a circuit. In a series circuit you find different values of the voltage depending on where you attach the voltmeter. You can assume that energy is only transferred when the current passes through electrical components such as lamps and motors – the energy transfer to thermal energy as the current flows through copper connecting wire is very small indeed. Therefore it is only possible to measure a p.d. or voltage across a component.

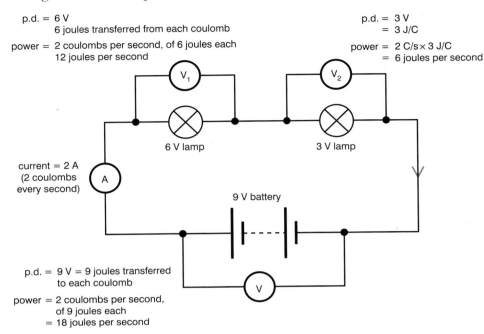

p.d. = 6 V
  6 joules transferred from each coulomb

power = 2 coulombs per second, of 6 joules each
    12 joules per second

V_1

6 V lamp

p.d. = 3 V
    = 3 J/C

power = 2 C/s × 3 J/C
    = 6 joules per second

V_2

3 V lamp

current = 2 A
(2 coulombs
every second)

A

9 V battery

V

p.d. = 9 V = 9 joules transferred
   to each coulomb

power = 2 coulombs per second,
    of 9 joules each
    = 18 joules per second

◁ Fig. 4.30 The potential difference across the battery equals the sum of the potential differences across each lamp. That is $V = V_1 + V_2$.

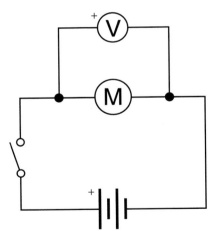

◁ Fig. 4.31 A voltmeter can be added after the rest of the circuit has been connected.

RESISTANCE

All components in an electrical circuit have a resistance to current flowing through them. The relationship between voltage, current and resistance in electrical circuits is given by this equation:

$V = IR$

where: V is the potential difference in volts (V)

    I is the current in amps (A)

    R is the resistance in ohms (Ω).

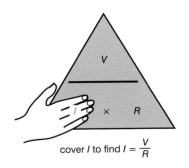

cover I to find $I = \dfrac{V}{R}$

△ Fig. 4.32 Equation triangle for voltage, current and resistance.

ELECTRICAL QUANTITIES

245

It is important to be able to rearrange this equation when performing calculations. Use the triangle in Fig. 4.32 to help you.

From this equation, you find that $R = V / I$. This is **Ohm's law.**

REMEMBER

The idea of resistance is useful because for a lot of objects their resistance does not change when you change the current through them. But there are many components, such as light bulbs, for which this is not true (see topic on electric circuits).

WORKED EXAMPLES

1. A heater element is connected to a 230 V supply. The current in the heater is 10 A. Calculate the resistance of the heater.

Write down the formula in terms of R: $\qquad$ $R = V / I$

Substitute the values for V and I: $\qquad$ $R = 230 / 10$

Work out the answer and write down the unit: $\quad R = 23\ \Omega$

2. A 6 V supply is applied to 1000 Ω resistor. What will be the current?

Write down the formula in terms of I: $\qquad$ $I = V / R$

Substitute the values for V and R: $\qquad$ $I = 6 / 1000$

Work out the answer and write down the unit: $\quad I = 0.006\ A$

QUESTIONS

1. Use the Ohm's law equation to calculate the potential difference across a 5 Ω resistor, which has a current of 2 A in it.

2. A lamp has a potential difference of 3.0 V across it and a current of 0.5 A in it. What is its resistance?

Measuring resistance

The resistance of a component can be found using the circuit in Fig. 4.30. The component (lamp, resistor or whatever) is placed in a circuit with an ammeter to measure the current in the component and a voltmeter to measure the potential difference across it. To take readings, the circuit is switched on and readings are made of the p.d. and the current.

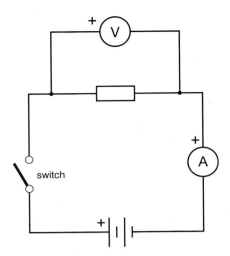

 Fig. 4.33 Measuring the resistance of a component. To power the circuit you could use a battery as shown (with a maximum of 3 V), or you could use a power supply with a suitable output. For safety, switch on for a maximum of 10 seconds only.

The resistance is calculated from the following equation:

$R = V / I$

Note that the readings may change a little over the first few seconds. If so, this is probably because the component is heating up and its resistance is changing. If this happens, you would have to decide whether to take the readings before the component has heated up, and so measure the resistance at room temperature, or to wait until the readings have stopped changing. This would give you the 'steady-state' resistance with the component at its usual running temperature.

You may wish to change the e.m.f. of the battery by changing the number of **cells** (or you may adjust the output of the power supply). When the component is a perfect resistor, then you will get the same answer for the resistance; but you will often find that the resistance of the component varies. (Modern multimeters measure resistance automatically and give a reading in ohms.)

For components like **resistors** and thick wires, the current through the component doubles when you double the voltage, triples when you triple the voltage, etc. The resistance of the component to the passage of electricity does not change, and the extra current is caused solely by the increased pressure of the extra voltage.
The current is directly proportional to the voltage and the graph is a straight line.

Take care. If you try using thick wire as the component, the current will be extremely high for a very low voltage. The wire can get very hot very quickly and there is a risk of injury.

Developing Investigative Skills

A student decides to find the resistance of a piece of fuse wire. He sets up the circuit in Fig. 4.34 and makes a note of the readings on the ammeter and the voltmeter for five different settings of the variable resistor. His measurements are shown in the table.

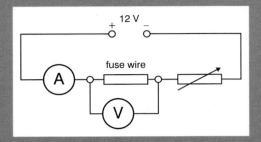

△ Fig. 4.34 A circuit diagram for the investigation.

Potential difference/V	Current /mA
0.0	0
0.5	44
1.0	88.5
1.5	137.5
2.0	181.5
2.5	225.5

Using and organising techniques, apparatus and materials

❶ The student did not measure the voltage of the supply or the particular settings of the variable resistor. Explain why these measurements were not required.

❷ The student should check the ammeter and voltmeter for zero errors. What are these?

Observing, measuring and recording

❸ Draw a graph of the student's results.

❹ Use your graph, with p.d. on the y-axis and current on the x-axis, to find the resistance of the wire.

Handling experimental observations and data

❺ Another student suggests that drawing a graph is not necessary. They say that you could use the equation $R = V / I$ for each pair of measurements and then find a mean of these values. Explain why calculating the gradient of the graph is a better method.

❻ To get an accurate value for the resistance of the wire, the student needed to avoid any heating effects in the wire. Describe how the student could reduce heating effects when carrying out the experiment.

Effects of length and cross-sectional area

For a particular conductor, the resistance is *proportional to length*. The longer the conductor, the further the electrons have to travel, the more likely they are to collide with the metal ions and so the greater the resistance. So a wire that is twice as long will have twice as much resistance.

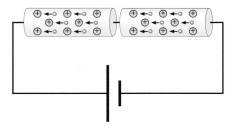

◁ Fig. 4.35 Two wires in series are like one long wire, because the electrons have to travel twice as far.

Resistance is *inversely proportional to the cross-sectional area* of the wire. The greater the cross-sectional area of the conductor, the more electrons there are available to carry the charge along the conductor's length, so the lower the resistance. Therefore a wire with twice the cross-sectional area will have half the resistance.

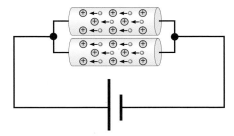

◁ Fig. 4.36 Two wires in parallel are like one thick wire, so the electrons have more routes to travel along the same distance.

REMEMBER

If the wire is of twice the diameter, then its cross-sectional area will be four times greater, so the resistance of the wire will be one quarter as much.

SCIENCE IN CONTEXT

SUPERCONDUCTORS

In 1908 the Dutch physicist Heike Kamerlingh Onnes became the first person to produce liquid helium, which meant reaching temperatures lower than −269 °C, the boiling point of helium. Having such a cold liquid meant that other low-temperature experiments became possible as he could now cool down the apparatus sufficiently.

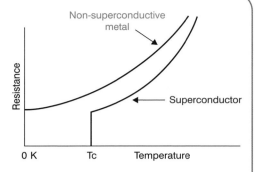

△ Fig 4.37 How resistance varies with temperature in a superconductor and a non-superconductor.

In particular, Kamerlingh Onnes looked at passing electric currents through extremely cold metals and in 1911 was measuring the resistance of a sample of mercury. He found that below a particular temperature, called the critical temperature, the mercury behaved as if it had no electrical resistance at all – he had discovered superconductivity.

Following this discovery, many more metallic elements were found to have superconducting properties, but it wasn't until the 1950s that a theory to explain their behaviour was developed. It requires energy for the electrons to scatter as they move through the metal lattice (these scatterings are the 'collisions' that lead to heating in a resistance) and at such low temperatures this energy is not available, so the electrons move smoothly – with zero resistance. The two key features of this are that no energy is wasted through heating the conductor, which leads to the ability to produce very large magnetic fields (see topic on Electromagnetic effects).

△ Fig. 4.38 A cross-section of a superconductor at CERN (Central European Organisation for Nuclear Research) in Geneva, Switzerland.

The search for superconductors has continued, with breakthroughs coming in the study of alloys rather than elements.

A particular milestone came in the discovery of materials that demonstrated superconductivity at temperatures up to −183 °C as this meant that liquid nitrogen could be used as the coolant – and liquid nitrogen is readily available commercially. The search for materials that superconduct at higher temperatures continues.

Superconductors are used in a variety of applications. They produce the strong magnetic fields required for MRI scanning in medicine and to confine beams of particles in accelerators such as the Large Hadron Collider. They even provide magnetic fields to support Maglev trains that 'float' above the track. On the small scale, superconductors are used in SQUID (superconducting quantum interference device) magnetometers, which can measure the fine magnetic fields associated with activity in the brain.

ELECTRICITY AND MAGNETISM

1. Explain why the resistance of a conductor is proportional to length.

2. Explain why the resistance of a conductor is inversely proportional to cross-sectional area.

3. EXTENDED The length of a resistor A is x. Resistor B is made of the same material and is of the same thickness, but its length is $3x$. The resistance of A is R. What is the resistance of B?

4. EXTENDED The area of cross-section of a resistor A is x. Resistor B is made of the same material, but its area of cross-section is $3x$. The resistance of A is R. What is the resistance of B?

EXTENDED

ELECTRICAL ENERGY

All electrical equipment has a **power rating**, which indicates how many joules of energy are supplied each second. The unit of power used is the **watt** (W). Light bulbs often have power ratings of 60 W or 100 W. Electric kettles have ratings of about 2 kilowatts (2 kW = 2000 W). A 2 kW kettle supplies 2000 J of energy each second.

The power of a piece of electrical equipment depends on the voltage and the current. The units watt, volt and amp are defined as follows:

- 1 watt = 1 J/s
- 1 volt = 1 J/C
- 1 amp = 1 C/s

From these definitions, we can see that 1 watt = 1 volt × 1 amp.

In other words: power = current × voltage

$$P = I \times V$$

where:

P = power in watts (W)

I = current in amps (A)

V = potential difference in volts (V)

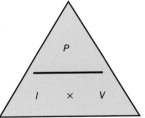

△ Fig. 4.39 Equation triangle for power, current and voltage to help with rearranging the equation.

You can use the triangle in Fig. 4.39 to help you to rearrange this equation.

1. What is the power of an appliance when a current of 7 A is obtained from a 230 V supply?

Write down the formula in terms of P: $P = V \times I$

Substitute the values: $P = 230 \times 7$

Work out the answer and write down the unit: $P = 1610$

2. An electric oven has a power rating of 2 kW. What will the current be when the oven is used with a 230 V supply?

Write down the formula in terms of I: $I = P / V$

Substitute the values: $I = 2000 / 230$

Work out the answer and write down the unit: $I = 8.7$ A

QUESTIONS

1. EXTENDED An appliance has 2 A of current in it and operates at 110 V. What is its power rating?

2. EXTENDED A 60 W lamp has a current of 5 A in it. At what voltage is it operating?

3. EXTENDED A 25 W lamp is designed to be used with a voltage of 230 V. Calculate the current in it.

Energy, current, voltage and time

If you switch on an electric kettle for a minute or a room heater for 5 minutes, then you can measure the temperature increase of the water in the kettle or of the room. The temperature will increase because energy has been given to the water or to the room. Energy is measured in **joules** (J). A heater rated at 1 watt will give out 1 joule of heat each second. A 2 kW heater will give out 2000 joules per second, and if the heater is switched on for 4 s, it will give out 8000 J.

energy = current × voltage × time

$E = I \times V \times t$

where: E = the energy transferred in joules (J)

I = current in amperes (A)

V = potential difference in volts (V)

t = time in seconds (s)

WORKED EXAMPLE

Calculate the energy transferred when a 12 V motor, running at a current of 0.5 A, is left on for 5 minutes.

Write down the formula: $\qquad$ $E = I \times V \times t$

Substitute the values: $\qquad$ $E = 0.5 \times 12 \times 300$

(Remember that the time *must* be in seconds.)

Work out the answer and write down the unit: $\qquad$ $E = 1800$ J

QUESTIONS

1. EXTENDED A laptop charger is designed for a country where the mains voltage is 230 V. The owner takes the charger to a country such as the USA, where the mains voltage is 110 V. Will they be able to charge their laptop?

2. EXTENDED How much energy is transferred when a current of 3 A flows in a circuit with a voltage of 12 V for 1 minute?

3. EXTENDED A heater which runs on 12 V transfers 4800 J of energy in 2 min. What is the current in the heater?

4. EXTENDED A bulb runs on a voltage of 110 V and has a current of 0.1 A in it. It transfers 2400 J of energy in a given time. What is this time?

5. EXTENDED A lamp transfers 24 J of energy and draws a current of 2 A for 1 s. What voltage is it operating at?

END OF EXTENDED

End of topic checklist

Key terms

ammeter, ampere (amp), battery, cell, conductor, electromotive force, electron cloud, electrostatic forces, insulator, microammeter, Ohm's law, potential difference, resistor, static charge, superconductor, voltage, voltmeter, volts

During your study of this topic you should have learned:

◯ How to describe simple experiments to show the production and detection of electrostatic charges.

◯ That there are positive and negative charges.

◯ That unlike charges attract and that like charges repel.

◯ How to describe an electric field as a region in which an electric charge experiences a force.

◯ How to distinguish between electrical insulators and conductors and give typical examples.

◯ EXTENDED That charge is measured in coulombs.

◯ EXTENDED About the direction of lines of force and how to describe simple field patterns, including the field around a point charge and the field around two parallel plates.

◯ EXTENDED How to give an account of charging by induction.

◯ EXTENDED How to use the simple electron model to distinguish between conductors and insulators.

◯ That current is related to flow of charge.

◯ How to use and describe the use of an ammeter.

◯ EXTENDED That current is a rate of flow of charge and how to use the equation $I = Q/t$.

◯ EXTENDED How to distinguish between the direction of flow of electrons and conventional current.

◯ That the e.m.f. of a source of electrical energy is measured in volts.

◯ EXTENDED That e.m.f. is defined in terms of energy supplied by a source in driving charge round a complete circuit.

○ That the potential difference across a circuit component is measured in volts.

○ How to use a voltmeter.

○ That resistance = p.d./current and understand qualitatively how changes in p.d. or resistance affect current.

○ How to use the equation $R = V/I$.

○ How to describe an experiment to determine resistance using a voltmeter and an ammeter.

○ How to relate (without calculation) the resistance of a wire to its length and to its diameter.

○ EXTENDED How to use quantitatively the proportionality between resistance and length, and the inverse proportionality between resistance and cross-sectional area of a wire.

○ EXTENDED How to use the equations $P = IV$ and $E = IVt$.

End of topic questions

Note: The marks awarded for these questions indicate the level of detail required in the answers. In the examination, the number of marks awarded to questions like these may be different.

1. A plastic rod is rubbed with a cloth.

   a) How does the plastic become positively charged? **(2 marks)**

   b) The charged plastic rod attracts small pieces of paper. Explain why this attraction occurs. **(2 marks)**

2. a) A car stops and one of the passengers gets out. When she touches a metal post she feels an electric shock. Explain why she feels this shock. **(2 marks)**

   b) Write down two other situations where people might get this type of shock. **(2 marks)**

3. Explain the following observations:

   a) You rub a plastic pen with a piece of dry kitchen paper, then put it a few millimetres away from a thin stream of water flowing from a tap. The stream of water is deflected by the pen. **(3 marks)**

   b) You rub an inflated balloon on a dry piece of cloth and hang it from the ceiling using a piece of sewing-thread. You rub a second balloon on the same piece of cloth, and find that it repels the first balloon when held near to it. **(3 marks)**

4. **EXTENDED** a) A charge of 10 coulombs flows through a motor in 30 seconds. What is the current in the motor? **(2 marks)**

   b) A heater uses a current of 10 A. How much charge flows through the lamp in:

   i) 1 second **(2 marks)**

   ii) 1 hour? **(2 marks)**

5. What units are equivalent to V? (1 mark)

6. What will the reading on a voltmeter across a component be when 3 J of energy are transferred to each coulomb of charge? **(1 mark)**

7. Calculate the following:

   a) the potential difference required to produce a current of 2 A in a 12 Ω resistor **(2 marks)**

   b) the potential difference required to produce a current of 0.1 A in a 200 Ω resistor **(2 marks)**

   c) the current produced when a potential difference of 12 V is applied to a 100 Ω resistor **(2 marks)**

d) the current produced when a potential difference of 230 V is applied to a 10 Ω resistor
(2 marks)

e) the resistance of a wire that under a potential difference of 6 V carries a current of 0.1 A
(2 marks)

f) the resistance of a heater, which under a potential difference of 230 V carries a current of 10 A.
(2 marks)

8. EXTENDED An electric motor drives a water pump that lifts water out of a well that is 10 m deep. It can deliver 360 kg of water per minute out of the tap at the top.

a) How much potential energy is given to the water each second? Hence, what power must be provided by the electric motor? Assume that the motor and pump have 100% efficiency.
(4 marks)

b) If the motor is designed to run on 12 V, what current will it take out of a 12 V supply when it is working?
(3 marks)

c) If the motor is designed to work on 220 V, what current will it take out of a 220 V supply when it is working? (Note: The 220 V will be an alternating current supply, but this does not affect the calculation.)
(3 marks)

d) Name one advantage and one disadvantage of the 220 V system over the 12 V system.
(2 marks)

9. Suggest why the diameter of a cable must be suitable for the current it has to carry. (Hint: current has a heating effect.)
(2 marks)

10. EXTENDED An appliance has a power rating of 1400 W. The potential difference of the mains is 230 V. Calculate the approximate current.
(3 marks)

11. EXTENDED The potential difference across a bulb is 5 V and the current through the bulb is 3 A. In 1 minute, how much energy will be transferred by charge passing through the bulb?
(2 marks)

12. EXTENDED A lamp has a power rating of 11 W and runs from a supply of 230 V. What is the current in the lamp?
(2 marks)

13. EXTENDED An appliance runs from a 110 V supply. It has a current of 3.2 A in it. What is its power rating?
(2 marks)

14. EXTENDED An appliance has a current of 2.7 A in it and has a power rating of 300 W. What is the voltage of the supply?
(2 marks)

Electric circuits

INTRODUCTION

Whenever you use an electrical appliance, electrical circuits operate. Some are visible to the eye but some have been etched on to microchips and are microscopic. The basic operation of all circuits relies on connecting components, the nature of the components and the energy supplied to the circuit. In this topic you will learn about different ways of connecting components in circuits, how to draw circuit diagrams that can be followed by anyone anywhere in the world, and how to carry out calculations to choose the right values for the components in a circuit.

△ Fig. 4.40 You can investigate electrical circuits in the classroom.

KNOWLEDGE CHECK

✓ Be able to use Ohm's law.
✓ Be able to use an ammeter and voltmeter in circuits.

LEARNING OBJECTIVES

✓ Draw and interpret circuit diagrams containing sources, switches, resistors (fixed and variable), lamps, ammeters, voltmeters, magnetising coils, transformers, bells, fuses and relays.
✓ **EXTENDED** Draw and interpret circuit diagrams containing diodes and transistors.
✓ Understand that the current at every point in a series circuit is the same.
✓ Give the combined resistance of two or more resistors in series.
✓ State that, for a parallel circuit, the current from the source is larger than the current in each branch.
✓ State that the combined resistance of two resistors in parallel is less than that of either resistor by itself.
✓ State the advantages of connecting lamps in parallel in a lighting circuit.
✓ **EXTENDED** Recall and use the fact that the sum of the p.d.s across the components in a series circuit is equal to the total p.d. across the supply.
✓ **EXTENDED** Recall and use the fact that the current from the source is the sum of the currents in the separate branches of a parallel circuit.
✓ **EXTENDED** Calculate the effective resistance of two resistors in parallel.
✓ Describe the action of a variable potential divider (potentiometer).
✓ Describe the action of thermistors and light-dependent resistors and show understanding of their use as input transducers.
✓ Describe the action of a capacitor as an energy store and show understanding of its use in time-delay circuits.

✓ Describe the action of a relay and show understanding of its use in switching circuits.

✓ EXTENDED Describe the action of a diode and show understanding of its use as a rectifier.

✓ EXTENDED Describe the action of a transistor as an electrically operated switch and show understanding of its use in switching circuits.

✓ EXTENDED Recognise and show understanding of circuits operating as light-sensitive switches and temperature-operated alarms (using a relay or a transistor).

✓ EXTENDED Explain and use the terms digital and analogue.

✓ EXTENDED State that logic gates are circuits containing transistors and other components.

✓ EXTENDED Describe the action of NOT, AND, OR, NAND and NOR gates.

✓ EXTENDED Design and understand simple digital circuits combining several logic gates.

✓ EXTENDED State and use the symbols for logic gates.

CIRCUIT DIAGRAMS

When people started using electricity, they quickly found that it was not convenient to draw accurate pictures of the circuits that they made. It was much easier to understand how the circuit worked, and to correct any faults, when they used standard symbols for the parts. It was also much easier when the wires were drawn in straight lines, rather than trying to copy the exact route taken.

Study the circuits used in this topic, and learn the symbols and what they represent.

Fig. 4.41 is a simple circuit diagram that shows how a torch is powered by a battery consisting of three 1.5 V cells, giving a total of 4.5 V. In the case of a torch, the cells are put in separately, but in the case of a 9 V battery for example, the six cells are pre-assembled by the manufacturer. The word 'battery' means an assembly of several cells, but people often use the word to refer to a single cell.

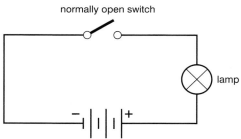

△ Fig. 4.41 A circuit diagram for a torch.

The '+' terminal of the cell is indicated by the long thin line, and the '−' terminal by the short thick line. To help you remember, imagine yourself cutting the long thin line into two shorter pieces and turning them into a + sign.

The other symbols in the circuit are the normally open switch, and the lamp.

The direction of the current in a lamp does not matter, but a pocket calculator, say, could be destroyed if the battery is not inserted correctly. One way to prevent this is to add a **diode** to the circuit. A diode allows current to flow in one direction but not in the other.

In this circuit (Fig. 4.42) the calculator is represented as a resistor. A calculator is far more complicated than that, but it does behave to the battery *as if* it were a resistor, drawing a small current, *I*, out of the battery.

EXTENDED

As you can see, the arrow on the diode shows the direction of a conventional current. When the battery is inserted the wrong way round, there is no current.

END OF EXTENDED

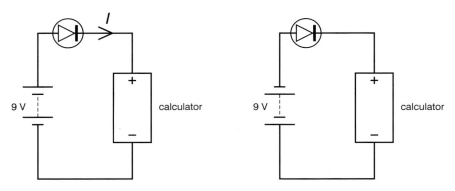

△ Fig. 4.42 A diode only allows current to pass through it in one direction.

Fig. 4.43 shows the circuit symbols that you need to know.

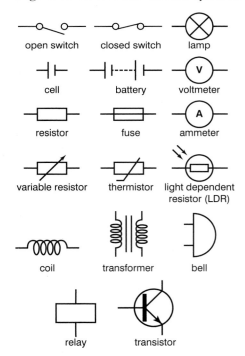

△ Fig. 4.43 Important circuit symbols for you to learn.

SERIES AND PARALLEL CIRCUITS

There are two different ways of connecting two lamps (or other components) to the same battery (or other power source). Two very different kinds of circuit can be made. These circuits are called **series** and **parallel circuits**.

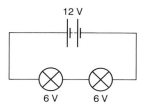

△ Fig. 4.44 A simple series circuit diagram.

When they are in series, then there is exactly the same electric current in each of the components in the circuit. The voltage is shared between the units in the circuit. Thus it is possible to join in series two identical lamps designed for 6 V and then to connect them to a 12 V battery (Fig. 4.44).

In a parallel circuit (Fig. 4.45), the current splits, with part of it going through each component. All of the appliances in a house are connected in parallel to the mains supply, and each one receives the full 110 V or 230 V of the mains supply when it is switched on. The two great advantages of the parallel arrangement are that each appliance can be designed to work with the mains voltage supply, and that the appliances can be switched on and off individually.

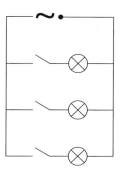

△ Fig. 4.45 A parallel circuit diagram.

△ Fig. 4.46 All of these lights are in parallel. If they were in series then they would all go off if any one of them failed or was switched off.

	Series	Parallel
Circuit diagram		
Appearance of the lamps	Both lamps have the same brightness, both lamps are dim.	Both lamps have the same brightness, both lamps are bright.
Battery	The battery is having a hard time pushing the same charge first through one bulb, then another. This means less charge flows each second, so there is a low current and energy is transferred slowly from the battery.	The battery pushes the charge along two alternative paths. This means more charge can flow around the circuit each second, so energy is transferred quickly from the battery.
Switches	The lamps cannot be switched on and off independently.	The lamps can be switched on and off independently by putting switches in the parallel branches.
Advantages/ disadvantages	A very simple circuit to make. The battery will last longer. If one lamp 'blows' then the circuit is broken so the other one goes out too.	If one lamp 'blows' the other one will keep working. The battery will not last as long.
Examples	Tree lights are often connected in series.	Electric lights in the home are connected in parallel.

△ Table 4.2 A comparison of series and parallel circuits for two identical 3 V lamps supplied from a 3 V battery.

QUESTIONS

1. If one bulb in a string of tree lights does not work, why does the rest of the string not work either?

2. A battery running two bulbs in parallel runs out of energy before the same battery running the same two bulbs in series. Explain why.

3. Why are electric lights in the home connected in parallel?

4. What is the difference in brightness in two bulbs connected: a) in series; b) in parallel with a given battery? Give a reason for your answer.

Current in a series circuit

The current in a circuit can be measured using an ammeter. When you want to measure the current in a particular component, such as a lamp or motor, the ammeter must be connected in series with the component. Figure 4.47 shows an ammeter in series with a motor. In a series circuit, the current is the same no matter where the ammeter is placed in the circuit. This is not the case with a parallel circuit.

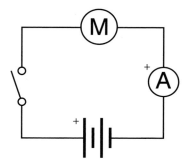

◁ Fig. 4.47 A circuit has to be broken to connect an ammeter.

The voltage across a component can be measured using a voltmeter, as shown in Figure 4.48.

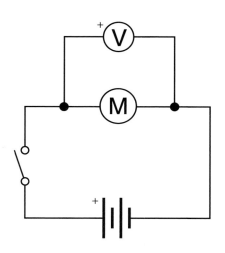

◁ Fig. 4.48 A voltmeter can be connected across the motor after the rest of the circuit has been completed.

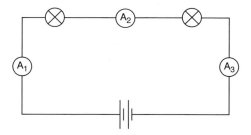

◁ Fig. 4.49 In this series circuit, the current will be the same throughout the circuit so $A_1 = A_2 = A_3$.

In a series circuit, the current is the same throughout the circuit (Fig. 4.49). In a parallel circuit, the current splits between the two branches of the parallel circuit. This means that the current from the source is larger than the current in each branch.

In a parallel circuit, the current from the source is the sum of the currents in the separate branches of the circuit, so in Fig. 4.50 $A_1 = A_2 + A_3$.

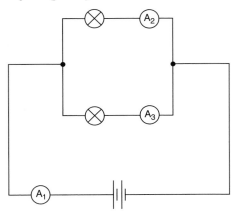

◁ Fig. 4.50 The current flow splits between the two branches of the parallel circuit so $A_1 = A_2 + A_3$.

Combining resistors

Two resistors can be replaced by a single resistor that has the same effect in the circuit. Calculating the value of the resistor needed depends on whether the original resistors are connected in series or parallel.

When the resistors R_1 and R_2 are in series, then the combined resistance, R_C, is:

$$R_C = R_1 + R_2$$

For resistors in parallel, the combined resistance is less than the value of either of the two resistors. This is because there are more paths for the charge to flow along, so the current is higher.

When the resistors R_1 and R_2 are in parallel, then R_C is:

$$\frac{1}{R_C} = \frac{1}{R_1} + \frac{1}{R_2} \text{ or } R_C = \frac{R_1 \times R_2}{R_1 + R_2}$$

WORKED EXAMPLES

1. Two resistors, 1000 Ω and 3000 Ω, are connected in series. What is their combined resistance?

   Write down the formula: $R_C = R_1 + R_2$

   Substitute the values: $R_C = 1000 + 3000$

   Work out the answer and add the unit: $R_C = 4000 \ \Omega$

   Note that the combined resistance is greater than the value of either of the two resistors.

2. **EXTENDED** Two resistors, 20 Ω and 30 Ω, are connected in parallel. What is their combined resistance?

   Write down the formula: $R_C = \dfrac{R_1 \times R_2}{R_1 + R_2}$

   Substitute the values $R_C = \dfrac{20 \times 30}{20 + 30}$

   Work out the answer and add the unit: $R_C = \dfrac{600}{50} \ \Omega$

   $= 12 \ \Omega$

QUESTIONS

1. In a series circuit, what can you say about the current at different points in the circuit?

2. Give two advantages of a parallel circuit in a house.

3. Two resistors, 100 Ω and 22 Ω, are connected in series. What is their combined resistance?

4. **EXTENDED** Two resistors, 147 kΩ and 220 kΩ, are connected in parallel. What is their combined resistance?

ACTION AND USE OF CIRCUIT COMPONENTS

Now that you have seen how circuits can be connected, it is time to consider how components may be put together to make useful circuits. In this section you will consider the action and use of some electrical components.

The variable resistor

A variable resistor contains a length of resistance wire and an adjustable sliding contact. One end of the wire and the contact are connected into the circuit. Because the contact can be moved from one end of the wire to the other, the resistance of the variable resistor can be set to any value from nearly zero to the total resistance of the resistance wire inside the device. As we have noted, using more voltage across a component will increase the current in it. The amount of current in a circuit can also be controlled by changing the resistance of the circuit using a variable resistor or **rheostat**. Adjustment of the rheostat changes the length of the wire the charge has to flow through. Variable resistors are often used, for example, to change the brightness of the lighting in a car.

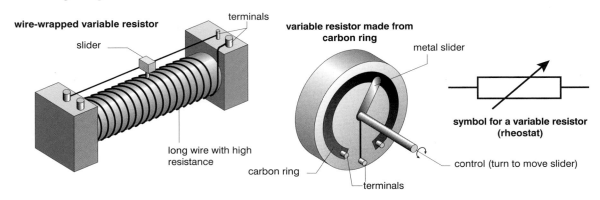

△ Fig 4.51 Variable resistors are commonly used in electrical equipment, for example in the speed controls of model racing cars or in volume controls on radios and audio systems.

In the circuit in Fig. 4.52 a variable resistor is used to control the speed of an electric motor, which has a resistance of 12 Ω. If it is a 24 V electric motor, and a battery with e.m.f. of 24 V, then with the variable resistor set to 0 Ω, the potential difference (p.d.) across the motor will be 24 V and the motor will run at full speed. The p.d. across the variable resistor will be 0 V. The resistance of the whole circuit is 12 Ω and so the current through the motor will be 2.0 A.

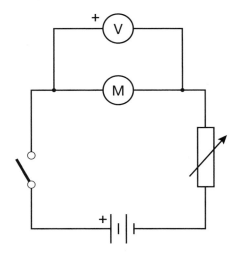

△ Fig. 4.52 The voltmeter can be added after the circuit has been made.

If the variable resistor is set to 12 Ω, then the total resistance in the circuit is now 24 Ω, and the total current can be calculated:

$I = V / R$

$I = 24 / 24$

$\quad = 1.0 \, A$

The current through the motor will have halved and the motor will run slower. Note that we can now work out the p.d. across the motor.

Current through the motor = 1.0 A

Its resistance   = 12 Ω

p.d.   = $I \times R$

$\quad\quad\quad\quad\quad\quad\quad = 1.0 \times 12$

$\quad\quad\quad\quad\quad\quad\quad = 12 \, V$

Likewise, the p.d. across the resistor is 12 V and the p.d. values around the circuit add up to 24 V, which is the same as the e.m.f. of the battery, as always.

Potentiometer and potential divider

A **potentiometer** is very similar in design to a variable resistor, and in fact the same component can normally be used as either device. In a potentiometer, all three points – both ends of the resistance wire and the adjustable contact – are connected into the circuit. The two ends of the resistance wire are connected to both ends of the battery or power supply. So when the battery is 5 V, then the p.d. across the potentiometer is 5 V. When the slider is set to the top, then the p.d., V_{out}, across the two output wires will again be 5 V. However, when the slider is set to minimum, the two output wires are connected to the same point and the p.d. will be 0 V.

This is a major difference between a potentiometer and a variable resistor: the voltage output of the potentiometer can be set to zero. This is one reason why the volume control on most audio equipment is a potentiometer, as it gives full control over the output volume.

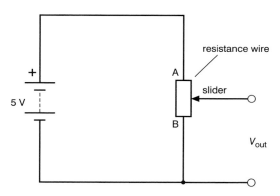

◁ Fig. 4.53 The potentiometer acts as a potential divider: it divides up the p.d. supplied by the power source.

It is also possible to make a **potential divider** using two resistors as shown in Fig. 4.54.

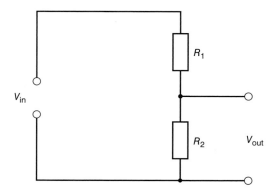

◁ Fig. 4.54 Using two resistors to create a potential divider.

When $R_1 = R_2$, then the output p.d., V_{out}, will be just half the input p.d., V_{in}. Note that it does not really matter what value R_1 and R_2 have; it is more important to note their *relative* values. So when R_1 is very small compared with R_2, then the output will be high, it will be approaching the value of V_{in}. When R_2 is very small compared with R_1, then the output will be close to zero, because the two output wires will almost be joined together.

QUESTIONS

1. Give one major difference between a potentiometer and a variable resistor.

2. Calculate V_{out} in this circuit.

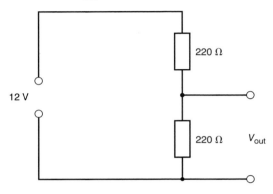

3. In the circuit in question 2, when R_1 is small compared with R_2, will the output be low or high?

4. Explain your answer to question 3.

Thermistor and LDR

In some substances, increasing the temperature actually lowers the resistance. This is the case with **semiconductors** such as silicon. A semiconductor is a material that does not conduct electricity as well as, for example, a metal, but conducts electricity better than an insulator, such as plastic. Silicon has very few free electrons (free electrons are necessary for there to be an electric current in a material) and so behaves more like an insulator than a conductor. However, when silicon is heated, more electrons are removed from the outer electron shells of the atoms, producing an increased electron cloud. The released electrons can move throughout the structure, allowing an electric current to pass more easily. This effect is large enough to outweigh the increase in resistance that might be expected from the increased vibration of the silicon ions in the structure as the temperature increases.

Semiconducting silicon is used to make **thermistors**, which are used as temperature sensors, and **light-dependent resistors (LDRs)**, which are used as light sensors.

In LDRs it is light energy that removes electrons from the silicon atoms, increasing the electron cloud. So LDRs have a very high resistance in the dark, and a very low resistance in the light. LDRs are used in street lamps that switch on automatically at night, and in the type of burglar alarm that sets a light beam (usually an infra-red beam so that it is invisible) across the path of the burglar.

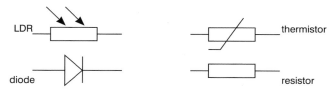

△ Fig. 4.55 Components made using semiconductor materials.

REMEMBER

In a thermistor, increasing temperature actually reduces the resistance. This is the opposite effect to that in a normal resistor. In an LDR an increase in brightness reduces the resistance.

QUESTIONS

1. What is a semiconductor material?

2. A student connects a battery, an ammeter and an LDR to make a simple light meter. Will the reading on the ammeter increase or decrease when the light gets brighter? Explain your answer.

3. Describe how the resistance of a thermistor changes with temperature.

Input transducers

A transducer is a device that transfers energy from one form to another. An **input transducer** may be needed to transfer, for example, heat or light energy to electrical energy. Many machines have to take action if exposed to light or heat or some other input. The controls of a boiler will light the flame if the water is too cold; the computer controlling the house will close the curtains when it gets dark. LDRs and thermistors are suitable electrical transducers for giving an electrical signal for this purpose. They are best used as part of a potentiometer.

In the circuit in Fig. 4.57, the LDR has a resistance of about 200 kΩ in the dark. This means that R_2 is much smaller than R_1, and the output will be small, (about 0.2 V). When the LDR is in the light, its resistance drops to about 3 kΩ, so the output voltage rises to something near to the input voltage (about 3.8 V).

Developing Investigative Skills

A student investigates how the resistance of a thermistor varies with temperature. She uses a multimeter as an ohmmeter. To measure the temperature of the thermistor she immerses it in a water bath. At the start of the experiment she fills the beaker with water at 50 °C. She takes measurements of the temperature and the resistance at various temperatures as the water cools down. The student adds ice to help achieve lower temperatures and stirs the water regularly. The student's measurements are shown in the table.

Temperature/°C	Resistance/kΩ
50	1.12
45	2.11
40	2.79
35	3.54
30	4.25
25	5.45
20	6.61
15	8.47
10	12.62

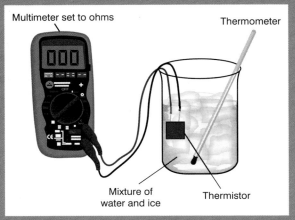

△ Fig. 4.53 Apparatus needed for the investigation.

Using and organising techniques, apparatus and materials

❶ Why is it important that the student stirs the water between readings?

❷ The student uses a thermometer that measures from – 10 °C to + 50 °C and is accurate to the nearest 2 °C.

   a) What is the range of this thermometer?

   b) When the thermometer reads 40 °C, what values could the true temperature be between?

Observing, measuring and recording

❸ Draw a graph of the student's results.

❹ Describe the pattern (if any) shown by the graph.

Handling experimental observations and data

❺ The student allowed the water to cool down slowly during the experiment. How did this improve the accuracy of her results?

❻ Use ideas about electron movement to suggest why the resistance of a thermistor changes in the way shown in this experiment.

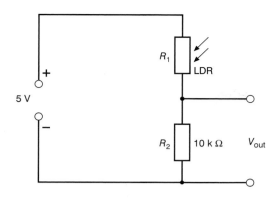

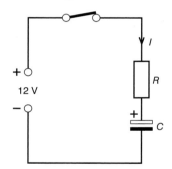

△ Fig. 4.57 With this circuit, light is detected by the output going from low to high. If the LDR had been put in the lower position, with a resistor above, then light would be detected by the output going from high to low.

Capacitor

A **capacitor** is designed to store electric charge (and hence electrical energy) temporarily. The energy is stored in an electric field between two plates. The space between the plates is filled with an insulator, so charge cannot flow through a capacitor. In some applications it is only stored for a fraction of a second, but be warned that large capacitors can hold on for many days to quantities of electricity that can kill. The following method should not be done with more than 12 V.

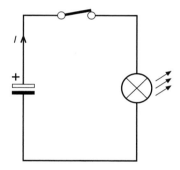

△ Fig. 4.58 Investigation to show how a capacitor can store energy.

1. Connect a 12 V d.c. power supply to the capacitor (as in Fig. 4.58 left).

Note that many capacitors are marked with + and − terminals. The symbol for a capacitor of this type has a rectangular box shape for the + terminal. When the terminals are connected the wrong way round the capacitor will be damaged or destroyed. Capacitors also have a voltage rating. This one must be rated for 12 V or higher.

When the switch is closed (step 1), charge flows *into* the capacitor as shown. A resistor, R, should be included to prevent a surge of current. Initially, the p.d. across the capacitor is 0 V, and the full 12 V is across the resistor. So when the resistor is 12 Ω, for example, the initial current will be 1 A. As the capacitor stores charge, the p.d. across it increases to 12 V. When the capacitor has a large value, then there will be a current for longer and more energy will be stored. Remember that a current of 1 amp for 1 second into the capacitor will store a charge of 1 coulomb. When it is fully charged, the p.d. across the capacitor will be 12 V, the p.d. across the resistor will be 0 V, and the current will be zero.

2. The charged capacitor is connected to a 12 V lamp (Fig. 4.58 right). Then when the switch is closed, the lamp will have 12 V of p.d. across it and will be lit with maximum brightness as the charge flows out of the capacitor. But the voltage of the capacitor will drop steadily and the lamp will get dimmer and dimmer until the current stops completely.

The capacitor can be used in a time-delay circuit (Fig. 4.59).

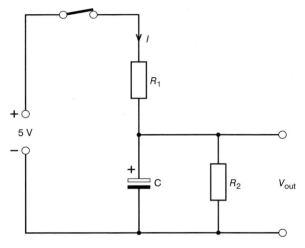

△ Fig. 4.59 A time-delay circuit.

In this circuit, when the switch is closed, the p.d. across the capacitor, C, will increase from zero. When the output is connected to an output transducer, such as a relay (see following section), that operates when the output voltage reaches, say, 3 V, then there will be a time delay between the switch closing and the relay operating. This delay could be a fraction of a second or many minutes, depending on the resistance of R_1 and the capacitance of the capacitor, C. For a long delay you want a high value of R_1 (to give a low current, I) and a large capacitor, C (to make it charge up more slowly).

You may need to add a resistor, R_2, so that the p.d. across the output is returned to zero when the switch is opened. R_2 must have a high resistance, or the capacitor will never be able to charge up (because the current would just flow through R_2 instead).

Relay

A **relay** is an electromagnet (see topic on Electromagnetic effects) that can operate one or more switch contacts. For example, the contacts in the relay in Fig. 4.60 join points A and B when the switch is open. When the electromagnet is energised, it attracts a piece of soft iron and joins points A and C. Points B and C are never joined. A relay like this can be used as an output transducer, as you can choose a relay that operates at a particular voltage. The relay transfers electrical energy to mechanical energy.

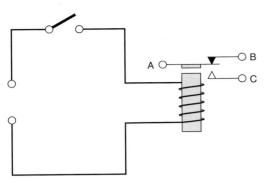

◁ Fig. 4.60 A relay can be used as
an output transducer.

Another application for a relay is to allow you to use a small current in
a control circuit to close the contacts for a very large current in a
second circuit. For example, the starter motor in a car is connected to
the battery by wires that are about 10 mm in diameter, so high is the
current that flows to the starter motor. It would be completely
impractical to have wires of this size to the switch operated by the car's
key, so the key controls only the current to the coil, and the relay
contacts control the current to the motor (Fig. 4.61).

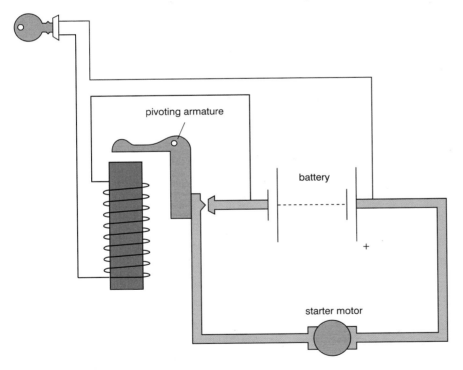

pivoting armature

battery

+

starter motor

△ Fig. 4.61 A relay used to switch on a starter motor.

QUESTIONS

1. What is a transducer? Give two examples of suitable electrical
transducers.

2. Where is electrical energy stored in a capacitor?

3. What is the basic component in a relay?

DIRECT AND ALTERNATING CURRENTS

A battery produces a steady current. The electrons are constantly flowing from the negative terminal of the battery around the circuit and back to the positive terminal. This produces a **direct current (d.c.)**.

The mains electricity used in houses is quite different. The electrons in the circuit move backwards and forwards. This kind of current is called **alternating current (a.c.)**. In some countries, mains electricity moves forwards and backwards 50 times each second, that is, with a frequency of 50 hertz (Hz). The frequency chosen varies from country to country.

The advantage of using an a.c. source of electricity rather than a d.c. source is that it can be transmitted from power stations to the home at very high voltages, which reduces the amount of energy that is lost in the overhead cables (see topic on Electromagnetic effects).

Fig. 4.62 shows a circuit in which the current in and the p.d. across an electric kettle are being monitored.

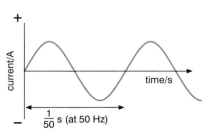

△ Fig. 4.62 In this circuit, the p.d. across the heater will have the same value as the e.m.f. of the a.c. supply to which it is connected.

As you can see, the current is being monitored through the 26.5 Ω heater in the kettle and the potential difference across it.

When the normally open switch is closed, the p.d. and the current will have the waveforms shown in Fig. 4.63. They will both alternate positive and negative at the same time.

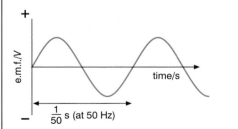

△ Fig. 4.63 Waveforms for the p.d. (left) and the current (right).

To drive the current back and forth, the e.m.f. has to change direction repeatedly. It is almost as if the circuit is being driven by a battery, but the wires to the two terminals on the battery are swapped over a hundred times per second.

The diode as a rectifier

If the power source in the circuit in Fig. 4.33 is a.c., the current will keep on changing direction. When a diode is added to the a.c. circuit, then although the e.m.f. will stay as before, there will be a current in only one direction.

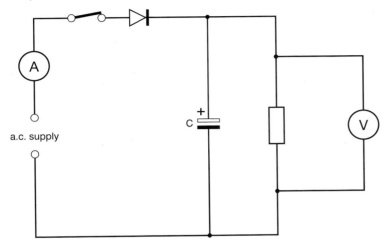

△ Fig. 4.64 The direction of conventional current is shown by the arrow in the diode symbol.

The left-hand graph in Fig. 4.65 show what you will measure across the resistor when the capacitor is *not* fitted. Only the positive p.d. will appear across the resistor. We say that the diode has rectified the alternating current. However, the p.d. and current fluctuate – they do not have a steady value.

When you fit a capacitor, C, as well (see Fig. 4.64), then you have a much 'smoother' d.c. power supply. Note that the capacitor must be fitted this way round. The capacitor will be charged up by the pulses of electricity, and will be able to deliver a steadier forward current through the resistor even when the e.m.f. is backwards.

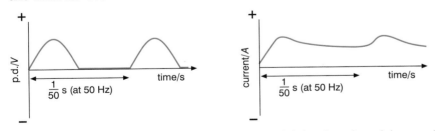

△ Fig. 4.65 The diode rectifies the p.d., as shown in the left-hand graph, and the capacitor smoothes it, as shown in the right-hand graph.

The transistor as a switch

The **transistor** is another output transducer. It is a semiconductor device made of silicon. It is the building block of electronics and the processor of a computer contains millions of them. Most transistors are small and run at a few volts, but modern electric trains are started and stopped by semiconductor devices that control hundreds of volts and thousands of amps.

The transistor has three wires coming out of it. These are labelled:

- b = base
- c = collector
- e = emitter.

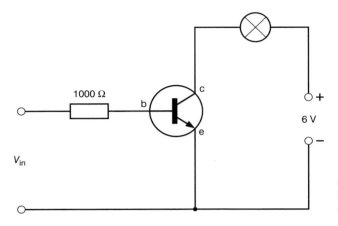

There are really two circuits in Fig. 4.66: one with the base and the emitter, which are in the input circuit, and one with the collector and the emitter, which are in the output circuit. (This overall circuit is known as a common-emitter circuit.)

In this circuit, if no voltage is applied to the base, or if the two input connections are joined together, then almost no current will flow through the output circuit and the lamp will not light. When the input to the base is raised above 0.6 V, then the lamp will switch on. The 1000 Ω resistor is there to protect the input of the transistor and allows the input to be set higher than 0.6 V, to 5 V or more, without harming the transistor. Very little current is needed in the input circuit (and some transistors require no current at all). The output circuit can handle much higher currents, the exact current depending on the transistor chosen.

Light-sensitive switch

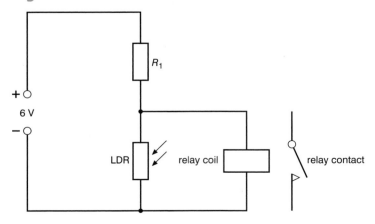

△ Fig. 4.67 The circuit of a light-sensitive switch, using a relay output.

In the circuit shown in Fig. 4.67, the relay is not energised so long as the resistance of the LDR stays low. When the illumination reduces, the resistance of the LDR increases and the p.d. across the coil goes up. When the illumination is sufficiently low, the relay will close the contact. Note that the circuit controlled by the relay does not need to have any connection whatsoever to the relay coil circuit. This can be an important safety feature of the circuit.

Temperature-operated alarm

In the circuit shown in Fig. 4.68, the transistor will start to conduct electricity, and the bell will sound, when the p.d. across resistor R_2 goes to more than 0.6 V. This will happen when the resistance of the thermistor drops sufficiently. Its resistance drops when the temperature goes up, so the alarm sounds to warn of a high temperature. The value of R_2 must be set at the correct temperature to make this occur. If R_2 was made a variable resistor, then the temperature of the alarm could be adjusted.

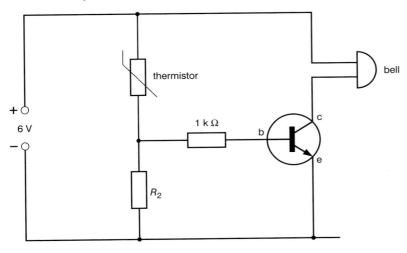

△ Fig. 4.68 A circuit for a temperature-operated alarm.

QUESTIONS

1. EXTENDED What effect does adding a diode have on the current in a circuit where the supply is a.c.?

2. What effect does a capacitor have when it is added to a rectification circuit?

3. Which two pins on an n-p-n transistor form the input circuit and which two form the output circuit?

4. EXTENDED Explain how a transistor operates as a switch.

DIGITAL ELECTRONICS

In the last part of this topic you learned about some circuits that can be used as control circuits. Here you will explore the action of **logic gates**, which can also be used in control circuits.

An **analogue** signal varies continuously. A **digital** signal can only have one of two states: high or low. In analogue electronics, as used by an amplifier driving a loudspeaker, the current through the loudspeaker varies in a complex way that accurately describes the way that the loudspeaker should move. All of the human senses are analogue, so there must always be analogue-to-digital converters between humans and machines. However, most equipment is now digital, as it gives good quality and the ability to add many extra features at low cost.

In digital electronics, the circuit is only allowed to be in one of two states: *on* or *off* (also called *high/low*). These two states are represented by the numbers 1 and 0. In practice, to make the circuit reliable, any low voltage is taken to indicate zero, and any high voltage is taken to represent 1. Information is sent from one place to another as a long stream of 1 and 0 numbers. Each number is known as a bit. Computers and DVD players use digital electronics. A DVD player has to read about 5 million bits per second to display the movie picture on the screen.

◁ Fig. 4.69 Some DJs still prefer vinyl records. If you look at the record closely you can see the analogue signal. The loudspeaker cone accurately follows these sideways movements of the groove.

◁ Fig. 4.70 Each DVD contains about 4.7 gigabytes of data in the form of the numbers 1 and 0. If the numbers out of one DVD were printed in paper books, you would need over 3000 books of 1000 pages each.

What are logic gates?

A logic gate is an electronic circuit that has one or more *input* signals and one *output* signal. These signals are voltages that can be *high* (about 5 V) or *low* (about 0 V). Logic gates are digital circuits as they can only have certain values of input and output – high or low. The output signal depends on the combination of signals at the inputs.

REMEMBER

Logic gates have a threshold value – usually between 2 V and 3 V. Input voltages below the threshold value are treated as low (0 V) and voltages above the threshold are treated as high (5 V).

What are truth tables?

Truth tables summarise the way in which a logic gate operates. Truth tables usually use 1 for a *high* signal and 0 for a *low* signal.

AND gate: the output is high only when input A AND input B are high.

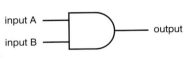

Δ Fig. 4.71 An AND gate.

Inputs		Output
A	B	
0	0	0
0	1	0
1	0	0
1	1	1

OR gate: the output is high when input A OR input B is high, OR both.

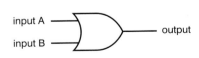

Δ Fig. 4.72 An OR gate.

Inputs		Output
A	B	
0	0	0
0	1	1
1	0	1
1	1	1

NOT gate: this gate is also called an inverter. It has only one input. The output is high when the input is NOT high.

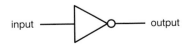

Δ Fig. 4.73 A NOT gate.

Inputs	Output
0	1
1	0

1. For safety, a car engine will not start unless the door is closed and the seat belt is fastened. Which type of logic gate is needed?

For the engine to start, both input conditions must be met. This circuit will need an AND gate.

2. A doorbell has switches at the front door and the back door of a house. Which type of logic gate is needed?

The bell needs to ring if either switch is pressed (or both). This circuit will need an OR gate.

More logic gates

A **NOR gate** combines an OR gate and a NOT gate. The output is high when *neither* A *nor* B is high (Fig. 4.74).

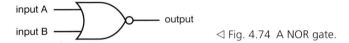

◁ Fig. 4.74 A NOR gate.

A **NAND gate** combines an AND gate and a NOT gate. The output is high when *both* inputs are *not* high (Fig. 4.75).

◁ Fig. 4.75 A NAND gate.

Logic gate circuits

Logic gates can be combined – the output signal from one gate can be used as the input signal to another.

Bistable circuits

The circuits in Fig. 4.76 are made by cross-linking NOR gates or NAND gates.

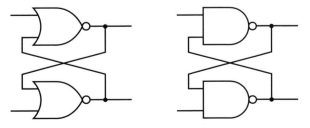

△ Fig. 4.76 Examples of bistable circuits.

A **bistable circuit** has two states that are stable. The output depends on the *sequence* of changes at the inputs – the circuits act as a simple 'memory'. If only one output is used, the circuit is called a **latch**.

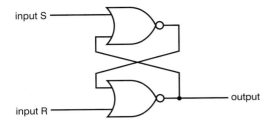

input S

input R

output

△ Fig. 4.77 A NOR gate latch.

Switch	Input voltage to logic gate
Open	LOW
Closed	HIGH

△ Table 4.3 The input to the logic gate depends on whether the switch is open or closed.

In a NOR gate latch such as that shown in Fig. 4.77:

- initially, both inputs are low and the output is low
- input S (the *set* input) goes high, so the output goes high
- input S returns to low, but the output stays high – it is *latched on*
- input R (the *reset* input) goes high, so the output returns to low
- input R returns to low and the output stays low – it is *latched off*.

This is useful in circuits such as burglar alarms where the input sensor may only send a signal for a short time. The latch circuit keeps the alarm on until the reset is used.

In a NAND gate latch, the sequence is the same except that:

- both inputs and the output are high at the start
- moving the set input briefly to low changes the output to low
- moving the reset input briefly to low returns the output to high.

How do we provide signals for logic gates?

The simplest way to provide an input signal for a logic gate is to use a switch and a resistor (Fig. 4.78).

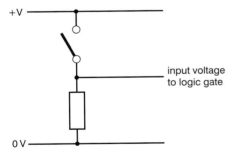

+V

input voltage
to logic gate

0 V

◁ Fig. 4.78 A switch and a resistor used as an input for a logic gate.

QUESTIONS

1. EXTENDED What does the output signal from a logic gate depend on?

2. EXTENDED The inputs at an OR gate are low and high. What is the output?

3. EXTENDED Explain the operation of a NOR gate latch.

4. EXTENDED What two components are used to provide signals to a logic gate?

END OF EXTENDED

End of topic checklist

Key terms

alternating current (a.c.), analogue, bistable circuit, capacitor, digital, diode, direct current (d.c.), input transducer, latch, light-dependent resistor, logic gate, NAND gate, NOR gate, parallel circuit, potential divider, potentiometer, relay, rheostat, semiconductor, series circuit, thermistor, transistor, truth table

During your study of this topic you should have learned:

○ How to draw and interpret circuit diagrams containing sources, switches, resistors (fixed and variable), lamps, ammeters, voltmeters, magnetising coils, transformers, bells, fuses and relays.

○ EXTENDED How to draw and interpret circuit diagrams containing diodes and transistors.

○ That the current at every point in a series circuit is the same.

○ How to give the combined resistance of two or more resistors in series.

○ That, for a parallel circuit, the current from the source is larger than the current in each branch.

○ That the combined resistance of two resistors in parallel is less than that of either resistor by itself.

○ About the advantages of connecting lamps in parallel in a lighting circuit.

○ EXTENDED How to use the fact that the sum of the p.d.s across the components in a series circuit is equal to the total p.d. across the supply.

○ EXTENDED How to use the fact that the current from the source is the sum of the currents in the separate branches of a parallel circuit.

○ EXTENDED How to calculate the effective resistance of two resistors in parallel.

○ How to describe the action of a variable potential divider (potentiometer).

○ How to describe the action of thermistors and light-dependent resistors and show understanding of their use as input transducers.

○ How to describe the action of a capacitor as an energy store and show understanding of its use in time-delay circuits.

○ How to describe the action of a relay and show understanding of its use in switching circuits.

○ EXTENDED How to describe the action of a diode and show understanding of its use as a rectifier.

○ EXTENDED How to describe the action of a transistor as an electrically operated switch and show understanding of its use in switching circuits.

○ EXTENDED About circuits operating as light-sensitive switches and temperature-operated alarms (using a relay or a transistor).

○ EXTENDED How to explain and use the terms 'digital' and 'analogue'.

○ EXTENDED That logic gates are circuits containing transistors and other components.

○ EXTENDED How to describe the action of NOT, AND, OR, NAND and NOR gates.

○ EXTENDED How to design and understand simple digital circuits combining several logic gates.

○ EXTENDED How to state and use the symbols for logic gates.

End of topic questions

Note: The marks awarded for these questions indicate the level of detail required in the answers. In the examination, the number of marks awarded to questions like these may be different.

1. Draw a circuit showing a resistor connected to a diode with an ammeter in the circuit and a voltmeter across the resistor. The power supply should be a 9 V battery and there should be a switch in the circuit as well. **(4 marks)**

2. Look at the following circuit diagrams. They show a number of ammeters and in some cases the readings on these ammeters. All the lamps are identical.

   a) For circuit X, what readings would you expect on ammeters A_1 and A_2?

   (2 marks)

   b) For circuit Y, what readings would you expect on ammeters A_4 and A_5?

   (4 marks)

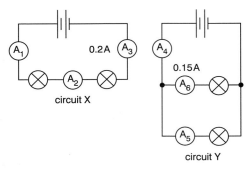

circuit X

circuit Y

3. Look at the circuit diagram. It shows how three voltmeters have been added to the circuit. What reading would you expect on V1? **(2 marks)**

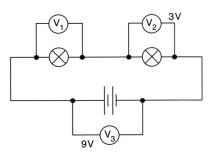

4. Look at the circuit diagram and answer the following questions:

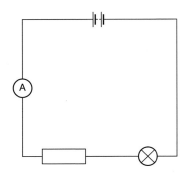

a) What supplies the voltage in this circuit? (1 mark)

b) What will happen to the current if another cell is added? (1 mark)

c) If the resistance of the circuit is increased, what will happen to the current in the circuit? (2 marks)

d) If the ammeter shows 0.3 A and the resistor is 5 Ω, what is the voltage of the cell? (2 marks)

5. An engineer was testing the resistance of a component and obtained the table of data shown.

Voltage/V	Current/A
0.5	0.14
1	0.29
1.5	0.43
3	0.86
4	1.14
5	1.43
5.5	1.57
6.5	1.86

a) What type of graph should he draw, and which quantity should be plotted on which axis? (2 marks)

b) Which was his independent variable? (1 mark)

c) Do you consider these results to be reliable? (2 marks)

d) How could he have improved the accuracy of his measurements? (2 marks)

e) Plot the graph and use the slope to calculate the resistance. (3 marks)

6. Copy and complete the following table.

Potential difference/V	Current/A	Resistance/Ω
	0.15	2
6	0.2	
	0.5	12
12	3	
240		18.5

(5 marks)

7. EXTENDED In the circuits shown here, what you would expect to read on each ammeter and voltmeter? All lamps are the same, and each cell produces 1.5 V. What *could* happen to these values if the bulbs had different resistances? **(12 marks)**

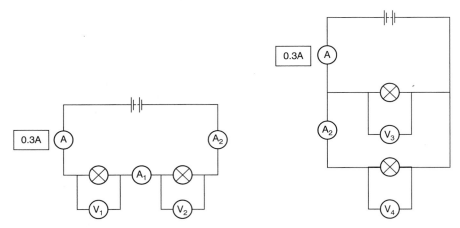

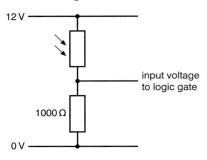

8. Describe how a potentiometer works. **(5 marks)**

9. Here is a light sensor circuit. It detects light and dark.

a) Explain how it works. **(4 marks)**

b) State two reasons why a relay must be used when the output from the logic gate needs to control a room heater. **(2 marks)**

Dangers of electricity

INTRODUCTION

Electricity is a clean and effective method of generating heat and movement. When a domestic appliance (such as a washing machine or a fridge) is switched on, a circuit is completed between the local substation and the appliance. Electrical energy travels from the substation to the appliance through the 'live' and 'neutral' wires. Some appliances have a third wire, the 'earth' wire. You will also meet the American word 'ground' instead of 'earth'. This wire does not normally carry any current, but it is there for safety.

△ Fig. 4.79 Electricity travels from power stations to our homes on pylons like these.

KNOWLEDGE CHECK

✔ Know some advantages of using mains electricity to transfer energy.
✔ Know some safety precautions to take when dealing with mains electricity.

LEARNING OBJECTIVES

✔ State the hazards of damaged insulation, overheating of cables and damp conditions.
✔ Show an understanding of the use of fuses and circuit-breakers.

ELECTRICAL HAZARDS

Electricity can cause hazards in domestic situations. Table 4.4 gives some examples.

Hazard	Possible consequences
Frayed cables	Wiring can become exposed
Long trailing cables	These might cause a trip or a fall
Damaged plugs	Wiring can become exposed
Water around sockets	Water conducts electricity, so can connect a person into the mains supply
Pushing metal objects into sockets	This connects the holder to the mains supply and is likely to be lethal
Overloading of sockets	Causes too high a current, which might melt the insulation and cause a fire
Long, coiled cable to an electric heater	Cable can heat up because of the coiling and start a fire

△ Table 4.4 Examples of domestic electrical hazards.

If there is a fault in an electrical appliance, it could take too much electrical current. This might make the appliance itself dangerous, or it could cause the flex between the appliance and the wall to become too hot and start a fire.

Insulation, fuses and circuit-breakers

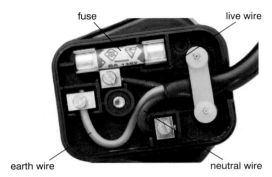

fuse   live wire

earth wire   neutral wire

△ Fig. 4.80 A three pin plug has a built-in safety device, the fuse.

There are several ways to make appliances safer to use and protect the user if a fault should develop. In some countries a **fuse** is fitted into the plug of the appliance. The fuse fits between the brown live wire and the pin. The brown **live wire** and the blue **neutral wire** carry the current. The green and yellow striped **earth wire** is needed to make metal appliance safer.

The laws for the safe use of electricity are constantly being improved by governments, and electricians learn to work to the latest standards. The most important aids to the safe use of electricity are **insulation** and fuses or **circuit-breakers**.

Insulation these days is generally a plastic such as PVC, which is used to cover the copper wires. This prevents them from touching each other, and also prevents the operator from touching them. In parts of appliances where the temperature goes above 100 °C, other plastics, glass or ceramic are used.

The electric current usually has to pass through a fuse or circuit-breaker before it reaches the appliance. If there is a sudden surge in the current, the wire in the fuse will heat up and melt – it 'blows'. This breaks the circuit and stops any further current flowing. When a circuit-breaker is used, then the circuit-breaker springs open (trips) a switch if there is an excessive current in the circuit. This can be reset easily after the fault in the circuit has been corrected.

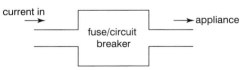

current in   appliance

fuse/circuit breaker

△ Fig. 4.81 How a fuse or circuit-breaker protects an appliance.

REMEMBER

Many students misunderstand the role of a fuse. It does not 'provide' current, nor does it 'allow' a certain amount of current to go through. It is just a wire that melts if the current gets too high.

In all houses with mains electricity, there is a distribution box (sometimes called a consumer unit) that takes all of the electricity for the house and sends it to the different rooms. In old houses this box may still contain fuses, but in modern installations the box has miniature circuit-breakers, often known as MCBs.

Where a fuse is fitted to a plug, it must have a higher current rating than the appliance needs, but should have the smallest current rating available above this. The most common ratings for plug fuses are 3 A, 5 A and 13 A. Any electrical appliance with a heating element in it should be fitted with a 13 A fuse. An appliance working at 3.5 A should have a 5 A fuse.

Metal-cased appliances, such as washing machines or electric cookers, must have an earth wire as well as a fuse. If the live wire works loose and comes into contact with the metal casing, the casing will become live and the user could be electrocuted.

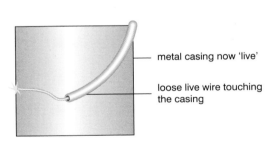

△ Fig. 4.82 A loose live wire can be dangerous if the metal casing of an appliance is not 'earthed'.

metal casing now 'live'

loose live wire touching the casing

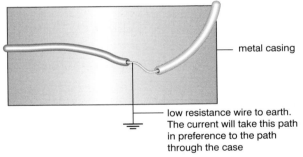

metal casing

low resistance wire to earth. The current will take this path in preference to the path through the case

△ Fig. 4.83 An earth wire provides a path for current to flow to ground.

The earth wire provides a very low resistance route to the 0 V earth. This low resistance means that a large current passes from the live wire to earth, causing the fuse to melt and break the circuit. This disconnects the appliance from the live connection, making it safe to touch (Fig. 4.83). If the earth wire is not fitted correctly, or if it has broken, the appliance will be extremely dangerous! If there is any doubt about the earthing of the appliance, or of the whole house, it must be checked by an electrician.

Appliances that are made with plastic casing such as kettles do not need an earth wire. The plastic is an insulator and so can never become live. Appliances like this are said to be **double insulated**.

In some situations people may be unexpectedly exposed to electricity: for example, using an electric drill, especially drilling into a wall with hidden power cables, or using power tools out of doors, perhaps in wet conditions. In these cases, a special type of circuit breaker called a **residual current circuit-breaker** (RCCB) must be used in the power socket on the wall. If any of the electricity starts to leak, through a short circuit (for example because the device has got wet), the RCCB will turn off the power in 30 ms or less. The RCCB cannot be guaranteed to save the user's life, but it gives them a much better chance of surviving.

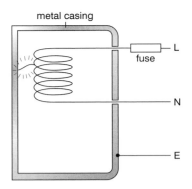

△ Fig. 4.84 The earth wire and fuse work together to make sure that the metal outer casing of this appliance can never become live and electrocute someone.

EXTENDED

Choosing the correct fuse is important when fitting one to an electrical appliance. The fuse is there to protect the user from electric shock, and to protect the appliance from damage.

For this task, take the mains supply to be 230 V.

How do you select the correct fuse? You need to understand the relationship between the power supplied and the potential difference (p.d.) across the appliance.

power = p.d. × current

An example of the fuse required for a lawnmower that has a 500 W rating and is connected to the 230 V mains would be:

power = p.d. × current

500 W = 230 V × current

current = 500 / 230

= 2.2 A

A 3 A fuse should therefore be fitted to the lawnmower.

1. Calculate the fuses required for the appliances listed here:

a) a vacuum cleaner of 360 W

b) a television of 80 W

c) a table lamp of 100 W

d) a kettle of 2100 W

e) an iron of 900 W.

Assume that the mains supply is 230 V.

Use an Excel spreadsheet to produce a printed table for your teacher to mark. For each appliance you should show:

- the power rating
- the p.d. supplied
- the current produced
- the current rating of fuse required (use the internet or textbook to identify suitable fuses).

END OF EXTENDED

QUESTIONS

1. Describe the wiring of a three-pin plug. You should explain what each of the wires in the plug is connected to and the colour of the insulation.

2. Explain the function of a fuse.

3. A student wants to run an appliance that requires a current of 6 A. He chooses a fuse of 5 A 'because it's the nearest available'. Explain why this is not a good choice.

4. The earth wire connection to the ground is usually quite a thick piece of copper wire. Explain why.

5. Explain why appliances with plastic casing do not need to be earthed.

SCIENCE IN CONTEXT — DEVELOPMENT OF MAINS ELECTRICITY

Electrical discoveries and techniques were made throughout the 19th century but the use of electricity in wider society developed only slowly. From the late 1830s onwards electricity was used for communications, but this only required the low power that batteries could provide. The invention of the incandescent light bulb in the 1870s was the key, as it led to the possibility of electric street lighting and this meant that electrical supplies would need to be sent across larger distances.

As local companies and authorities developed electricity supply systems sometimes a direct current (d.c.) system was used; sometimes an alternating current (a.c.) system. As the distances became greater, however, the power losses in the cables became more significant and it became clear that higher voltages would be more economic. Since d.c. systems had no straightforward way to convert to higher voltages, a.c. became the standard that has developed into the systems we use today.

Different countries have different standards for mains supply, reflecting the historical development of the networks across the world. For example, the UK, Sri Lanka, India and Australia use a 230 V supply, China uses 220 V and the USA uses 120 V.

What does the quoted voltage value refer to in an a.c. supply?

The voltage alternates between positive and negative. Where on the voltage axis (if we refer to the UK value) should the '230' go? The mean value of the voltage is 0 (being equally spread in positive and negative values). If we label the highest value (called the 'peak' value) then that doesn't seem very representative of the voltage since the supply would only be at that value for very short times.

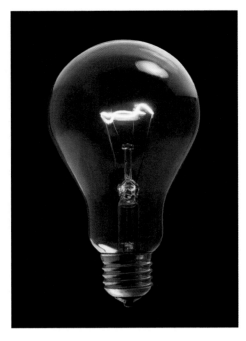

△ Fig. 4.85 A modern incandescent light bulb.

A value called the root mean square (RMS) value is calculated in three stages. Firstly, all values of voltage are *squared* – this makes all the values on the graph positive. Secondly, now that all the values are positive, a *mean* is calculated – this will not be zero. Finally, since this mean value is in (volts)^2, the *square root* is taken to give a value in volts. It is this final value – the RMS value – that is quoted as 230 V.

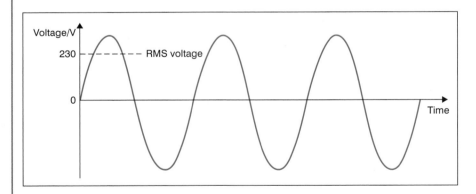

△ Fig. 4.86 Alternating and RMS voltages.

The particular advantage of using the RMS value is that an a.c. supply of 230 V RMS would provide the same *heating effect* as a 230 V d.c. battery, so the two systems can be compared easily.

End of topic checklist

Key terms

circuit-breaker, double insulated, earth wire, fuse, insulation, live wire, neutral wire, residual current circuit-breaker

During your study of this topic you should have learned:

○ About the hazards of:

- damaged insulation
- overheating of cables
- damp conditions.

○ About the use of fuses and circuit-breakers.

End of topic questions

Note: The marks awarded for these questions indicate the level of detail required in the answers. In the examination, the number of marks awarded to questions like these may be different.

1. EXTENDED **a)** A hairdryer works on 230 V mains electricity and takes a current of 4 A. Calculate the power of the hairdryer. **(2 marks)**

   b) In some countries it is illegal to have power sockets in a bathroom to stop you using electrical devices such as hairdryers near the wash basin or bath. Why would it be foolish to use a hairdryer near to water? **(2 marks)**

2. Why should a fuse always be connected in series with the live wire? **(1 mark)**

3. EXTENDED An appliance has a power rating of 1400 W. The potential difference of the mains is 230 V. Calculate the approximate current. Explain what size standard fuse you would use. **(3 marks)**

4. EXTENDED In her living room, Felicity has the following items:

   - three 100 W lamps
   - a TV that takes 2 A
   - an audio system that takes 1 A
   - a 2 kW electric heater
   - a 3 kW air conditioning unit.

   The whole room is supplied from a 220 V a.c. power supply through one miniature circuit breaker (MCB). What rating of MCB should she fit, if values of 10 A, 20 A, 30 A, 40 A, 50 A and 60 A are available? **(2 marks)**

5. EXTENDED What rating of fuse would you use in a microwave of power rating 800 W with:

   a) a 240 V mains supply **(2 marks)**

   b) a 120 V mains supply? **(2 marks)**

6. EXTENDED What potential problems might there be with the fuse in question 5?

The current used by the transformer must change as well. No transformer is 100 per cent efficient, because all transformers produce some heat when they are working. However if it *were* 100 per cent efficient, then the electrical power going in would equal the electrical power going out. In other words:

$$\text{primary coil voltage } (V_p) \times \text{primary coil current } (I_p) = \text{secondary coil voltage } (V_s) \times \text{secondary coil current } (I_s)$$

For example, if the output is 12 V, 10 A, that is 120 watts of power going out of the transformer. If you know that the input voltage is 240 V, then the input current will be 0.5 A.

A bathroom shaver socket contains an isolating transformer. The socket has an output voltage that is the same as the input voltage. It sometimes has an alternative output voltage. This means that people who travel around the world can use their electric shavers in their hotel rooms.

Your task is to do some research into how shaver sockets work in a way that makes electricity safe to use in a bathroom.

1. Prepare revision notes to share with your classmates.

2. Use plenty of diagrams and colour to help them remember your points.

Use the information given here to get you started.

- The mains supply is hidden behind the socket face.

- The only 'bare' terminals exposed are the two holes that the shaver plugs into.

- Neither of these holes is connected directly to the mains 'live', so there is no risk of being electrocuted if you touch either or both of them with damp hands.

END OF EXTENDED

QUESTIONS

1. Describe the difference between a step-up transformer and a step-down transformer.

2. A transformer has an input voltage of 2 V. There are 20 turns on the primary and 200 turns on the secondary. What is the output voltage?

3. A transformer has an input of voltage 1.5 V. There are 60 turns on the primary and 240 turns on the secondary. What is the output voltage?

4. A transformer has an input voltage of 2 V. There are 50 turns on the primary coil. The secondary coil has 600 turns.

   a) What is the output voltage?

   b) The secondary coil has a resistance of 12 Ω. What is the secondary currwent?

   c) The transformer is perfectly efficient. What is the primary current?

Transmitting electricity

Most power stations *burn fuel* to heat water and produce high-pressure steam, which is used to drive a **turbine**. The turbine turns an a.c. generator, which produces the electricity.

To minimise the power loss in transmitting electricity, the current has to be kept as low as possible. The higher the current, the more the transmission wires will be heated by the current, causing more energy to be wasted as heat.

This is where transformers are useful. This is also the reason that mains electricity is generated as alternating current. When a transformer steps up a voltage, it also steps down the current and vice versa. Power stations generate electricity with a voltage of 25 000 V. Before this is transmitted, it is converted by a step-up transformer to 400 000 V. This is then reduced by a series of step-down transformers to 230 V before it is supplied to homes.

△ Fig. 4.94 A hydroelectric power station doesn't need to burn fuel. This turbine will be turned by water taken from a reservoir behind a dam. The a.c. generator will be fitted to the top of a turbine.

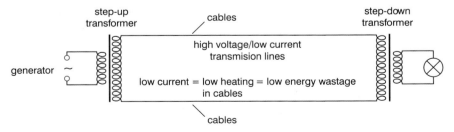

△ Fig. 4.95 Mains electricity is a.c. so that it can be easily stepped up and down. High-voltage/low current transmission lines waste less energy than low-voltage/high-current lines.

Energy losses in cables

With the exception of some lengths of superconducting cable (which has zero resistance but needs to be kept at a temperature below −200 °C) the distribution cables used by the electricity companies do not have zero resistance. A typical cable with a length of 100 km may have a resistance of 4 Ω. Now consider the problem facing the company when they want to send 4 MW of power to a town 100 km away. They could send either 10 A at 400 000 V, or 160 A at 25 000 V, or 17 400 A at 230 V.

The 230 V solution will not work. To send 17 400 A through a resistor of 4 Ω requires a p.d. across the wire of 68 000 V. More power would be lost from the cables than was put into them by the power station. This would be impossible.

At 25 000 V, the p.d. across the cable would be:

$V = I \times R$

$\quad = 160 \times 4$

$\quad = 640 \text{ V}$

The power lost in the cables would be:

$P = V \times I$

$\quad = 640 \times 160$

$\quad = 102\ 000 \text{ W}$

Of the 4 000 000 W being sent, this is 2.6 per cent. This is not too bad, as electricity supply companies expect to lose a total of 5–10 per cent of the power that they generate between the power station and the customer.

At 400 000 V, 10 A, the power lost in the cables is just 400 W, which is 0.01 per cent of the power being sent. These cables will cost more, and so the electricity company will have to work out which high voltage solution is best.

For the same power, the current will be lower for a higher voltage transmission. With a lower current there will be much lower heating in the cable.

power = voltage × current = current × resistance × current
$$= \text{current}^2 \times \text{resistance}$$

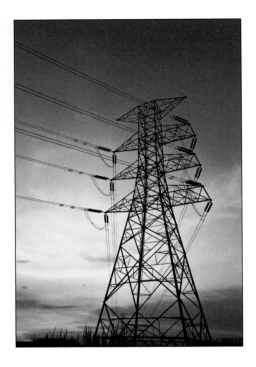

◁ Fig. 4.96 This 400 000 V distribution power line absorbs very little of the power that it carries, but it cost perhaps US$ 500 000 per km to build.

QUESTIONS

1. Explain why electricity is transmitted at high voltages when the distances involved are large.

2. Describe how transformers help in the transmission of high-voltage electricity.

3. Practise using the formulae given earlier.

   a) How much power would be lost if the electricity were sent at 50 000 V with a resistance of 4 Ω and a current of 80 A?

   b) What percentage of the 4 MW that the company want to send is this?

THE MAGNETIC EFFECT OF CURRENT

You have seen that moving a wire in a magnetic field induces an e.m.f. In this part of the topic you shall see that currents produce magnetic fields.

When a wire is carrying electric current it produces a magnetic field around itself. The higher the current, the stronger the field generated. Some people believe that this field is a health hazard, particularly around high voltage transmission lines, but research into the topic has been unable to demonstrate any risk so far.

By changing the magnitude of the current, you can change the strength of the magnetic field; and by reversing the current you reverse the direction of the magnetic field.

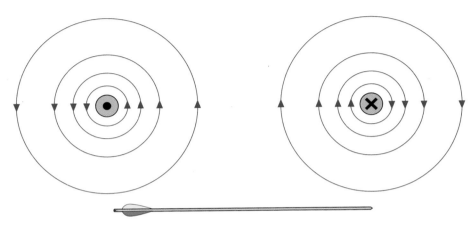

△ Fig. 4.97 The field pattern for a straight current-carrying conductor.

The dot in the centre of the wire indicates that the current is directed towards you; the cross indicates that the current is directed away. To remember this, think of an arrow. The ● ○ ✕ is the tip of the arrow coming towards you, the 'X' is the flights on the tail of the arrow. We are using the conventional current, so remember that the electrons are *actually* going in the opposite direction.

The field lines form continuous rings around the wire all along its length.

The lines are shown closest together near to the wire, because the field is strongest there and quickly gets smaller further away from the wire.

If the current is travelling towards you, the magnetic field lines are going in an anticlockwise direction, and if away from you they are going clockwise. To remember this, think of a woodscrew. In this case, if the screw is travelling away from you it is going clockwise.

Fig. 4.99 shows the magnetic field due to current in a **solenoid** (a coil of wire).

EXTENDED

To make the field stronger you need more turns in the solenoid, and more current through the turns. (And adding a soft iron core makes a big difference as well.) If you reverse the current, the N and S poles will change ends.

END OF EXTENDED

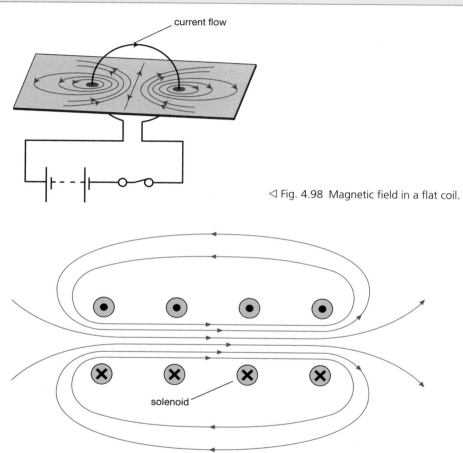

◁ Fig. 4.98 Magnetic field in a flat coil.

Δ Fig. 4.99 Magnetic field in a solenoid.

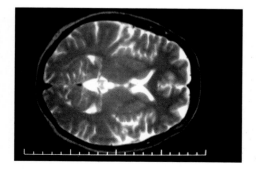

◁ Fig. 4.100 MRI image of a human brain.

The magnetic field inside a solenoid is remarkably uniform, and this is used in MRI scanners to allow doctors to produce images of the inside of the body like that in Fig. 4.100. To do this the whole body has to be placed inside the solenoid.

An electric current in a conductor produces a magnetic field around it. **Electromagnets** are made out of a coil of wire. Fig. 4.101 shows a coil of wire before a current is switched on. Electromagnets are used in relays.

However, when an electric current is passed through the coil as shown in Fig. 4.102, a magnet is formed with the N pole at one end of the coil and the S pole at the other end. If the coil is wrapped around a magnetically soft core as shown in Fig. 4.102, forming a solenoid (a coil of wire), then when the coil is magnetised, it magnetises the core as well, making a very much stronger magnetic field. When the current is switched off, the coil loses its magnetism, so the core does as well.

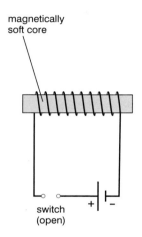

△ Fig. 4.101 Before the current is switched on, the coil does not produce a magnetic field.

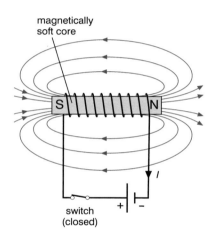

△ Fig. 4.102 The magnetic field produced when a current is passed through the coil.

QUESTIONS

1. Sketch the magnetic field produced by a solenoid. Describe how it is similar to the field of a bar magnet.

2. Describe how a coil can produce a uniform magnetic field. Which part of the field is uniform?

3. Sketch the field lines around a single wire where the current is a) into page b) out of page.

Developing Investigative Skills

A student wants to investigate the factors that affect the strength of an electromagnet. He makes the electromagnet by winding a coil of wire around a large iron nail. He then holds the electromagnet vertically in a clamp attached to a clamp stand. He uses a low-voltage power supply to provide the current for the electromagnet.

The student decides to investigate the effect of changing the current in the coil. To measure the strength of the electromagnet he finds out how many paper clips he can hang from the end of the electromagnet. His measurements are shown in the table.

Current/A	Number of paper clips held
0	0
0.3	2
0.5	5
0.7	6
0.9	9
1.0	9

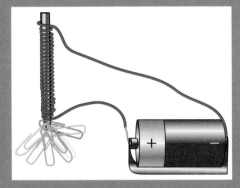

△ Fig. 4.103 When the circuit is complete, paperclips hang off the nail.

Using and organising techniques, apparatus and materials

❶ Describe how the student can vary the current in the electromagnet coil.

❷ What factors should the student keep constant during the investigation? Why do these factors need to be controlled?

Observing, measuring and recording

❸ Draw a graph of the student's results.

❹ Describe the pattern (if any) shown by the graph.

Handling experimental observations and data

❺ The student thought of three different ways to hang paper clips on the end of the nail.

   a) all the paper clips hanging on the nail together (Fig. 4.103)

   b) the paper clips hanging in a line from the end of the nail with the paper clips interlocked

   c) the paper clips hanging in a line from the end of the nail, but just held magnetically, not joined together.

Describe advantages and disadvantages of each method.

❻ How could the student change his method so that he could achieve more precise measurements of the strength of the electromagnet?

❼ The student wants to continue making measurements with higher values of current. Suggest a difficulty he will have as the current increases further.

FORCE ON A CURRENT-CARRYING CONDUCTOR

When a wire carrying an electric current passes through a magnetic field, with the field at right-angles to the wire, the wire will experience a force at right-angles both to the wire and to the magnetic field. The size of the force depends on the magnitude of the current and the strength of the magnetic field. **Fleming's left-hand rule**, which is shown in Fig. 4.104, predicts the direction of the force. You can demonstrate this using the apparatus in Fig. 4.105.

Remember that the current direction is that of the conventional current, and that the electrons are travelling the opposite way.

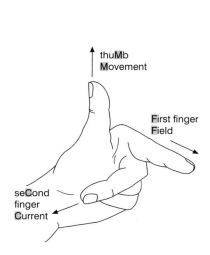

△ Fig. 4.104 Fleming's left-hand rule predicts the direction of the force on a current-carrying wire.

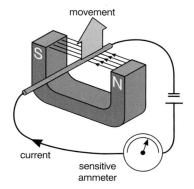

△ Fig. 4.105 Apparatus that can be used to demonstrate that if a wire carrying an electric current passes through a magnetic field, with the field at right-angles to the wire, then the wire will experience a force at right-angles both to the wire and to the magnetic field.

When you try applying Fleming's left-hand rule, you should be able to confirm that if you reverse either the magnetic field or the current then the force will be applied in the opposite direction, but that if you reverse *both* the field *and* the current then the force stays unchanged.

It is useful to look at the magnetic field lines for this set-up (Fig. 4.106).

△ Fig. 4.106 How the magnetic field lines are changed by a wire in a uniform magnetic field.

The field lines from the magnet are dragged downwards by the direction of the field lines that are around the wire. If you imagine that the lines are made of stretched elastic, then it is clear why the wire feels an upwards force.

The direction of an induced e.m.f.

Take the wire and the magnet described at the beginning of this section, with no current. If the wire is moved upwards in the magnetic field, then there will be a current in the wire (if the circuit is complete). The direction of the current in the wire will be towards you, which will give you a resultant force downwards. So as the wire is moved upwards, it will resist you by generating a force downwards. Even if there is no current, an e.m.f. will be induced in the wire that will try to generate this current.

More generally, 'the direction of an induced e.m.f. opposes the changes causing it'.

Force on a charged particle in a magnetic field

When a charged particle, usually an electron, is stationary in a magnetic field, it does not experience any force from the field. So when a copper wire that is full of electrons is placed near a magnet, nothing happens. When you move the wire parallel to the magnetic field, nothing happens. However, when the charged particle starts to move through the field at an angle to the field, then it will experience a sideways force that will try to push it off its path.

The deflection of a beam of charged particles in a magnetic field can be demonstrated using the particle generator in Fig. 4.107.

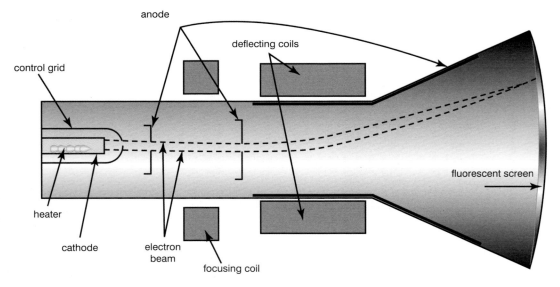

△ Fig. 4.107 In this particle generator, a beam of electrons is produced at the cathode. The beam is focused by a focusing coil and then passes through a pair of deflecting coils. The beam is detected on a fluorescent screen.

DC MOTOR

An **electric motor** transfers electrical energy to kinetic energy. It is made from a coil of wire positioned between the poles of two permanent magnets. When a current flows through the coil of wire, it creates a magnetic field, which interacts with the magnetic field produced by the two permanent magnets. The two fields exert forces on the sides of the coil, at right angles to the permanent magnetic field.

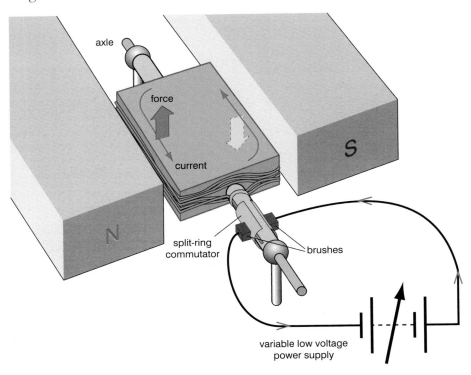

△ Fig. 4.108 An electric motor. These are used to transfer electrical energy to kinetic energy.

A motor coil as set up in Fig. 4.108 will be forced round as indicated by the arrows. One side of the coil experiences a force upwards while the other side experiences a force downwards. The **split-ring commutator** ensures that the motor continues to spin. Without the commutator, the coil would rotate 90° from the position shown and then stop. This would not make a very useful motor. The commutator reverses the direction of the current so that the forces on the coil are reversed and continue the rotating motion.

In Fig. 4.109, a length of wire has been connected across a power supply and coiled around one pole of a permanent magnet. A magnetic field is produced around the coil when a current is passed through the wire. The magnetic field of the permanent magnet repels that of the coil, causing the wire to jump off the magnet. You can see the wire jumping off the magnet in Fig. 4.110.

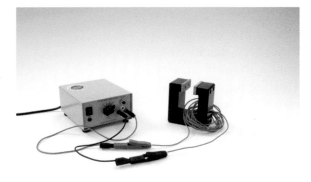

△ Fig. 4.109 Coil around pole of permanent magnet.

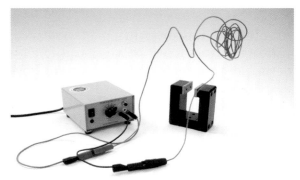

△ Fig. 4.110 Coil jumps off pole of permanent magnet.

△ Fig. 4.111 Inside a d.c. motor.

Fig. 4.111 shows the internal construction of a direct current motor. You can see the curved magnets attached to the inside of the cover. You can see the armature, coils, commutator and brushes on the right.

QUESTIONS

1. Describe simply how a force is created on the sides of the coil of a motor.

2. Explain what the commutator does in a motor.

Force increases with field and current

The motor can be used to show how the force on the current-carrying wires varies when you change the conditions.

EXTENDED

When you increase the current or you increase the strength of the magnetic field, then the force on each side is larger and the motor spins faster. When you change the direction of the current or you reverse the magnetic field, the direction of the forces is reversed and the motor spins in the opposite direction.

END OF EXTENDED

QUESTIONS

1. Describe how Fleming's left-hand rule can be used to predict the direction of a resulting force when a wire carries a current perpendicular to a magnetic field.

2. Describe *two* ways to increase the force created (and so increase the speed at which a motor spins).

3. Describe *two* ways to reverse the direction in which a motor spins.

End of topic checklist

Key terms

dynamo, electric motor, electromagnet, electromagnetic induction, Fleming's left-hand rule, flux, solenoid, split-ring commutator, step-down transformer, step-up transformer, transformer, turbine

During your study of this topic you should have learned:

○ How to describe an experiment that shows that a changing magnetic field can induce an e.m.f. in a circuit.

○ EXTENDED About the factors affecting the magnitude of an induced e.m.f.

○ EXTENDED That the direction of an induced e.m.f. opposes the change causing it.

○ How to describe a rotating-coil generator and about the use of slip rings.

○ How to sketch a graph of voltage output against time for a simple a.c. generator.

○ How to describe the construction of a basic iron-cored transformer as used for voltage transformations.

○ How to use the equation $(V_p/V_s) = (N_p/N_s)$.

○ How to describe the use of the transformer in high-voltage transmission of electricity.

○ About the advantages of high-voltage transmission.

○ EXTENDED How to describe the principle of operation of a transformer.

○ EXTENDED How to use the equation $V_p I_p = V_s I_s$ (for 100% efficiency).

○ EXTENDED Why energy losses in cables are lower when the voltage is high.

○ How to describe the pattern of the magnetic field due to currents in straight wires and in solenoids.

○ How to describe applications of the magnetic effect of current, including the action of a relay.

○ EXTENDED How the strength of the magnetic field varies over the pattern of the field.

○ EXTENDED How to describe the effect on the magnetic field of changing the magnitude and direction of the current.

○ How to describe an experiment to show that a force acts on a current-carrying conductor in a magnetic field, including the effect of reversing the current and the direction of the field.

○ EXTENDED How to describe an experiment to show the corresponding force on beams of charged particles.

○ EXTENDED About the relative directions of force, field and current and how to use them.

○ That a current-carrying coil in a magnetic field experiences a turning effect and that the effect is increased by increasing the number of turns on the coil.

○ How to relate this turning effect to the action of an electric motor.

○ EXTENDED How to describe the effect of increasing the current.

End of topic questions

Note: The marks awarded for these questions indicate the level of detail required in the answers. In the examination, the number of marks awarded to questions like these may be different.

1. Describe what is meant by electromagnetic induction.　**(4 marks)**

2. The diagram shows a simple electromagnet made by a student.

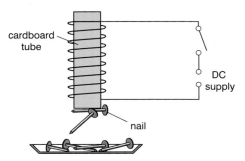

Suggest two ways in which the electromagnet can be made to pick up more nails.

(2 marks)

3. The diagram shows an electric bell.

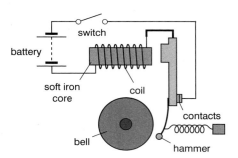

Explain how the bell works when the switch is closed.　**(4 marks)**

4. **EXTENDED** Two students are using the equipment shown in the diagram. They cannot decide whether it is an electric motor or a generator. Explain how you would know which it is.

(4 marks)

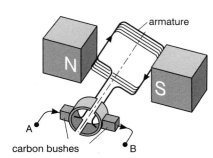

5. How can a cyclist increase the voltage supplied to his bicycle light by the dynamo? Explain your answer in terms of electromagnetic induction. **(3 marks)**

6. A householder has asked an engineer to design a small generator to generate electricity when the main supply fails. After the first design, the householder finds that he is relocating to a country where the mains voltage supplied to houses is lower. How could the design be modified to take this into account? **(4 marks)**

7. The diagram shows a transformer.

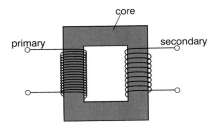

a) What material is used for the transformer core? **(1 mark)**

b) What happens in the core when a current is switched on in the primary coil? **(3 marks)**

c) What happens in the secondary coil when the primary current is switched on? **(3 marks)**

d) When the primary coil has 12 turns and the secondary coil has 7 turns, what will the primary voltage be when the secondary a.c. voltage is 14 V? **(3 marks)**

8. List three devices that use an electromagnet. **(4 marks)**

9. **EXTENDED** How can you show that a force acts on a current-carrying conductor when in a magnetic field? **(6 marks)**

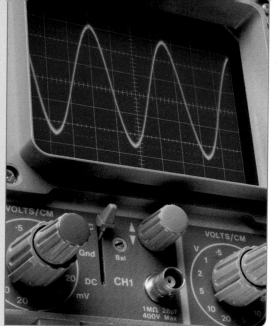

Cathode-ray oscilloscopes

INTRODUCTION

Cathode rays were discovered in the 1890s. Old-fashioned televisions and radios were based around cathode-ray tubes.

Nowadays cathode rays are mainly used in oscilloscopes, which are used in laboratories to display waveforms.

In this topic you will learn how cathode rays are controlled to produce the display shown on the oscillicope screen in Fig. 4.112.

△ Fig. 4.112 Waveforms displayed on an oscilloscope screen.

KNOWLEDGE CHECK

✓ Be able to describe the deflection of charged particles in a magnetic field.

LEARNING OBJECTIVES

✓ Describe the production and detection of cathode rays.
✓ Describe their deflection in electric fields.
✓ State that the particles emitted in thermionic emission are electrons.
✓ **EXTENDED** Describe (in outline) the basic structure and action of a cathode-ray oscilloscope.
✓ **EXTENDED** Use and describe the use of a cathode-ray oscilloscope to display waveforms.

CATHODE RAYS

Cathode rays were discovered in the late 1800s. J.J. Thomson discovered that these rays consisted of a stream of electrons emitted from a heated **cathode** (a negative terminal).

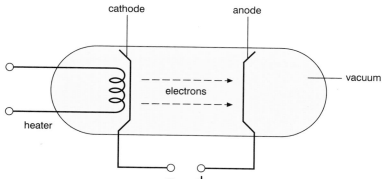

◁ Fig. 4.113 The structure of a cathode ray tube.

The positive terminal (the **anode**) in a cathode ray tube attracts the electrons from the cathode. The cathode is heated to increase the average energy of the free electrons within it, which means that electrons will spontaneously jump out of the surface of the metal. The process of emitting electrons from a heated cathode is called **thermionic emission**. This is similar to molecules of water evaporating from a water surface.

If there is a hole in the anode, a beam of electrons shoots through. The whole arrangement is then called an **electron gun**.

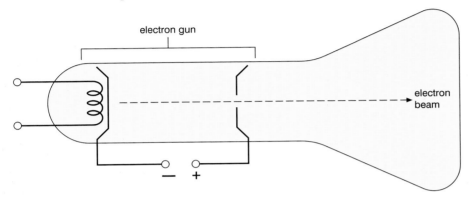

△ Fig. 4.114 The structure of an electron gun.

Deflecting the beam

An electron beam is equivalent to an electric current in the opposite direction, but without the wire. The beam can be deflected by *other electric charges* or by magnetic fields. In Fig. 4.109, the magnetic field is at right angles to the electron beam, so the beam is deflected. This is an example of the **motor effect** (see topic on electromagnetic effects). Check that it is obeying Fleming's left-hand motor rule, with First finger for Field, seCond finger for Current and thuMb for movement. Be careful over the question of which way the current is flowing.

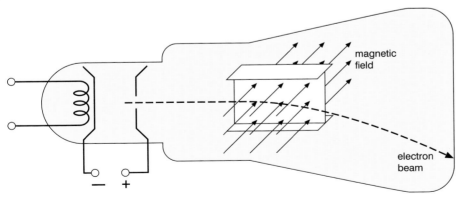

△ Fig. 4.115 An electron beam is deflected by a magnetic field at right angles to the beam.

In Fig. 4.116, the metal plates are charged, attracting the electron beam towards the positive plate and repelling it away from the negative plate.

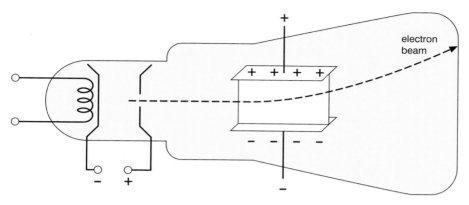

△ Fig. 4.116 An electron beam is attracted towards a positively charged metal plate and away from a negatively charged one.

QUESTIONS

1. What are cathode rays?

2. How are cathode rays produced?

3. Are cathode rays deflected towards the negative or positive plate? Give a reason for your answer.

EXTENDED

SIMPLE TREATMENT OF CATHODE-RAY OSCILLOSCOPE

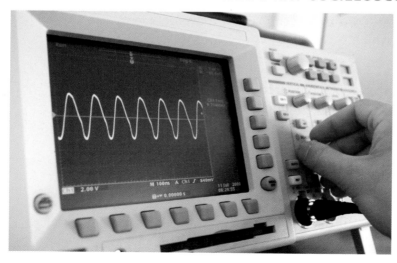

△ Fig. 4.117 A cathode-ray oscilloscope in use.

In a **cathode-ray oscilloscope** (CRO) the electron beam is directed towards a **fluorescent screen**. Where the beam hits the screen, the coating on the screen absorbs the energy from the electrons and releases the energy as light – a dot appears on the screen (Fig. 4.118).

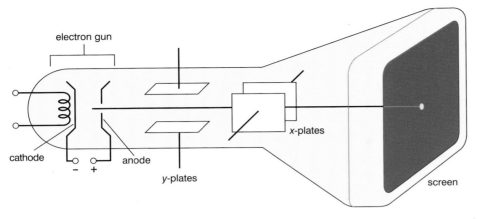

△ Fig. 4.118 Two sets of metal plates are used to deflect the beam – one pair in the *vertical* direction (called the *y*-plates) and one pair in the *horizontal* direction (called the *x*-plates). By controlling the voltages on these sets of plates, the dot can be moved to any position on the screen.

A CRO has a circuit – the **timebase circuit** – that moves the dot across the screen, from left to right, at a constant speed and then returns the dot very quickly to the start. Repeating this process quickly means the dot appears as a *line* across the screen.

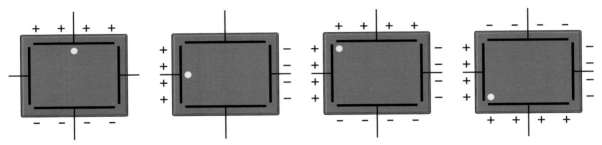

△ Fig. 4.119 By controlling the voltages on the plates, the dot can be moved to any position on the screen.

A CRO can be used as a very high resistance voltmeter. When an unknown voltage is connected to the *y*-plates, the deflection produced in the beam can be compared to reference measurements and a value for the voltage obtained.

With the timebase circuit switched on and a variable signal connected to the *y*-plates, a CRO can be used to show how a waveform varies. This can be used to measure the frequency of a signal.

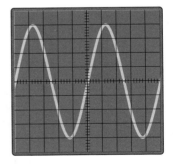

△ Fig. 4.120 The screen on the CRO when it is used as a voltmeter.

END OF EXTENDED

QUESTIONS

1. **EXTENDED** What happens when the electron beam hits the screen of the CRO?
2. **EXTENDED** How is the dot moved to any position on the screen?
3. **EXTENDED** What is the timebase circuit of a CRO?

End of topic checklist

Key terms

anode, cathode, cathode-ray oscilloscope, electron gun, fluorescent screen, motor effect, thermionic emission, timebase circuit

During your study of this topic you should have learned:

○ How to describe the production and detection of cathode rays.

○ How to describe their deflection in electric fields.

○ That the particles emitted in thermionic emission are electrons.

○ **EXTENDED** How to describe (in outline) the basic structure and action of a cathode-ray oscilloscope.

○ **EXTENDED** How to use and describe the use of a cathode-ray oscilloscope to display waveforms.

End of topic questions

Note: The marks awarded for these questions indicate the level of detail required in the answers. In the examination, the number of marks awarded to questions like these may be different.

1. What is thermionic emission? **(3 marks)**

2. EXTENDED The diagram shows a CRO. Copy the diagram and add the following labels in the correct places:

screen	x-plates	y-plates	anode	cathode	electron gun

(6 marks)

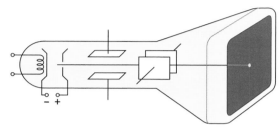

3. The diagram shows a trace on a CRO screen. The vertical setting is 0.2 V per division (square) and the timebase setting is 10 ms per division (square). 10 ms = 0.01 s.

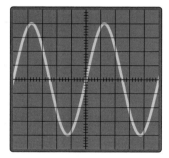

a) What is the amplitude of the signal in volts? **(2 marks)**

b) What is the time period of the signal (the time for one complete cycle)? **(2 marks)**

4. EXTENDED Describe how you would display a waveform on a cathode-ray oscilloscope **(2 marks)**

Exam-style questions

Note: The questions, sample answers and marks in this section have been written by the authors as a guide only. The marks awarded for these questions indicate the level of detail required in the answers. In the examination, the number of marks awarded to questions like these may be different.

Sample student answers

Question 1

This question is about electrostatics.

a) There are two kinds of electric charge.

Write down the names of both types of electric charge.

positive and negative ✓ ① **(1)**

b) Leon wants to charge his plastic comb.

Write down one way he could do this.

He could rub it. ✓ ① **(2)**

c) Leon holds his charged comb near some small pieces of paper.

Suggest what might happen to the papers.

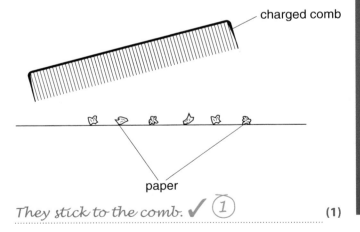

charged comb

paper

They stick to the comb. ✓ ① **(1)**

TEACHER'S COMMENTS

a) The correct response has been given. The symbols '+' and '−' would also be acceptable.

b) 'He could rub it' scores one mark, although 'by friction' would have been a stronger phrase to use. There is a second mark for saying that the comb should be rubbed against an insulator (or you could give an example of an insulator, such as cloth). Always check the number of marks available.

c) One mark has been awarded for the correct response. The student indicates correctly that there will be an attraction between the comb and the pieces of paper.

d) This is a very vague answer. There are three marks available. The correct response needs to state that Leon has become charged (perhaps by friction against a carpet) and that these charges move when he touches the radiator, from Leon to the radiator. The third mark is for using correct scientific words. Relevant words here are: charging, electrons, earth, earthing.

e) i) One mark has been awarded. Alternative correct responses would include inkjet printers, dust precipitators or crop spraying.

ii) Two marks have been awarded. The student seems to have an idea of what is happening, but has failed to use the correct scientific terms accurately. One mark has been awarded for the idea that opposite charges attract, but saying that the paint 'sticks' to the car is not accurate enough to gain a second mark – the student needed to say that the paint is attracted to the car. In a similar way, saying the paint covers 'much better' is too vague. At this level, the student should refer to the paint being attracted to the whole object, even parts not in direct line, or that less paint is wasted. Another approach would be to state that like charges repel (one mark), which produces an even coat (one mark).

d) Leon touches a metal radiator. He gets an electric shock.

Describe how Leon gets an electric shock. (One mark would be awarded for the correct use of scientific words.)

The metal radiator is electric and gives Leon a shock. ✗ ✗ ✗ **(3)**

e) Leon paints cars.

Static electricity is useful in spraying paint.

i) Write down **one other** use of static electricity.

A photocopier ✔ ①   **(1)**

ii) Explain why static electricity is useful in spraying cars.

Use ideas about electric charge in your answer. (One mark is for linking ideas.)

The paint is charged when it comes out of the sprayer. The car is also charged with the opposite charge. ✔
This makes the paint stick to the car much better. ✔ ②   **(4)**

(Total 12 marks)

Question 2

An electric iron has a power rating of 1100 W.

It is designed to run from a 230 V a.c. supply.

a) Explain why an electric current causes the iron to become hot. .... (2)

  i) State the equation linking power, current and voltage. .... (1)

  ii) Calculate the current in the iron when it is operating normally. .... (2)

b) The mains plug attached to the iron contains a fuse rated at 13 A.

  Describe the purpose of the fuse. .... (3)

c) The mains connection for the iron also contains an earth wire.

  i) Why is an earth wire needed for an electric iron? .... (2)

  ii) Describe the operation of an earth wire. .... (3)

d) Explain the difference between an alternating current (a.c.) and a direct current (d.c.). .... (2)

(Total 15 marks)

Question 3

A student investigates how the current varies with voltage in a filament lamp.

This is the student's circuit diagram.

The lamp is fully bright when 12 V is applied.

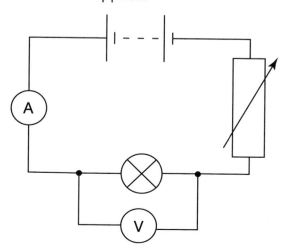

a) Describe how the student should use the circuit to carry out the investigation. (2)

   i) Sketch the graph the student should obtain if the lamp operates normally.
   Put the voltage on the vertical axis and the current on the horizontal axis. (3)

   ii) Explain the shape of the graph you have drawn. (3)

   The student carries out the experiment again using a lamp that is designed to be fully bright when 24 V is applied.

b) Suggest how the graph obtained would be different if the student carried out the test using the same 12 V supply.

   Explain your answer. (3)

c) The variable resistor used in the investigation has a resistance of 15 Ω.

   i) State the equation linking voltage, current and resistance. (1)

   ii) Calculate the current in the variable resistor if the voltage across it is 3 V. (2)

   iii) State the equation linking charge, current and time. (1)

   iv) Calculate the charge that passes through the variable resistor in 10 minutes when the voltage across it is 3 V.

   State the correct unit. (3)

(Total 18 marks)

Question 4

A student investigates electrostatic charges.

She has some insulating rods made of different types of plastic.

She rubs each one with a cloth to create the electrostatic charge.

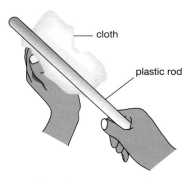

cloth

plastic rod

a) Using ideas about electrons, explain how an insulating rod can gain a positive or a negative electrostatic charge. (2)

b) A metal rod cannot gain an electrostatic charge in this way.

Explain why not. .... (2)

c) Describe an experiment the student could do to find out if two insulating rods had the same charge or opposite charges.

You should describe the equipment the student would need and how she should use it. .... (4)

d) Describe a situation where electrostatic charges can potentially be dangerous.

You should include:

what the hazard is

how the risk can be reduced. .... (3)

(Total 11 marks)

Question 5

A student uses a 12 V low-voltage power supply in the classroom.

It plugs into the 230 V mains supply.

a) The student realises that the power supply must contain a step-down transformer.

    i) Describe the operation of a transformer. .... (4)

    ii) Why does the power supply contain a step-down transformer? .... (1)

b) The student wants to use the power supply to provide a current of 3 A.

    i) Write down the equation linking input power and output power of a transformer, assuming 100% efficiency. .... (1)

    ii) Calculate the input current from the 230 V mains supply if the student is to use an output current of 3 A at 12 V. .... (3)

c) Step-up and step-down transformers are also used in the large-scale transmission of electrical energy.

    i) Explain the benefits of using transformers in this way. .... (4)

    ii) Describe a potential hazard in transmitting electrical energy this way and describe how this risk can be reduced. .... (2)

(Total 15 marks)

Question 6

The diagram shows two bar magnets.

a) Copy the diagram. Draw the magnetic field pattern on your diagram. .... **(3)**

b) Describe how you could test the area near a bar magnet to find the magnetic field pattern. .... **(3)**

c) The diagram shows a simple electric motor.

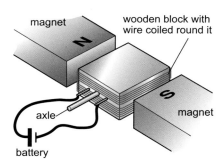

i) Explain why the coil spins when an electric current is supplied to it. .... **(4)**

ii) The motor spins faster when the current is increased.

Explain why. .... **(2)**

iii) When the current is reversed, the motor spins in the opposite direction.

Explain why. .... **(2)**

(Total 14 marks)

What have treatment for cancer, finding leaks in underground pipes, and dating archaeological specimens got in common? The answer is that they all use radioactivity in some way. Cancer is created by targeting the tumour with radioactive substances that destroy the cells of the tumour but do minimal damage to the surrounding tissues. Leaks in underground pipes can be detected by adding a radioactive substance to the fluid flowing in the pipe and then using a detector above the ground to trace the amount of radioactivity emitted at any point. Archaeological specimens can be dated using the fact that everything that lives, or once lived, contains some radioactive carbon atoms.

STARTING POINTS

1. What is an atom?

2. What happens when moving charged particles pass through a magnetic field?

3. What is meant by: a) proton number; b) nucleon number of a nuclide?

4. What do you have to do to balance any equation?

5. What do you understand by the term 'radioactivity'?

CONTENTS

a) The nuclear atom

b) Radioactivity

c) Exam-style questions

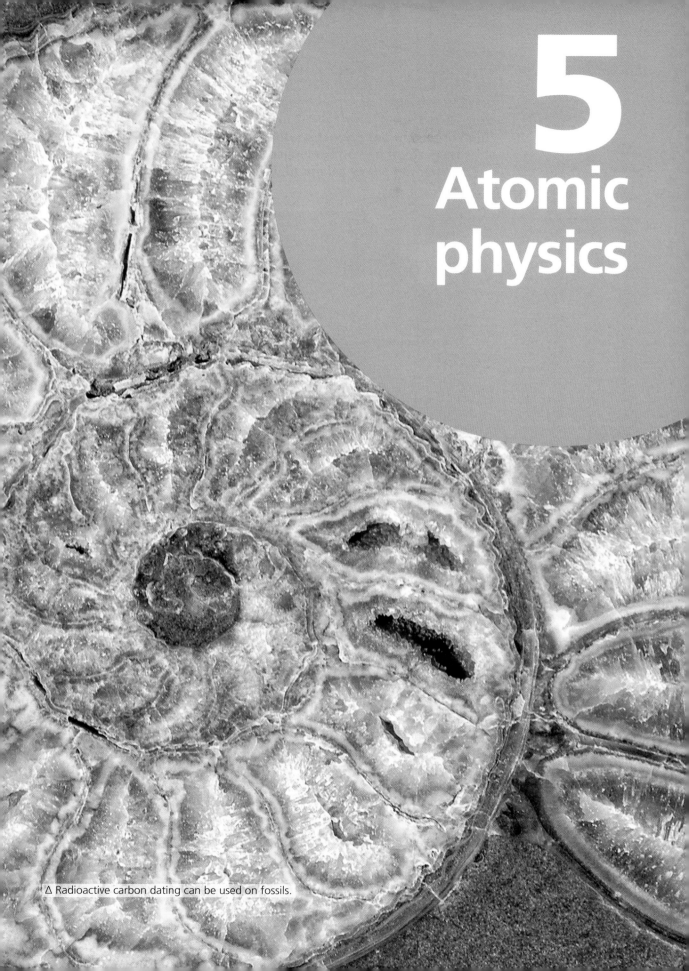

5
Atomic
physics

△ Radioactive carbon dating can be used on fossils.

The nuclear atom

INTRODUCTION

To understand radioactivity, you first need to know about the structure of the atom. Understanding of atomic structure has developed over time. The model that we use now was first developed as a result of an experiment by Geiger and Marsden in the 1910s. In this topic you will learn about the basic building blocks of atoms and about some uses of isotopes.

Δ Fig. 5.1 This submarine gets its energy from a small nuclear reactor inside it.

KNOWLEDGE CHECK

✓ Know that matter is made from atoms and molecules.

LEARNING OBJECTIVES

✓ Describe the structure of an atom in terms of a nucleus and electrons.
✓ **EXTENDED** Describe how the scattering of alpha particles by thin metal foils provides evidence for the nuclear atom.
✓ Describe the composition of the nucleus in terms of protons and neutrons.
✓ Use the term 'proton number Z'.
✓ Use the term 'nucleon number A'.
✓ Use the term 'nuclide' and use the nuclide notation $^A_Z X$.
✓ **EXTENDED** Use the term 'isotope'.
✓ **EXTENDED** Give and explain examples of practical applications of isotopes.

ATOMIC MODEL

All elements are made up of atoms, consisting of protons, neutrons and electrons. The protons and electrons have electrical charges that are exactly equal in size but opposite in sign. Because atoms generally do not have an electric charge, they usually contain the same number of protons and electrons.

The nucleus is made of protons and neutrons, bound together by an extremely strong force, far stronger than gravity, or electromagnetic forces, and completely different from any of them. The electrons form a loose cloud on the outside of the atom with the nucleus in the middle. Table 5.1 summarises this.

Particle:	proton	neutron	electron
Relative mass:	1.007	1.008	0.0005
Relative Charge:	+1	0	−1

△ Table 5.1 Atomic structure.

Geiger and Marsden's experiment

In the first decade of the 20th century, scientists knew that the atom contained positive and negative charges but the structure was a great mystery. An experiment suggested by Rutherford discovered the strange scattering of **alpha particles** when they get close to atoms (Fig. 5.2), and this cast great light on the structure. (The actual work was done by two students of Rutherford's – Geiger and Marsden.)

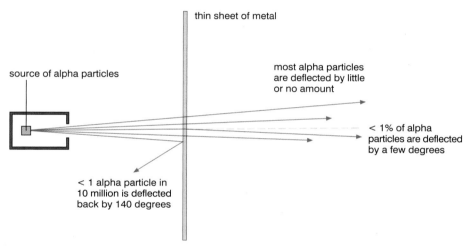

thin sheet of metal

source of alpha particles

most alpha particles are deflected by little or no amount

< 1% of alpha particles are deflected by a few degrees

< 1 alpha particle in 10 million is deflected back by 140 degrees

△ Fig. 5.2 Rutherford's scattering experiment, which revealed the structure of the atom.

What they discovered was that almost all of the alpha particles got through the thin metal sheet with no difficulty, but maybe one particle in a million hit a relatively large object that sent it off at a wide angle – perhaps even back the way it had come. This 'back scattering' was very surprising as it went against the existing model of the atom, proposed by Thomson (the 'plum pudding' model). The results told them that the atom has a nucleus that contains almost all of the mass of the atom. Because so few alpha particles hit the nucleus, it must be extremely small, surrounded by a cloud of extremely light electrons.

Rutherford's nuclear model

We are left with the slightly disturbing thought that almost all of a solid object is actually empty space, loosely filled with **electrons**, with a tiny nucleus at the centre of each atom. In a neutron star, where all of the atoms collapse, the whole star can end up perhaps no more than 10 km across, with a density of 300 *million* tonnes per cubic centimetre.

1. EXTENDED Explain how the results of the Rutherford scattering experiment provide evidence that the atom has a small, dense, positively charged nucleus.

2. EXTENDED Why do results from the scattering experiment suggest that electrons are not part of the central nucleus?

3. EXTENDED Why do the results also suggest that electrons are very small?

THE NUCLEUS

We know that the nucleus is made up of protons and neutrons, bound by an extremely strong force.

Atomic number and mass number

The behaviour of the atom is fixed by the nucleus. Each nucleus is represented by its chemical symbol with two extra numbers written before it.

The symbol for radium-226 is $^{226}_{88}\text{Ra}$.

The top number is the **nucleon number**, **A** (the total number of protons and neutrons)

The bottom number is the **proton number**, **Z** (the number of protons). The number of neutrons is therefore 138 (A minus Z) in the case of radium-226.

EXTENDED

ISOTOPES

It is common for several different nuclides (different nuclei) to have the same number of protons but different numbers of neutrons. Nuclides with the same number of protons but different number of neutrons are called **isotopes**. For example, there are two types of stable copper nuclei, $^{63}_{29}\text{Cu}$ and $^{65}_{29}\text{Cu}$. The first type contain 29 protons and 63 nucleons (particles in a nucleus: that is, protons and neutrons), hence (63 − 29 =) 34 neutrons. The second type is the same except it contains 36 neutrons (65 − 29).

In addition, there are various unstable isotopes of copper that are therefore radioactive. The different number of neutrons in their nuclei makes them

▷ Fig. 5.3 This copper roof contains 69 per cent $^{63}_{29}\text{Cu}$ nuclei and 31 per cent $^{65}_{29}\text{Cu}$ nuclei.

unstable. There are nine radioactive isotopes, with nucleon numbers that vary from 59 to 69. These two extremes are very unstable with half-lives (see the following topic) of a few minutes. $^{64}_{29}$Cu has a half-life of 12.7 hours. So all of the unstable isotopes of copper are extremely radioactive. Some radioactive isotopes of other elements are much less radioactive, and have half-lives measured in years, sometimes thousands of years.

END OF EXTENDED

QUESTIONS

1. What is in an atom?

2. Why are atoms electrically neutral?

3. Explain the meaning of the terms proton number, nucleon number.

4. EXTENDED Why are different isotopes of an element identical chemically?

End of topic checklist

Key terms

alpha particle, isotope, nucleon number, proton number, radioisotope

During your study of this topic you should have learned:

○ How to describe the structure of an atom in terms of a nucleus and electrons.

○ EXTENDED How to describe how the scattering of alpha particles by thin metal foils provides evidence for the nuclear atom.

○ How to describe the composition of the nucleus in terms of protons and neutrons.

○ How to use the term 'proton number Z'.

○ How to use the term 'nucleon number A'.

○ How to use the term 'nuclide' and use the nuclide notation $^A_Z X$.

○ EXTENDED How to use the term 'isotope'.

○ EXTENDED About examples of practical applications of isotopes.

End of topic questions

Note: The marks awarded for these questions indicate the level of detail required in the answers. In the examination, the number of marks awarded to questions like these may be different.

1. Describe the structure of the atom in terms of its nucleus and electrons. **(4 marks)**

2. **EXTENDED** How does an alpha particle scattering experiment provide evidence for the nuclear atom? **(4 marks)**

3. **EXTENDED** Give an example of isotopes. How do the atoms of these isotopes differ? **(3 marks)**

4. Copy and complete this table to show the particles in the atoms.

Atom	Symbol	Number of protons	Number of neutrons	Number of electrons
hydrogen	$^{1}_{1}H$			
carbon	$^{12}_{6}C$			
calcium	$^{40}_{20}Ca$			
uranium	$^{238}_{92}U$			

(12 marks)

5. Sodium-24 has a proton number of 11 and a nucleon number of 24. What is the composition of the nucleus of a sodium-24 atom? **(3 marks)**

Radioactivity

△ Fig. 5.4 Workers painting luminous watch dials with uranium salts in the early 20th century.

INTRODUCTION

The discovery of radioactivity in the late 1800s came at a time of great development in our knowledge of the atom. Far from being the 'fundamental building blocks of nature' as had first been thought, atoms were revealed as collections of particles in many different combinations.

Piecing the whole puzzle together took many years as the properties of unstable atoms were studied and entirely new atoms were discovered. Unfortunately, many of the early experimenters suffered from the harmful effects of the radiation before the dangers were recognised.

Now that the danger is well understood, radioactive materials are used in a carefully controlled manner in a number of everyday applications such as smoke alarms.

KNOWLEDGE CHECK

✓ Know the basic structure of an atom in terms of protons, neutrons and electrons.
✓ Have some background knowledge of some issues relating to radioactivity in everyday life – waste from nuclear power stations, etc.

LEARNING OBJECTIVES

✓ Show awareness of the existence of background radiation.
✓ Describe the detection of α-particles, β-particles and γ-rays.
✓ State that radioactive emissions occur randomly over space and time.
✓ State, for radioactive emissions: their nature; their relative ionising effects; their relative penetrating abilities.
✓ EXTENDED Describe their deflection in electric fields and magnetic fields.
✓ EXTENDED Interpret their relative ionising effects.
✓ State the meaning of radioactive decay, using equations to represent changes in the composition of the nucleus when particles are emitted.
✓ Use the term 'half-life' in simple calculations, which might involve information in tables or decay curves.
✓ Describe how radioactive materials are handled, used and stored in a safe way.

CHARACTERISTICS OF THE THREE KINDS OF EMISSION

Inside the atom the central nucleus of positively charged protons and neutral neutrons is surrounded by shells, or orbits, of electrons. Most nuclei are very stable, but some are unstable and 'decay', emitting particles or waves to form more stable nuclei. This process is called **radioactive decay**. Radioactive decay occurs spontaneously and randomly over space and time. Atoms whose nuclei do this are radioactive.

When a radioactive nucleus decays it may emit one or more of the following:

- **alpha (α) particles**
- **beta (β) particles**
- **gamma (γ) rays.**

A stream of these rays is referred to as **ionising radiation** (often called nuclear radiation, or just 'radiation' for short).

DETECTION OF RADIOACTIVITY

All ionising radiation is invisible to the naked eye but it affects photographic plates. Individual particles of ionising radiation (α-particles, β-particles and γ-rays) can be detected using a Geiger–Müller tube as shown in Fig. 5.5. You can distinguish between the types of radiation using their properties (see Fig. 5.7 and Table 5.2).

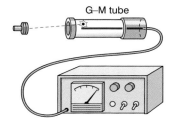

G–M tube

△ Fig. 5.5 Radioactivity is measured using a Geiger–Müller tube linked to a counter.

There is *always* ionising radiation present. This is called **background radiation**. Background radiation comes from both natural and manmade sources. Background radiation is caused by radioactivity in soil, rocks and materials like concrete; radioactive gases in the atmosphere; and cosmic rays, which come from somewhere in outer space, though we are still not sure *exactly* where.

△ Fig. 5.6 GM tube.

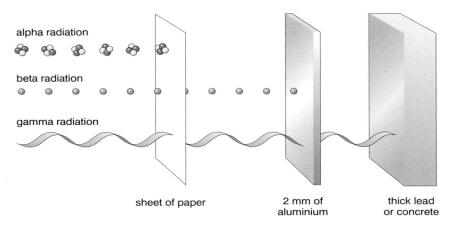

alpha radiation

beta radiation

gamma radiation

sheet of paper   2 mm of aluminium   thick lead or concrete

△ Fig. 5.7 Different radiations have different penetration power.

	alpha (α)	beta (β)	gamma (γ)
Description	A positively charged particle, identical to a helium nucleus (two protons and two neutrons)	A negatively charged particle, identical to an electron	Short wavelength electromagnetic radiation; electrically neutral
Penetration	4–10 cm of air; stopped by a sheet of paper	About 1 m of air; stopped by a few mm of aluminium	Almost no limit in air; intensity greatly reduced by several cm of lead or several metres of concrete
EXTENDED Effect of electric and magnetic fields	Deflected* in opposite direct to β	Deflected* considerably in opposite direct to α	Unaffected – not deflected*

△ Table 5.2 Properties of the different types of radiation.

*Note: Alpha particles and beta particles are deflected by magnetic and electric fields in the same manner that electrons are deflected in a cathode-ray oscilloscope (see topic on cathode-ray oscilloscopes). The particles from radioactive decay are travelling much faster so the deflections are smaller than in a cathode ray oscilloscope. Beta particles are actually electrons, so they are bent the same way. Alpha particles carry a positive charge, so they are bent the opposite way, but their deflection is much smaller than beta particles because the mass of the alpha particle is much greater than a beta particle.

An alpha particle contains two protons and two neutrons. So, with four nucleons and two protons, it is written as $^4_2\alpha$. Radiations are ionising, which means that when the radiation collides with an atom, it removes electrons from the atom, causing it to become charged. Alpha particles are more ionising than beta, which are more ionising than gamma.

This means that alpha particles can do more damage to living cells than beta, which in turn can do more damage than gamma. However, alpha particles are less penetrating than beta particles, which are in turn less penetrating than gamma.

Developing Investigative Skills

A researcher has a radioactive source but does not know what type of radiation the source is emitting.

Plan an investigation to find out what type of radiation the source is emitting. You have the following equipment:

- radioactive source
- GM tube and meter
- sheet of paper
- 2 mm thick sheet of aluminium
- sheet of thick lead

Using and organising techniques, apparatus and materials

❶ Plan your experiment, describing clearly the following:

  a) the aim of your investigation

  b) what you will measure

  c) the number and range of readings that you will take

❷ Draw out a results table that you would use in your investigation.

QUESTIONS

1. What is radioactive decay?

2. Is a radioactive isotope stable or unstable before it decays?

3. Use the descriptions of alpha, beta and gamma radiation given in Table 5.2 to explain why they have different penetrating powers.

4. Why are alpha and beta particles deflected by electric and magnetic fields, but gamma rays are unaffected?

5. EXTENDED The Rutherford scattering experiment was carried out in a chamber where the air had been removed. Use ideas about how far alpha particles travel to explain why this was necessary.

RADIOACTIVE DECAY

Ionising radiation is emitted from nuclei of unstable atoms/isotopes in order for them to become more stable. This process is known as radioactive decay. An alpha particle contains two protons and two neutrons. So, with four nucleons and two protons, it is written as $_2^4\alpha$. It is the same particle as the nucleus of a helium atom, which is written $_2^4$He.

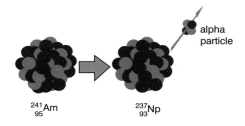

△ Fig. 5.8 Alpha decay.

When a nucleus emits an alpha particle it loses four nucleons, and its nucleon number decreases by 4. It loses two protons and its proton number decreases by 2 (Fig. 5.8).

A beta particle is written $_{-1}^0\beta$ to show that it is not a nucleon and has a mass so small that it can be ignored and is of exactly the opposite charge to a proton. A beta particle is the same as an electron, and could be written $_{-1}^0$e.

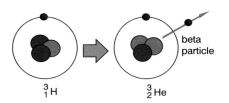

△ Fig. 5.9 Beta decay.

When a nucleus emits a beta particle, a neutron inside the nucleus has changed into a proton (that stays in the nucleus) plus an electron. The total charge before and after the reaction is unchanged, but the nucleus has lost a neutron and gained a proton. The electron, of course, is emitted as the beta particle (Fig. 5.9). The nucleon number of the nucleus is unchanged by beta emission, but the proton number increases by 1.

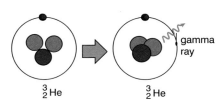

△ Fig. 5.10 Gamma ray emission.

When a nucleus emits a gamma ray, it is just a wave (carrying energy) that is emitted as the unstable nucleus (which has excess energy) reorganises itself internally. No particles are emitted, and so the nucleon number and the proton number do not change (Fig. 5.10).

Table 5.3 summarises these changes.

Nucleus emits	Nucleon number	Proton number
Alpha particle	Decreases by 4	Decreases by 2
Beta particle	Does not change	Increases by 1
Gamma ray	Does not change	Does not change

△ Table 5.3 Emission of different particles.

NUCLEAR EQUATIONS

You can write down nuclear changes as **nuclear equations**. The rules are as follows:

- The numbers in the top row must be balanced on each side of the equation, because the number of nucleons will not change. (For example, you could get 231 on the left and 227 + 4 for an alpha emission, and 231 on the left and 231 + 0 on the right for beta emission.)
- The numbers in the lower row must be balanced on each side of the equation, because the total electrical charge will stay unchanged.

Fig. 5.11 shows two more examples. Note particularly what happens when a beta particle is emitted. Because a neutron has changed into a proton, the atomic number has increased by 1!

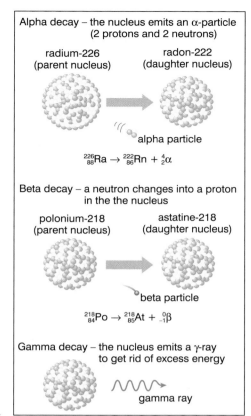

Alpha decay – the nucleus emits an α-particle (2 protons and 2 neutrons)

radium-226 (parent nucleus)   radon-222 (daughter nucleus)

alpha particle

$$^{226}_{88}Ra \rightarrow {}^{222}_{86}Rn + {}^{4}_{2}\alpha$$

Beta decay – a neutron changes into a proton in the the nucleus

polonium-218 (parent nucleus)   astatine-218 (daughter nucleus)

beta particle

$$^{218}_{84}Po \rightarrow {}^{218}_{85}At + {}^{0}_{-1}\beta$$

Gamma decay – the nucleus emits a γ-ray to get rid of excess energy

gamma ray

▷ Fig. 5.11 Examples of radioactive decay.

QUESTIONS

1. How does alpha decay affect a nucleus?

2. How does beta decay affect a nucleus?

3. Describe how emitting gamma radiation affects the nucleus.

4. After emitting alpha or beta radiation, the atom has changed to be a different element. Explain why.

HALF-LIFE

The **activity** of a radioactive source is the number of ionising particles it emits each second. Over time, fewer nuclei are left in the source to decay, so the activity drops. The time taken for half the radioactive nuclei to decay is called the **half-life**. Note that this time is the same whenever you choose to start measuring the source of radioactivity.

The level of radioactivity is measured in **becquerels**. A source that is one becquerel (written as 1 Bq) has one nucleus decay and emit radiation per second. A source in a laboratory may be a few hundred Bq, but industrial sources can be several kBq, sometimes MBq or GBq.

Starting with a pure sample of radioactive nuclei, after one half-life half the nuclei will have decayed. The remaining undecayed nuclei still have the same chance of decaying as before, so after a second half-life half of the remaining nuclei will have decayed. After two half-lives a quarter of the nuclei will remain undecayed (Fig. 5.12).

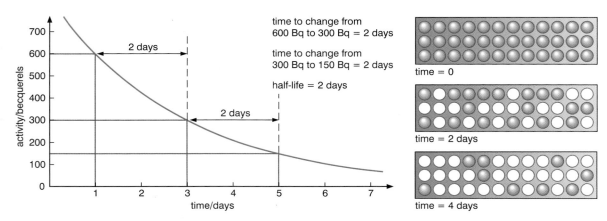

△ Fig. 5.12 The half-life is 2 days. Half the number of radioactive nuclei decays in 2 days.

WORKED EXAMPLE

A radioactive element is detected by a Geiger–Müller tube and counter as having an activity of 400 counts per minute. Three hours later the count is 50 counts per minute. What is the half-life of the radioactive element?

Write down the activity and progressively halve it. Each halving of the activity is one half-life:

0	400 counts
1 half-life	200 counts
2 half-lives	100 counts
3 half-lives	50 counts

It takes 3 hours to get to 3 half lives so one half-life is one hour.

QUESTIONS

1. What does the term 'half-life' mean?

2. A radioactive sample has a half-life of 8 hours. The activity is 800 Bq now. After how long will the activity be 100 Bq?

Developing Investigative Skills

A teacher demonstrates the radioactive decay of protactinium. Before starting the investigation, the teacher makes measurements to allow for background radiation. Then she sets a GM tube alongside a bottle containing the protactinium source. The GM tube is connected to a ratemeter. The teacher starts a stopclock and measures the activity of the source every 30 seconds for 5 minutes. The results are shown in the table.

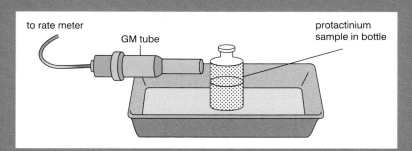

△ Fig. 5.13 Apparatus needed for the investigation.

Using and organising techniques, apparatus and materials

❶ Why does the teacher carry out this experiment, rather than a student?

❷ What measurements should the teacher make to correct for background radiation?

❸ What was the independent variable in this investigation? What was the dependent variable?

Time/minutes	Count rate corrected for background radiation/Bq
0	80
0.5	60
1.0	44
1.5	35
2.0	28
2.5	21
3.0	16
3.5	14
4.0	10
4.5	7
5.0	6

Observing, measuring and recording

❹ Draw a graph of the results.

❺ Use your graph to find the half-life of the sample.

Handling experimental observations and data

❻ Radioactivity is a random process. What does this mean? Is there any evidence from the graph to support the idea?

❼ Why was it important to correct for background radiation?

❽ Would repeating the experiment and taking an average give a more accurate value of the half-life? Explain your answer.

SAFETY PRECAUTIONS

Alpha, beta and gamma radiation can all damage living cells. Alpha particles, due to their strong ability to ionise other particles, are particularly dangerous to human tissue. However, they cannot penetrate skin, so when alpha sources are outside the body they are relatively harmless. If they are swallowed, inhaled, etc. they cause a lot of cell damage. Gamma radiation is dangerous because of its high penetrating power. However, the cell has repair mechanisms that make ordinary levels of gamma radiation relatively harmless.

Nevertheless, radiation can be very useful – it just needs to be used *safely*.

Safety precautions for handling radioactive materials include:

- Use forceps when moving radioactive sources – don't hold them directly.
- Do not point radioactive sources at living tissue.
- Store radioactive materials in lead-lined containers – and lock the containers away securely.
- Check the surrounding area for radiation levels above normal background levels.

High levels of radiation are extremely hazardous. People who deal with highly radioactive materials must wear special film badges (containing photographic film) that monitor the dose they receive. They may need to wear protective clothing, perhaps containing sheets of lead, and at the end of each shift they will need to check for radioactivity on their bodies and may need to shower.

Uses of isotopes

Radioisotopes have the same chemistry as non-radioactive isotopes of the same element. This can be very valuable in research as well as medicine. A famous example is the use of radioactive iodine in treatment of cancer of the thyroid. The thyroid gland can become cancerous and the cancer then spreads through the body. Because the cells of the thyroid absorb far more iodine than other parts of the body, the cancer can be targeted by injecting the body with radioactive iodine. The iodine is absorbed by the cancerous cells wherever they are in the body, after which it kills them. Another example is carbon-11, which is used in a technique called positron emission

△ Fig. 5.14 Radioactive iodine is injected in the treatment of cancer.

tomography, which builds up images of the organs inside a human body. Phosphorus-32 is often used to amino acids and phosphoproteins in biochemical studies.

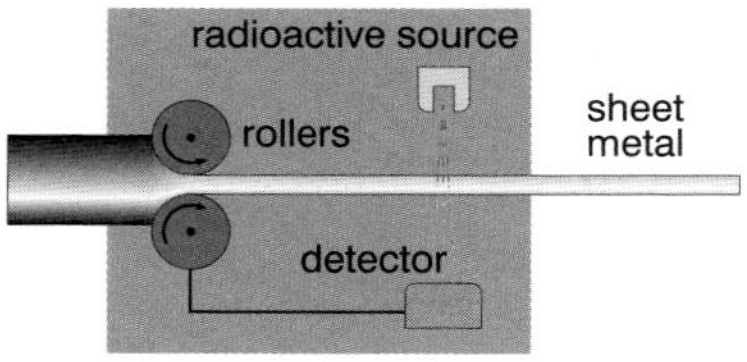

Gamma rays can be used to kill bacteria. This is used in sterilising medical equipment and in preserving food. The food can be treated after it has been packaged. A commonly used isotope is cobalt-60.

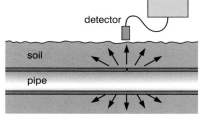

△ Fig. 5.15 Sheet thickness control.

A smoke alarm includes a small radioactive source that emits alpha radiation. The isotope used is usually americium-241. The radiation produces ions in the air, which conduct a small electric current. When smoke absorbs some of the alpha particles, it reduces the number of ions in the air and the current drops. This sets off the alarm.

Beta particles are used to monitor the thickness of paper or metal (Fig. 5.15). The number of beta particles passing through the material is reduced when the thickness of the material is increased. A commonly used isotope is strontium-90.

A gamma source is placed on one side of a weld and a photographic plate on the other side. Weaknesses in the weld will show up on the photographic plate in a similar way to an X-ray photograph of a broken bone.

In **radiotherapy** high doses of radiation are fired at cancer cells to kill them. Here, as in the case of X-rays (see topic on light), the radiation that can cause cancer is also an important tool in treating it.

△ Fig. 5.16 Tracers detect leaks.

Tracers are radioactive substances with half-lives and radiation types that suit the job they are used for. The half-life must be long enough for the tracer to spread out and be detected, but not so long that it stays in the system and causes irreparable damage.

- Medical tracers are used to detect blockages in vital organs. A gamma camera is used to monitor the passage of the radioactive material through the body. Some of the isotopes used are phosphorus-32, carbon-13 and iodine-123
- Agricultural tracers monitor the flow of nutrients through a plant. A commonly used isotope is tritium which is hydrogen-3.
- Industrial tracers can monitor the flow of liquid and gases through pipes to identify leakages (Fig. 5.16). There are many isotopes used. Some examples are bromine-82, iodine-131, and sodium-24.

END OF EXTENDED

SCIENCE IN CONTEXT

SCIENCE IN CONTEXT — HOW OLD IS THE EARTH?

We know that the Earth is about 4500 million years old, but how do we know that?

During the 19th century, the science of geology was growing. Rock samples and fossils were collected from all over the world, categorised, their similarities noted and a timeline for the different rock samples was worked out. However, the timeline was only relative – early geologists could only say that one rock was older than another; there was no way to put an actual figure on them in years.

Some geologists looked at the way in which rivers and seas washed fragments away – evidence of the land being broken down is all around us. 'The Earth cannot be very old', these people said, 'because if it was old the rivers would have smoothed it all out by now'.

Others said, 'No, that isn't a problem as long as there is a way to build the land back up again'. Unfortunately, at that time nobody knew exactly how mountains formed. The idea of plate tectonics, with huge land masses pushing on each other, was not developed until well into the 20th century.

Also during the 19th century, Charles Darwin had published his theory of evolution. This required changes to species to happen only gradually over long periods of time. So supporters of this theory also 'needed' the Earth to be ancient.

Another approach was necessary.

If you cannot work out the age of the Earth, what about working out the age of the Sun? Whatever that turns out to be, the Earth must be younger. Surprisingly, working out the age of the Sun is easier to do – or at least it seemed that way.

Firstly, you need to work out how much energy the Sun produces. To do this, all you need is a pan of water, a thermometer and a clock. Put your pan of water into the sunlight and measure how much the temperature goes up in a set amount of time. Because we know how much energy it takes to raise the temperature of water, we can work out how much energy arrived at our pan from the Sun in that time. Then we just need to work out what fraction of the Sun's total output that is – you should be able to figure out how to do that!

Now, because we already know the total mass of the Sun, it is easy to work out how long the Sun will take to burn up its fuel. The problem was that people assumed the Sun burned like a fire using a combustion reaction – the process of nuclear fusion was not known. This gave a final answer of only a few thousand years for the Sun's age – indicating the Sun had to be much younger than the Earth, which was not possible.

△ Fig. 5.17 The boundary of two tectonic plates in Iceland.

Rocks could only be dated when radioactivity and the idea of half-life had been understood in the 20th century. The technique for dating rocks compares the proportion of uranium now to that when rocks were formed. This led to convincing evidence for the true age of the Earth. The discovery of nuclear fusion allowed a true age for the Sun to be calculated too.

So now we know the age of both. However, getting this knowledge has been a longer story than you might think.

Radioactive dating

Igneous rock, which is formed through the cooling and solidification of magma and larva, contains small quantities of uranium-238, a type of uranium that decays with a half-life of 4500 million years, eventually forming lead. The ratio of lead to uranium in a rock sample can be used to calculate the age of the rock. For example, a piece of rock with equal numbers of uranium and lead atoms in it must be 4500 million years old – but this would be unlikely, as the earth itself is 4500 million years old.

Fig. 5.18 The Tollund Man in Denmark is the best example of a body preserved in a bog. Radioactive carbon dating showed that he had been there for over 2000 years.

Carbon in living material contains a constant, small amount of the radioactive isotope carbon-14, which has a half-life of 5700 years. When the living material dies the carbon-14 nuclei slowly decay. The ratio of carbon-14 nuclei to the non-radioactive carbon-12 atoms can be used to calculate the age of the plant or animal material. This method is called **radioactive carbon dating** (Fig. 5.18).

QUESTIONS

1. Explain why safety precautions need to be taken when handling radioactive materials.

2. List three uses of radioisotopes.

End of topic checklist

Key terms

alpha particle, background radiation, beta particle, gamma ray, half-life, ionising radiation, nuclear equation, radioactive carbon dating, radioactive decay, radiotherapy, tracer

During your study of this topic you should have learned:

○ About the existence of background radiation.

○ How to describe the detection of α-particles, β-particles and γ-rays.

○ That radioactive emissions occur randomly over space and time.

○ About, for radioactive emissions:
  - their nature
  - their relative ionising effects
  - their relative penetrating abilities.

○ EXTENDED How to describe their deflection in electric fields and magnetic fields.

○ EXTENDED How to interpret their relative ionising effects.

○ The meaning of radioactive decay, and how to use equations to represent changes in the composition of the nucleus when particles are emitted.

○ How to use the term 'half-life' in simple calculations, which might involve information in tables or decay curves.

○ How to describe how radioactive materials are handled, used and stored in a safe way.

End of topic questions

Note: The marks awarded for these questions indicate the level of detail required in the answers. In the examination, the number of marks awarded to questions like these may be different.

1. EXTENDED The diagram shows some of the results of an experiment using some very thin gold foil that was carried out by researchers working for Sir Ernest Rutherford.

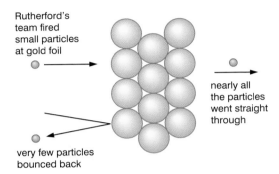

Rutherford's team fired small particles at gold foil

nearly all the particles went straight through

very few particles bounced back

   a) What type of radioactive particle did they use? (1 mark)

   b) What did Rutherford deduce from the observation that most of the particles passed straight through the foil? (2 marks)

   c) What did Rutherford deduce from the observation that some particles bounced back from the foil? (2 marks)

2. EXTENDED Scientists have a saying that 'most matter is empty space'. Explain what this means, using the ideas from Geiger and Marsden's experiment. (6 marks)

3. The following equation shows what happens when a nucleus of sodium-24 decays.
$$^{24}_{11}Na \longrightarrow {}^{x}_{y}Mg + {}^{0}_{-1}\beta$$

   a) What type of nuclear radiation is produced? (1 mark)

   b) What are the numerical values of x and y? (2 marks)

4. The graph shows how the activity of a sample of sodium-24 changes with time. Activity is measured in becquerels (Bq).

   Use the graph to work out the half-life of the sodium-24. (3 marks)

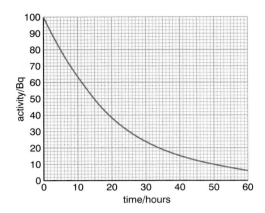

5. Describe the properties of beta particles. **(3 marks)**

6. What do you understand by ionisation? **(2 marks)**

7. Radon-220 is radioactive. It decays to polonium-216. Write the nuclear equation for its decay by alpha radiation. The atomic number of radon is 86 and the atomic number of polonium is 84. **(3 marks)**

8. Carbon-14 decays by emitting beta radiation. Write the nuclear equation. **(3 marks)**

9. A laboratory technician has three radioactive sources: cobalt-60, which is a source of gamma rays, strontium-90, which is a source of beta particles and americium-241, which is a source of alpha particles.

Suggest how the technician can tell which is which. **(6 marks)**

10. A sample of radioactive material has 800 active nuclei.

a) How many of the active nuclei are left after two half-lives? **(1 mark)**

b) How many half-lives does it take to reduce it to 50 active nuclei? **(2 marks)**

c) The material has a half-life of 30 minutes. How long does it take for the number of active nuclei to reduce to 100? **(3 marks)**

11. Iodine-131 has a half-life of 8 days. A sample has a count rate of 128 counts/minute.

a) What will the count rate be after 3 half-lives? **(2 marks)**

b) Calculate the time it will take for the activity rate to drop to 4 counts/minute. **(2 marks)**

12. The graph shows the decay curve for strontium-93. Determine its half-life. **(3 marks)**

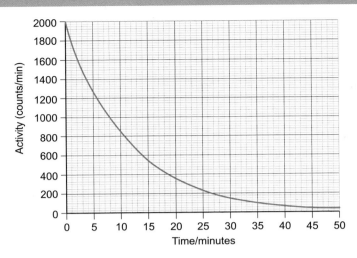

13. What type of radiation is used in:

a) smoke detectors   (1 mark)

b) thickness measurement   (1 mark)

c) weld checking?   (1 mark)

14. a) When uranium-238 in a rock sample decays, what element is
eventually produced?   (2 marks)

b) Explain how the production of this new element enables the age
of the rock sample to be determined.   (4 marks)

Exam-style questions

Note: The questions, sample answers and marks in this section have been written by the authors as a guide only. The marks awarded for these questions indicate the level of detail required in the answers. In the examination, the number of marks awarded to questions like these may be different.

Sample student answers

Question 1

Americium-241 is a radioactive isotope that decays mainly by emitting alpha particles.

It has a half-life of 432 years.

a) What are isotopes?

Atoms with the same number of protons ✓ ① *but a different number of neutrons.* ✓ ①　(2)

b) What are alpha particles?

The nucleus ✓ ① *of a helium atom* ✓ ①　(2)

c) What does 'It has a half-life of 432 years' mean?

The radiation loses half its power in 432 years. ✗ ✗　(2)

d) Americium-241 is used in smoke detectors. If there is no smoke present, the alpha particles ionise a path through the air and a small current can flow.

　i) Describe how alpha particles can ionise particles in the air.

　　The alpha particles hit the atoms in the air. ✗　(2)

　ii) Suggest what happens when particles of smoke enter the detector.

　　The smoke ✓ ① *blocks the radiation* ✗ *so the alarm goes off* ✗　(3)

TEACHER'S COMMENTS

a) Fine – standard definition. Answers in terms of atomic number or proton number and mass number or nucleon number would also be accepted.

b) Fine – answer in terms of protons and neutrons would also be accepted.

c) A very common mistake – this answer refers to the radiation given off (the alpha particles) and not the radioactive source itself. Half-life describes how the activity of the source will change over time; the radiation emitted does not decay.

d) These answers are typical of a candidate who knows about the situation but who does not give enough detail to gain the highest marks. Both answers here begin correctly but fail to develop the ideas sufficiently to gain full marks.

　i) the idea of removing electrons is required.

　ii) the consequences of blocking the radiation (no ionisation, no current) are missing.

e) i) 'Cause mutations' just about scores the mark, although it is a bit vague. 'Causes mutations in cells' would have been much better.

ii) The candidate has missed the point of the question –it is in part e) for a reason. The examiner wanted the idea given in part i) to be developed further – in this case explaining why these harmful effects are NOT caused by the smoke detector. 'It's on the ceiling' gives the correct idea, but more detail is needed at this level.

e) Radioactive emissions can be harmful to humans.

i) Describe one harmful effect that radioactive emissions can have on humans.

Cause mutations. ✔ ① (1)

ii) Suggest why it is safe to have a radioactive source in a smoke detector.

It doesn't last very long ✗ *and it's on the ceiling.* ✗ (2)

(Total 14 marks)

Question 2

a) A radioactive isotope emits only alpha particles.

    i) Draw a labelled diagram of the apparatus you would use to prove that no beta particles or gamma radiation are emitted from the isotope.   **(2)**

    ii) Describe the test you would carry out.   **(2)**

    iii) Explain how your results would show that only alpha particles are emitted   **(2)**

b) **EXTENDED** The diagram shows a stream of alpha particles about to enter the space between the poles of a very strong magnet.

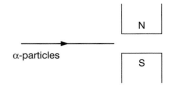

α-particles

Describe the path of the alpha particles in the space between the magnetic poles.   **(3)**

(Total 9 marks)

Question 3

a) A sodium nucleus decays by the emission of a beta particle to form magnesium.

   i) Copy and complete the decay equation: **(2)**

$$^{12}_{11}Na \rightarrow Mg+$$

   ii) EXTENDED The diagram shows beta particles from sodium nuclei moving into the space between the poles of a magnet.

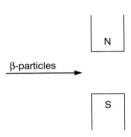

Describe the path of the beta particles between the magnetic poles.   **(3)**

b) Very small quantities of a radioactive isotope are used to check the circulation of blood by injecting the isotope into the bloodstream.

   i) Describe how the results are obtained.   **(2)**

   ii) Explain why a gamma emitting isotope is used for this purpose rather than one that emits either alpha particles or beta particles.   **(2)**

(Total 9 marks)

Doing well in examinations

INTRODUCTION

Examinations will test how good your understanding of scientific ideas is, how well you can apply your understanding to new situations and how well you can analyse and interpret information you have been given. The assessments are opportunities to show how well you can do these.

To be successful in exams you need to:

✓ have a good knowledge and understanding of science

✓ be able to apply this knowledge and understanding to familiar and new situations

✓ be able to interpret and evaluate evidence that you have just been given.

You need to be able to do these things under exam conditions.

OVERVIEW

Ensure you are familiar with the structure of the examinations you are taking. Consult the relevant syllabus of the year you are entering your examinations for details of the different papers and the weighting of each, including the papers to test practical skills. Your teacher will advise you of which papers you will be taking.

You will be required to perform calculations, draw graphs and describe, explain and interpret ideas and information about physics. In some of the questions the content may be unfamiliar to you; these questions are designed to assess data-handling skills and the ability to apply physical principles and ideas in unfamiliar situations.

ASSESSMENT OBJECTIVES AND WEIGHTINGS

For the Cambridge IGCSE examination, the assessment objectives and weightings are as follows:

✓ A: Knowledge and understanding (50%)

✓ B: Handling information and problem solving (30%)

✓ C: Experimental skills and investigations (20%).

The types of questions in your assessment fit the three assessment objectives shown in the table.

ASSESSMENT

Assessment objective	Your answer should show that you can...
A Knowledge and understanding	Recall, select and communicate your knowledge and understanding of science.
B Handling information and problem solving	Apply skills, including evaluation and analysis, knowledge and understanding of scientific contexts.
C Experimental skills and investigations	Use the skills of planning, observation, analysis and evaluation in practical situations.

EXAMINATION TECHNIQUES

To help you maximise your chances in exams, there are a few simple steps to follow.

Check your understanding of the question

✓ **Read the introduction to each question carefully before moving on to the questions themselves**.

✓ Look in detail at any **diagrams, graphs** or **tables**.

✓ Underline or circle the **key words** in the question.

✓ **Make sure you answer the question that is being asked** rather than the one you wish had been asked!

✓ Make sure that you understand the meaning of the '**command words**' in the questions.

REMEMBER

Remember that any information you are given is there to help you to answer the question.

EXAMPLE

✓ **'Give', 'state', 'name'** are used when recall of knowledge is required. For example, you could be asked to give a definition, or provide the best answers from a list of options.

✓ **'Describe'** is used when you have to give the main feature(s) of, for example, a biological process or structure.

✓ **'Explain'** is used when you have to give reasons, for example for some experimental results or a biological fact or observation. You will often be asked to 'explain your answer', i.e. give reasons for it.

✓ **'Suggest'** is used when you have to come up with an idea to explain the information you're given – there may be more than one possible answer, no definitive answer from the information given, or it may be that you will not have learnt the answer but have to use the knowledge you do have to come up with a sensible one.

✓ **'Calculate'** means that you have to work out an answer in figures.

✓ **'Plot'** and **'Draw a graph'** are used when you have to use the data provided to produce graphs and charts.

Check the number of marks for each question

✓ Look at the **number of marks** allocated to each question.

✓ Look at the **space provided** to guide you as to the length of your answer.

✓ Make sure you include at least as many points in your answer as there are marks.

✓ Do not use any more space than the space that has been provided in the examination paper.

REMEMBER

Beware of continually writing too much because it probably means you are not really answering the questions.

Use your time effectively

✓ Don't spend so long on some questions that you don't have time to finish the paper.

✓ If you are really stuck on a question, leave it, finish the rest of the paper and come back to it at the end.

✓ Even if you eventually have to guess at an answer, you stand a better chance of gaining some marks than if you leave it blank.

ANSWERING QUESTIONS

Multiple choice questions

✓ Select your answer by placing a cross (not a tick) in the box.

Short- and long-answer questions

✓ In short-answer questions, **don't write more than you are asked for**.

✓ You may not gain any marks, even if the first part of your answer is correct, if you've written down something incorrect later on or which contradicts what you've said earlier. This might give the impression that you haven't really understood the question or are guessing.

✓ In some questions, particularly short-answer questions, answers of only one or two words may be sufficient, but in longer questions you should aim to use **scientific language** to make your answer as clear as possible.

✓ Present the information in a logical sequence.

✓ Don't be afraid to also use **labelled diagrams** or **flow charts** if it helps you to show your answer more clearly.

Questions with calculations

✓ **In calculations always show your working**.

✓ Even if your final answer is incorrect you may still gain some marks if part of your attempt is correct.

✓ If you just write down the final answer and it is incorrect, you will get no marks at all.

✓ Write down your answers to as many **significant figures** as are used in the numbers in the question (and no more). If the question doesn't state how many significant figures, then a good general rule is to quote 3 significant figures.

✓ Don't round off too early in calculations with many steps – it's always better to give too many significant figures than too few.

✓ You may also lose marks if you don't use the correct **units**. In some questions the units will be mentioned (e.g. calculate the mass in grams) or the units may also be given on the answer line. If numbers you are working with are very large, you may need to make a conversion (e.g. convert joules into kilojoules, or kilograms into tonnes).

Finishing your exam

✓ When you've finished your exam, **check through** your paper to make sure you've answered all the questions.

✓ Check that you haven't missed any questions at the end of the paper or turned over two pages at once and missed questions.

✓ Cover over your answers and read through the questions again and check that your answers are as good as you can make them.

Developing experimental skills

INTRODUCTION

As part your Physics course, you will develop practical skills and have to carry out investigative work in science. This will either be done as coursework, a practical test or a written paper, depending on your school.

This section provides guidance on carrying out an investigation.

The experimental and investigative skills are divided into four parts as follows (each of the four sections carry equal weighting):

1. Using and organising techniques, apparatus and materials
2. Observing, measuring and recording
3. Handling experimental observations and data
4. Planning and evaluating investigations

1. USING AND ORGANISING TECHNIQUES, APPARATUS AND MATERIALS

Learning objective: to demonstrate and describe appropriate experimental and investigative methods, including safe and skillful practical techniques.

Questions to ask:

How shall I use the equipment safely to minimise the risks — what are my safety precautions?

✓ When writing a Risk Assessment, investigators need to be careful to check that they've matched the hazard with the technique used.

✓ In the exam, you may be asked to describe the precautions taken when carrying out an investigation.

How much detail should I give in my description?

✓ You need to give enough detail so that someone else who has not done the experiment would be able to carry it out to reproduce your results.

How should I use the equipment to give me the precision I need?

✓ You should know how to read the scales on the measuring equipment you are using.

✓ You need to show that you are aware of the precision needed.

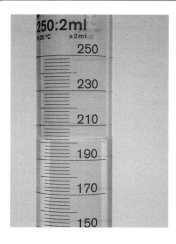

◁ Fig. 8.1 The volume of liquid in a measuring cylinder must be read to the bottom of the meniscus. The volume in this measuring cylinder is 202 cm³ (ml), not 204 cm³.

EXAMPLE 1

This is an extract from a student's notebook. It describes the precautions he took when investigating Hooke's law.

Precautions taken to improve reliability

It's important to take precautions in order to make the readings as reliable as possible. I will view the scale at right angles in order to prevent a parallax error.

Safety measures

Potential risk: The spring may break or the masses may fall off. The spring may flick and could damage face/eyes.

Safety measure: I will wear eye protection to protect my eyes in case the spring flicks up.

The student has identified a risk and described the precautions to be taken when carrying out the investigation.

EXAMPLE 2

This is an extract from a student's notebook. It describes how she investigated terminal velocity.

Experimental detail

The student's method is given below

1 *The tube was marked every 10 cm using tape.*

2 *The ball was released carefully from the surface of the oil.*

3 *At the same time, a stopclock was started.*

4 *As the ball passed each mark, the time was noted.*

5 *Since the marks are 10 cm apart, the speed of the ball in each section of the tube can be calculated.*

Precision and accuracy

An example from the notebook is:

> *The speed measured to the nearest 0.1 cm/s*

COMMENT

The method is well written and detailed. Point 1 could have been improved if the student had noted the width of the tape used.
The student has appreciated the accuracy that can be achieved using this method.

---

2. OBSERVING, MEASURING AND RECORDING

Learning objective: to make observations and measurements with appropriate precision, record these methodically, and present them in a suitable form.

Questions to ask:

How many different measurements or observations do I need to take?

✓ Sufficient readings have been taken to ensure that the data are consistent.

✓ It is usual to repeat an experiment to get more than one measurement. If an investigator takes just one measurement, this may not be typical of what would normally happen when the experiment was carried out.

✓ When repeat readings are consistent they are said to be **repeatable**.

Do I need to repeat any measurements or observations that are anomalous?

✓ An **anomalous result** or **outlier** is a result that is not consistent with other results.

✓ You want to be sure a single result is accurate (as in Example 3). So you will need to repeat the experiment until you get close agreement in the results you obtain.

✓ If an investigator has made repeat measurements, they would normally use these to calculate the arithmetical mean (or just mean or average) of these data to give a more accurate result. You calculate the mean by adding together all the measurements, and dividing by the number of measurements. Be careful though, anomalous results should not be included when taking averages.

- ✓ Anomalous results might be the consequence of an error made in measurement. But sometimes outliers are genuine results. If you think an outlier has been introduced by careless practical work, you should omit it when calculating the mean. But you should examine possible reasons carefully before just leaving it out.

- ✓ You are taking a number of readings in order to see a changing pattern. For example, measuring the speed every 10 cm for 60 cm (so six different readings). It is likely that you will plot your results onto a graph and then draw a **line of best fit**.

- ✓ You can often pick an anomalous reading out from a results table (or a graph if all the data points have been plotted, as well as the mean, to show the range of data). It may be a good idea to repeat this part of the practical again, but it's not necessary if the results show good consistency.

- ✓ If you are confident that you can draw a line of best fit through most of the points, it is not necessary to repeat any measurements that are obviously inaccurate. If, however, the pattern is not clear enough to draw a graph then readings will need to be repeated.

How should I record my measurements or observations – is a table the best way? What headings and units should I use?

- ✓ A table is often the best way to record results.

- ✓ Headings should be clear.

- ✓ If a table contains numerical data, do not forget to include units; data are meaningless without them.

- ✓ The units should be the same as those that are on the measuring equipment you are using.

- ✓ Sometimes you are recording observations that are not quantities. Putting observations in a table with headings is a good way of presenting this information.

EXAMPLE 3

The student from Example 2 has recorded the results in a table as shown below.

Distance fallen through oil/cm	Speed 1st experiment	Speed 2nd experiment	Speed 3rd experiment
0	0.0	0.1	0.1
10	2.4	2.4	2.3
20	4.4	4.3	4.4
30	5.6	5.6	5.7
40	6.0	5.9	5.9
50	6.4	6.4	6.3
60	6.4	6.3	6.4

△ Table 8.1 Readings from investigation.

EXAMPLE 4

In an experiment to investigate the efficiency of a small motor the student has sensibly recorded her results in a table. Notice each column has a heading *and* units.

Mass lifted/g	Distance lifted/m	Useful work done/J	Voltage of motor/V	Current in motor/A	Time to lift the mass/s	Electrical energy supplied/J
0.01	1.0		2.4	0.20	22.0	
0.03	1.0		2.4	0.22	24.4	
0.05	1.0		2.4	0.25	26.5	
0.07	1.0		2.3	0.28	27.6	
0.09	1.0		2.3	0.29	28.7	

△ Table 8.2 Table of results

EXAMPLE 5

In another experiment the student has recorded his results obtained in an experiment to investigate the strength of an electromagnet as the current in the coil varies.

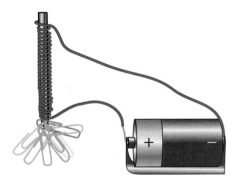

△ Fig. 8.2 Apparatus for experiment.

Current/A	Number of paper clips held
0	0
0.3	2
0.5	5
0.7	6
0.9	9
1.0	9

△ Table 8.3 Results of experiment.

COMMENT

In this table of results:

the description of each measurement is clear.

the units are given in each case.

3. HANDLING EXPERIMENTAL OBSERVATIONS AND DATA

Learning objective: to analyse and interpret data to draw conclusions from experimental activities which are consistent with the evidence, using physics knowledge and understanding, and to communicate these findings using appropriate specialist vocabulary, relevant calculations and graphs.

Questions to ask:

What is the best way to show the pattern in my results? Should I use a bar chart, line graph or scatter graph?

✓ Graphs are usually the best way of demonstrating trends in data.

✓ A bar chart or bar graph is used when one of the variables is a **categoric variable**, for example when the melting points of the oxides of the group 2 elements are shown for each oxide, the names are categoric and not continuous variables.

✓ A line graph is used when both variables are continuous, for example time and temperature, time and volume.

✓ Scatter graphs can be used to show the intensity of a relationship, or degree of *correlation*, between two variables.

✓ Sometimes a line of best fit is added to a scatter graph, but usually the points are left without a line.

When drawing bar charts or line graphs:

✓ Choose scales that take up most of the graph paper

✓ Make sure the axes are linear and allow points to be plotted accurately. Each square on an axis should represent the same quantity. For example, one big square = 5 or 10 units; not 3 units

✓ Label the axes with the variables (ideally with the independent variable on the x-axis)

✓ Make sure the axes have units

✓ If more than one set of data is plotted use a key to distinguish the different data sets.

If I use a line graph should I join the points with a straight line or a smooth curve?

✓ When you draw a line, do not just join the dots!

✓ Remember there may be some points that don't fall on the curve – these may be incorrect or anomalous results.

✓ A graph will often make it obvious which results are anomalous and so it would not be necessary to repeat the experiment (see Example 7).

Do I have to calculate anything from my results?

✓ It will be usual to calculate means from the data.

✓ Sometimes it is helpful make other calculations, before plotting a graph, for example you might calculate 1/time for a rate of reaction experiment.

✓ Sometimes you will have to make some calculations before you can draw any conclusions.

Can I draw a conclusion from my analysis of the results, and what physics knowledge and understanding can be used to explain the conclusion?

✓ You need to use your physics knowledge and understanding to explain your conclusion.

✓ It is important to be able to add some explanation which refers to relevant scientific ideas in order to justify your conclusion.

What is the best way to show the pattern in my results?

✓ If the experiment involves **continuous variables,** a line graph is needed.

Straight line or a smooth curve?

✓ The results obtained will either require a smooth curve or a straight line of best fit. The shape of the results should show you which is needed. In physics experiments you will often need to draw a line of best fit.

Do I have to calculate anything from my results?

✓ If you have to calculate a quantity you will often be able to do this by looking at the change in steepness/ gradient of the curve.

Can I draw a conclusion from my analysis of the results?

✓ You need to write a sentence summarising what you have learnt from your investigation.

✓ Make sure that you write a clear statement. You might refer, for example, to 'the gradient of the line' at points 1, 2 and 3 to make your conclusion even more precise.

What physics knowledge and understanding can be used to explain the conclusion?

✓ You need to be able to explain your results using your knowledge of the physics of the situation.

COMMENT

A good conclusion will make direct links to scientific knowledge in relation to the topic.

4. PLANNING AND EVALUATING INVESTIGATIONS

4a Planning

Learning objective: to devise and plan investigations, drawing on physics knowledge and understanding in selecting appropriate techniques.

Questions to ask:

What do I already know about the area of physics I am investigating and how can I use this knowledge and understanding to help me with my plan?

✓ Think about what you have already learned and any investigations you have already done that are relevant to this investigation.

✓ List the factors that might affect the process you are investigating.

What is the best method or technique to use?

✓ Think about whether you can use or adapt a method that you have already used.

✓ A method, and the measuring instruments, must be able to produce **valid** measurements. A measurement is valid if it measures what it is supposed to be measuring.

You will make a decision as to which technique to use based on:

✓ The accuracy and precision of the results required.

✓ Investigators might require results that are as accurate and precise as possible but if you are doing a quick comparison, or a preliminary test to check a range over which results should be collected, a high level of accuracy and precision may not be required.

✓ The simplicity or difficulty of the techniques available, or the equipment required; is this expensive, for instance?

✓ The scale, for example using standard laboratory equipment or on a micro-scale, which may give results in a shorter time period.

✓ The time available to do the investigation.

✓ Health and safety considerations.

What am I going to measure?

✓ The factor you are investigating is called the **independent variable**. A **dependent variable** is affected or changed by the independent variable that you select.

✓ You need to choose a range of measurements that will be enough to allow you to plot a graph of your results and so find out the pattern in your results.

✓ You might be asked to explain why you have chosen your range rather than a lower or higher range.

How am I going to control the other variables?

✓ These are **control variables**. Some of these may be difficult to control.

✓ You must decide how you are going to control any other variables in the investigation and so ensure that you are using a fair test and that any conclusions you draw are valid.

What equipment is suitable and will give me the accuracy and precision I need?

✓ The **accuracy** of a measurement is how close it is to its true value.

✓ **Precision** is related to the smallest scale division on the measuring instrument that you are using, for example when measuring a distance, a rule marked in millimetres will give greater precision that one divided into centimetres only.

✓ A set of precise measurements also refers to measurements that have very little spread about the mean value.

✓ You need to be sensible about selecting your devices and make a judgement about the degree of precision. Think about what is the least precise variable you are measuring and choose suitable measuring devices. There is no point having instruments that are much more precise than the precision you can measure the variable to.

What are the potential hazards of the equipment and technique I will be using and how can I reduce the risks associated with these hazards?

✓ In the exam, be prepared to suggest safety precautions when presented with details of a physics investigation.

EXAMPLE 7

You have been asked to design and plan an investigation to explore the motion of a trolley down a ramp. In a previous investigation you have investigated such motion using ticker tape so you are familiar with what happens and the measurements you need to take.

What do I already know?
Previously you have investigated the motion of a trolley down a ramp. You know that you can use ticker tape to measure the distance the trolley travels in a given time.

What is the best method or technique to use?

The technique you used in your previous investigation can be re-used. You set up the apparatus as shown in the diagram.

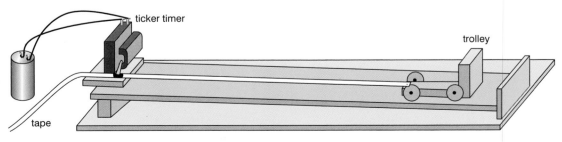

△ Fig. 8.3 Trolley and ramp apparatus for the investigation.

What am I going to measure?

You are investigating the motion of a trolley down a ramp. You will measure the length of each 5-dot strip of ticket tape with a ruler.

How am I going to control the other variables?

It is important that you decide on the angle at which to set the ramp at the start. As you have carried out this investigation before you can look back and see what angle you used previously and decide whether you will use the same angle, or increase or decrease it.

What equipment is suitable and will give me the accuracy and precision I need?

You now know what you will need to measure and so can decide on your measuring devices.

Measurement	Quantity	Device
Length of ticket tape	5-dot strips	Ruler so can measure to nearest cm

△ Table 8.4 Suitable equipment for experiment.

Choosing a ruler which can measure to nearest mm would not be appropriate as the width of the ticker tape dots is of the order of mm.

What are the potential hazards and how can I reduce the risks?

The hazards are as follows:

✓ trolley and ramp

These indicate that there are no specific hazards you need to be aware of.

In terms of the equipment and technique, the major hazard will be the trolley rolling off the end of the ramp. You can limit this hazard by putting a buffer at the end of the ramp as shown in the diagram above.

4b Evaluating

Learning objective: to evaluate data and methods.

Questions to ask:

Do any of my results stand out as being inaccurate or anomalous?

✓ You need to look for any anomalous results or outliers that do not fit the pattern.

✓ You can often pick this out from a results table (or a graph if all the data points have been plotted, as well as the mean, to show the range of data).

What reasons can I give for any inaccurate results?

✓ When answering questions like this it is important to be specific. Answers such as 'experimental error' will not score any marks.

✓ It is often possible to look at the practical technique and suggest explanations for anomalous results.

✓ When you carry out the experiment you will have a better idea of which possible sources of error are more likely.

✓ Try to give a specific source of error and avoid statements such as 'the measurements must have been wrong'

Your conclusion will be based on your findings, but must take into consideration any uncertainty in these introduced by any possible sources of error. You should discuss where these have come from in your evaluation.

Error is a difference between a measurement you make, and its true value.

The two types of errors are:

✓ random error

✓ systematic error.

With **random error**, measurements vary in an unpredictable way. This can occur when the instrument you're using to measure lacks sufficient precision to indicate differences in readings. It can also occur when it's difficult to make a measurement.

With **systematic error**, readings vary in a controlled way. They're either consistently too high or too low. One reason could be down to the way you are making a reading, e.g., taking a burette reading at the wrong point on the meniscus, or not being directly in front of an instrument when reading from it.

What an investigator *should not* discuss in an evaluation are problems introduced by using faulty equipment, or by using the equipment inappropriately. These errors can, or could have been, eliminated, by:

✓ checking equipment

✓ practising techniques before the investigation, and taking care and patience when carrying out the practical.

Overall was the method or technique I used precise enough?

✓ If your results were good enough to provide a confident answer to the problem you were investigating, the method probably was good enough.

✓ If you realise your results are not precise when you compare your conclusion with the actual answer, it may be that you have a **systematic error** (an error that has been made in obtaining all the results.) A systematic error would indicate an overall problem with the experimental method.

✓ If your results do not show a convincing pattern then it is fair to assume that your method or technique was not precise enough and there may have been a **random error** (i.e. measurements vary in an unpredictable way).

If I were to do the investigation again what would I change or improve upon?

✓ Having identified possible errors it is important to say how these could be overcome. Again you should try and be absolutely precise.

✓ When suggesting improvements, do not just say 'do it more accurately next time' or 'measure the volumes more accurately next time'.

✓ For example, if you were measuring small lengths, you could improve the method by using a vernier scale to measure the lengths rather than a ruler.

EXAMPLE 8

A student was measuring how current varies with voltage. He used the circuit shown in Fig. 8.4.

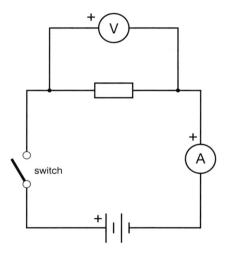

△ Fig. 8.4 Circuit used to measure how current varies with voltage.

Do any of my results stand out as being inaccurate or anomalous?

The student plotted his results on a graph, as shown in Fig.8.5. An inaccurate result stands out from the rest, as shown by the circle on the graph. Given the pattern obtained with the other results there is no real need to repeat the result – you could be very confident that the result should have followed the pattern set by the others. A result like this is referred to as an anomalous result. It was an error but not a systematic error.

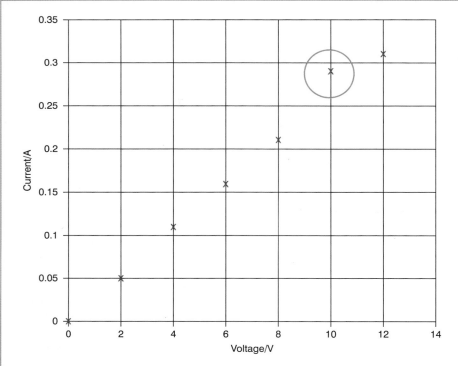

△ Fig. 8.5 Graph of results.

What reasons can I give for any inaccurate results?

The possible source of the error is that one of the variables was noted incorrectly.

Was the method or technique I used precise enough?

You can be reasonably confident that using digital meters for the current and voltage readings will give you precise measurements.

How can I improve the investigation?

For example, you could say, take readings after the component has heated up so that the steady state resistance is noted.

Glossary

acceleration A change in speed divided by the time taken to change.

air resistance The drag caused by something moving through air.

alpha particle A particle emitted from the nuclei of radioactive atoms, consisting of two protons and two neutrons.

alternating current (a.c.) Electrical current that repeatedly reverses its direction, like mains electricity.

ammeter An instrument that measures electrical current in amperes.

ampere A unit of current measuring the electric charge that flows during one second.

amplitude The maximum change of the medium from normal in a wave. For example, the height of a water wave above the level of calm water.

analogue Describes a quantity that can change smoothly, like the position of a pointer over a dial (the opposite of digital).

angle of incidence The angle between the incident light ray and the normal to the surface.

angle of reflection The angle between the reflected light ray and the normal to the surface of the material.

angle of refraction The angle between the refracted light ray and the normal to the surface inside the material.

anode A positive electrode.

atomic number The number of protons found in the nucleus of an atom.

average speed The distance an object has moved, divided by the time taken.

background radiation The level of radiation found due to natural processes in the environment.

becquerel The units for the radioactivity of a substance. One becquerel is one decay per second.

beta particle A type of nuclear radiation emitted as an electron by a radioactive nucleus.

biomass (fuel) The mass of living material, including waste wood and other natural materials.

boiling point The temperature at which a substance changes state from a liquid to a gas.

Boyle's law If the temperature of the gas stays constant, then the volume of the gas is inversely proportional to the pressure.

Brownian motion The random motion of pollen grains on the surface of water (also the random motion of smoke particles in air).

centre of mass The point in a body from which the force of gravity appears to be acting on the body.

centripetal force The force that acts towards a centre. A centripetal force is needed to move in a circle.

charge A fundamental property of matter that produces all electrical effects. It is equal to current × time.

Charles' law If the pressure of the gas stays constant, then the volume of the gas is proportional to its absolute temperature.

chemical energy Energy stored in molecules. Batteries and fuels contain stored chemical energy.

circuit breaker A device that breaks a circuit when there is an increase in current.

commutator The part of an electric motor that allows the coils to be connected to the opposite terminals each time the motor rotates through 180°.

compression The squashing together of particles in a particular region.

condensation The change of state from a gas to a liquid.

conduction The transfer of heat energy through a material.

conductors, heat Substances that conduct heat very well.

conductors, electricity Substances that conduct electricity well.

convection Heat transfer in a liquid or gas – when particles in a warmer region gain energy and move into cooler regions carrying this energy with them.

conventional current Movement of positive charge that is imagined to move from the positive terminal to the negative terminal of a battery. Equivalent in effect to the real flow of negative charge in the opposite direction.

coulomb The unit of electric charge.

crest The highest part of a wave.

current, electric A flowing electric charge caused by the flow of electrons.

density The mass, in kilograms, of a one metre cube of a substance: mass divided by volume.

diffraction Waves spreading into the shadow when they pass an edge.

diffusion Molecules moving from an area of high concentration to an area of low concentration.

digital Describes quantities that can only be displayed as numbers (the opposite of analogue).

diode A device that lets electricity flow through it one way only.

direct current (d.c.) Current that always flows in the same direction.

dispersion Splitting white light into the colours that it is made of.

distance–time graph A visual representation of how distance travelled varies with time.

double-insulated When a device has a casing that is made of an insulator and does not need an earth wire.

dynamo A simple current generator.

efficiency Useful energy output divided by total energy output.

earth wire A wire connecting the case of an electrical appliance, through the earth pin on a three-pin plug, to earth.

elastic Describes materials that go back to their original shape and size after you stretch them.

elastic strain energy A form of stored energy from stretching or compressing an object like a spring.

electric current Flowing electric charge.

electric field A region in which any electrical charges will feel a force.

electromagnetic induction A changing magnetic force can induce electric current in a wire.

electromagnetic spectrum The 'family' of electromagnetic radiations (from longest to shortest wavelength): radio, microwave, infra-red, visible light, ultraviolet, X-rays, gamma rays. In order of frequency, the order is reversed. They all travel at the same speed in a vacuum.

electromagnetic wave A wave that transfers energy – it can travel through a vacuum and travel at the speed of light.

electromagnets Magnets made from a coil of wire. The magnetic force is made when electric current flows in the coil. The magnetic force is stronger when the coil is wrapped around a piece of iron.

electron Negatively charged particles with almost no mass that form the outer portion of all atoms.

electrostatic effects Effects caused by having extra electrons or a shortage of electrons. They happen when insulators have gained or lost electrons.

evaporation The change of state from a liquid to a gas.

extension The increase in length when something is stretched.

Fleming's left-hand rule Predicts the direction of the force on a wire that is carrying a current when the thumb, and first and second fingers are held at right angles. The first finger points in the direction of the field, the second finger in the direction of the current and the thumb gives the direction of the force (movement).

fluid Any liquid or gas.

force Change in momentum divided by time taken.

fossil fuel Non-renewable energy resource such as coal, oil or natural gas.

free fall Movement under the effect of the force of gravity alone.

frequency The number of vibrations per second or number of peaks or troughs that pass a point each second, measured in hertz (Hz). It is equal to 1/time period.

friction The force that resists when you try to move something. It can cause insulators to become charged.

fuse A special wire that protects an electric circuit. If the current gets too large, the fuse melts and stops the current.

gamma ray Ionising electromagnetic radiation – radioactive and dangerous to human health.

gradient The slope of a curve.

gravitational field strength The force of gravity on a mass of one kilogram. The unit is the newton per kilogram, and it is different on different planets.

gravitational potential energy A form of stored energy given by mass × g × height

gravity A force that causes objects in the Solar System to travel in repeating cycles of motion called orbits.

half-life The time it takes for half of the radioactive nuclei in a sample to decay.

Hooke's law The extension of a spring is in direct proportion to the force applied to it, as long as the force is smaller than the material's elastic limit.

induction When something is affected without touching it. An electric force can induce charge in a conductor. A changing magnetic force can induce electric current in a wire.

infra-red The part of the electromagnetic spectrum that has a slightly longer wavelength than the visible spectrum.

ion An atom (or group of atoms) with a positive or negative charge, caused by losing or gaining electrons.

ionising radiation Charged particles or high-energy light rays that ionise the material they travel through.

insulators (of electricity) Substances that do not conduct electricity.

insulators (of heat) Substances that do not conduct heat very well.

interference When waves combine with each other as they collide.

internal energy The energy inside an object.

inversely proportional The relationship between two quantities if one doubles when the other halves.

isotope Atoms of the same element that contain different numbers of neutrons. Isotopes have the same atomic number but different mass numbers.

joule The unit of energy. One joule is the energy needed to push an object through one metre with a one newton force.

kinetic energy The energy of moving objects, equal to $\frac{1}{2} \times$ mass $\times$ (speed)^2.

kinetic molecular model The theory describing the movement of particles in solids, liquid and gases.

latent heat (or energy) The energy required for a substance to change state.

law of conservation of energy Energy cannot be created or destroyed.

light-dependent resistor A resistor with a resistance that decreases when light is shone on it.

longitudinal wave A wave in which the change of the medium is parallel to the direction of the wave. Sound is an example.

magnetic field The region in which magnetic materials feel a force.

magnetic field lines The lines that show the path a free North pole would follow.

magnetic materials Materials that are attracted to magnets and can be made into magnets. Iron, cobalt and nickel are magnetic materials.

magnetic hardness When materials retain their magnetism.

magnetic softness When materials lose their magnetism.

mass The amount of material in an object, measured in kilograms.

mass number The number of protons and neutrons in the nucleus of an atom.

melting The change of state from a solid to a liquid.

moment Force × perpendicular distance from the pivot.

momentum Mass × velocity.

neutron A particle in the nucleus of atoms that has mass but no charge.

Newton's first law of motion For a body to change the way it is moving, a resultant force needs to act on it.

Newton's second law of motion When a force acts on a body, the body is accelerated in the direction of the force. It is given by the equation $F = ma$.

Newton's third law of motion Forces always come in pairs that are equal in size and opposite in direction.

non-renewable (resources) An energy resource that will run out, such as oil or natural gas.

nuclear fission The process where a large nucleus absorbs a neutron and then splits into two large fragments, releasing energy and further neutrons.

nuclear fusion The process where the nuclei of small atoms such as hydrogen join together to form a larger nucleus, releasing energy.

nucleus, atomic The tiny centre of an atom, made up of protons and neutrons.

nuclide A nucleus that contains a particular number of protons and neutrons.

Ohm's law The current flowing through a component is proportional to the potential difference between its ends, providing temperature is constant.

orbital speed How fast one object orbits another. It is calculated from orbital speed = (2 × π × orbital radius)/time.

parallel Describes a circuit in which the current splits up into more than one path.

photons Particles of light and other electromagnetic radiations. Sometimes radiation behaves like waves, sometimes like particles.

pitch Whether a note sounds high or low to your ear.

polarity The polarity of an object is where it is a north pole or a south pole or positively or negatively charged.

potential difference (p.d.) The energy transferred from one coulomb of charge between two points. Measured in volts. Often called the 'voltage'.

potential energy A form of stored energy.

power The amount of energy transferred every second, equal to work done/time taken. Power can be transferred from somewhere (such as a power station) or to somewhere (such an electric kettle).

pressure The effect of a force spread out over an area. Pressure is equal to force/area.

pressure difference (in a fluid) Equal to density $\times$ g $\times$ height difference.

pressure law If the volume of the gas stays constant, then the pressure of the gas is proportional to its absolute temperature.

primary coil The input coil of a transformer. You connect it to the voltage you want to change.

proton Positively charged, massive particles found in the nucleus of an atom.

radiation Energy, such as electromagnetic rays, that travels in straight lines.

radio wave The part of the electromagnetic spectrum that has a long wavelength and is used for communications.

radioactive decay Natural and random change of a nucleus.

radioactive Describes a substance that has nuclei that are not stable.

radioactivity The emission of particles or energy from an unstable nucleus.

rarefaction Region where particles are stretched further apart than normal.

reflection When waves bounce off a mirror. The angle of incidence is the same size as the angle of reflection.

refraction When waves change direction because they have gone into a different medium. They change direction because their speed changes.

refractive index Indicates how strongly a particular material changes the direction of light, where $n = \sin i/\sin r$ and $n = 1/\sin c$.

renewable (resource) An energy resource that is constantly available or can be replaced as it is used, such as solar power or wind power.

resistance The property of an electrical conductor that limits how easily an electric current flows through it. Measured in ohms.

resultant force A single imaginary force that is equivalent to all the forces acting on an object, equal to mass $\times$ acceleration.

rheostat A resistor whose resistance can be varied.

semiconductor A material that does not conduct electricity as well as metal, for example, but conducts electricity better than an insulator, such as plastic.

series Describes a circuit in which the current travels along one path through every component.

short circuit The unwanted branch of an electrical circuit that bypasses other parts of the circuit and causes a large current to flow.

solidification The change of state from a liquid to a solid.

speed A measure of how far something moves every second. Average speed = distance travelled ÷ time taken.

spectrum The 'rainbow' of colours that make up white light: red, orange, yellow, green, blue, indigo and violet.

thermistor A resistor made from semiconductor material: its resistance decreases as temperature increases.

transformer A machine that changes the voltage of a.c. electricity. The ratio of the number of turns in the coils is the same as the ratio of the voltages produced. A step-up transformer increases the voltage. A step-down transformer decreases the voltage.

transverse wave A wave in which the change of the medium is at 90 degrees to the direction of the wave. Light is an example.

trough The lowest part of a wave.

turbine A machine that rotates. It is pushed by the movement of a fluid such as air or water.

ultraviolet The part of the electromagnetic spectrum that has a slightly longer wavelength than the visible spectrum.

variable resistor A component with a resistance that can be manually altered.

velocity The speed and direction of an object.

velocity–time graph A graph of how velocity varies with time.

virtual image An image that cannot be projected onto a screen.

volt A unit of voltage. The energy carried by one coulomb of electric charge.

voltage A measure of the energy carried by an electric current.

watt A unit of power. One watt is one joule transferred every second.

wave equation Wave speed = frequency × wavelength.

wavefront The moving line that joins all the points on the crest of a wave.

wavelength The distance between the same points of successive waves, for example, the distance from one crest to the next.

wave speed Equal to frequency × wavelength.

weight The force of gravity on a mass, equal to mass × gravitational field strength. The unit of weight is the newton.

work The energy transferred when a job is done, equal to force × distance moved in the direction of the force.

Answers

The answers given in this section have been written by the author and are not taken from examination mark schemes.

SECTION 1 GENERAL PHYSICS

Speed, velocity and acceleration

Pages 18–19

1. a) The cars move along the road in the same direction, a constant distance apart.

    b) If they are moving towards each other, they will collide head on. If they are moving apart, they will continue to do so.

    c) The cars will move along the road, a constant distance apart in the opposite direction to a).

2. Average speed = distance/time = 2 × distance between home and school/2 × time taken to travel between home and school.

3. 10 000/15 × 60 = 10 000/900 = 11.1 m/s.

4. 22.5 m.

5. 3000 s = 50 minutes.

Page 19

1. The straight line will have a positive gradient for moving away, and a negative gradient for moving towards.

2. A graph will have axes which are labelled properly with a scale, plotted data points and the best line. A sketch graph is drawn to illustrate the main shape of the line. Only key values such as where the line changes direction, will be given on the axes.

3. Your graph is likely to be a curve, as shown in Fig. 1.9.

Page 21

1. 10 m/s^2.

2. −15 m/s^2.

Page 22

1. a) Athlete: 8 m/s. Fun runner: 6.25 m/s.

    b) Athlete: horizontal line at 8 m/s, starting at 0 s and finishing at 50 s. Fun runner: horizontal line at 6.25 m/s, starting at 0 s and finishing at 64 s.

Page 27

1. The velocity that an object, such as a skydiver, has when the forces are balanced so that the object travels at a maximum constant speed.

2. 10 m/s.

3. 15 N upwards.

4. 585 N downwards.

5. EXTENDED a) Velocity.

    b) Acceleration.

The velocity graph decreases from initial zero until it reaches a constant value, which is the terminal velocity. The force graph includes the constant weight (the drag), which increases with time and then becomes constant; and the resultant, which is found by adding the weight and the drag. The acceleration graph increases initially and then reaches zero because the velocity has reached terminal velocity, which is not changing, so there is no acceleration.

Density

Page 40

1. a) Volume = 2 cm × 4 cm × 5 cm = 40 cm^3.

    b) Density = mass/volume = 312 g/40 cm^3 = 7.8 g/cm^3.

2. The bread contains more air spaces, making the overall density less.

3. The block of wood is less dense than sea water.

Forces

Page 47

1. a) A force can change the speed of an object, the shape of an object and the direction the object is moving in.

    b) Any three from: gravitational, electric, magnetic, (electromagnetic), strong nuclear force.

2. a) Gravity.

    b) The mass of objects and the distance between their centres.

3. In a nucleus.

4. Electromagnetic.

Page 55

1. EXTENDED 0.01 N.

2. EXTENDED 0.2 N/cm or 20 N/m.

3. EXTENDED 20 cm.

Page 57

1. No resultant force so stationary or constant speed.

2. Resultant force speed or direction of motion will change.

3. The gymnast's weight.

1. **EXTENDED** **a)** force = mass × acceleration.

   b) The force must be a resultant force; the mass must remain constant.

2. **EXTENDED** 600 N.

3. **EXTENDED** 800 m/s^2.

Page 61 Extended

1. The Moon would move in a straight line in the direction it was travelling when gravity ceased.

2. The car would slide and carry on in a straight line.

3. The person would move in a straight line in the direction the person was travelling when gravity ceased.

Page 63

1. The size of the perpendicular force and the distance between the line of the force and the turning point (pivot).

2. **EXTENDED** 1.5 m.

Page 66 top

1. The point at which we can assume all the mass of an object is concentrated.

2. The heavy base means that the centre of mass is lower; the wide base means it has to tip further before the centre of mass falls outside the pivot, which would cause the vase to tip over.

Page 66 bottom

1. **EXTENDED** A scalar quantity has magnitude only, e.g. mass; a vector quantity has magnitude and direction, e.g. velocity.

2. **EXTENDED** Force is a vector because it has direction as well as magnitude associated with it.

3. **EXTENDED** Draw the two forces in correct direction and to suitable scale length. Find resultant by completing parallelogram formed by these two forces. Resultant is represented by diagonal of parallelogram. This gives its direction. The size can be found by measuring the length of the diagonal and then using the original scale to convert.

Energy, work and power

Page 74

1. **EXTENDED** 100 J.

2. **EXTENDED** 4 J.

Page 76

1. Gravitational → kinetic → gravitational.

2. Springs.

3. Bonds between atoms.

Page 77

1. Energy cannot be created or destroyed, only transferred from one form to another.

2. Electrical energy changes to light energy and heat.

3. **a)** Electrical.

   b) Kinetic.

   c) Sound, heat.

Page 84

1. Light to electric.

2. Kinetic to electric.

3. Fuel is burned and steam is produced in a boiler. The steam turns a turbine. The turbine drives a generator. The generator produces electricity. The electricity is supplied to homes, industry, etc.

4. In certain parts of the world, water forms hot springs that can be used directly for heating. Water can also be pumped deep into the ground to be heated.

Page 88

1. 250 J.

2. 500 N.

3. 80 J.

4. 50 m.

5. 400 N.

6. **EXTENDED** $8.45 \times 10^{12}/8 \times 10^6$ N $= 1.06 \times 10^6$ N.

7. **EXTENDED** **a)** The shuttle does a series of manoeuvres before landing to get rid of the excess energy.

   b) 1650 °C. The orbiter is covered with ceramic insulating materials designed to protect it from this heat. The materials include: reinforced carbon-carbon (RCC) on the wing surfaces and underside; high-temperature black surface insulation tiles on the upper forward fuselage and around the windows; white Nomex blankets on the upper payload bay doors, portions of the upper wing and mid/aft fuselage; low-temperature white surface tiles on the remaining areas.

Page 92

1. The man has twice the weight, so the force is double, but the time is the same.

2. The machine transfers energy at a great rate.

3. **EXTENDED** The watt (W).

4. **EXTENDED** 240 W.

5. **EXTENDED** **a)** 2940 J.

   b) 49 W.

Pressure

1. For the pin, the force is concentrated over a smaller area – there is a greater pressure.

2. EXTENDED Pressure = force/area = 100 N/0.2 m² = 500 Pa.

3. EXTENDED 80 N.

4. EXTENDED 1.28 m².

Page 106

1. EXTENDED Depth, density of the fluid, gravitational field strength.

2. EXTENDED Pressure difference = $h \times$ density $\times g$ = 8 m × 1000 kg/m³ × 10 N/kg = 80 000 Pa (= 80 kPa).

3. EXTENDED 1 030 000 Pa.

4. EXTENDED 400 kPa.

5. EXTENDED 20 400 Pa.

SECTION 2 THERMAL PHYSICS

Simple kinetic molecular model of matter

Page 123

1. It increases – either as faster and larger vibration in solids or as faster translational and vibrational motion in liquids and faster translational motion in gases.

2. Compressing a gas pushes the particles closer together; in a liquid they are already close to each other and will repel if pushed closer.

3. a) The particles are closely packed together in a regular arrangement in a solid.

   b) The particles are closely packed together in an irregular arrangement in a liquid.

   c) The particles are widely spaced in an irregular arrangement in a gas.

4. The volume of a gas depends on the shape of the container.

Page 124

1. The molecules are always moving about and spread out throughout the container.

2. Since volume inversely proportional to pressure increasing pressure means decreasing volume.

3. The mass of the gas must remain constant (that is, no particles move in or out of the system). The temperature must be measured using the kelvin scale. The gas must be ideal (not liquefy or solidify).

Page 126

1. The random motion of small particles in a gas or liquid brought about by molecular bombardment.

2. The small particles we can see are being hit by even smaller particles that we cannot see.

3. The particles are colliding with the walls of the container.

4. Faster molecules hit the walls harder and more often, so create a bigger force.

Page 127

1. Higher temperature, increased flow of air across the surface, larger surface area.

2. Smaller surface area, so rate of cooling lower.

Page 129

1. The pressure is inversely proportional to volume.

2. The mass of gas must remain constant (as well as the temperature).

3. EXTENDED 519.8 cm³.

Thermal properties

Page 137

1. Metals expand at different rates as their temperatures rise. So if strips of two metals are bound closely together, and are warmed, they bend as one metal expands more than the other.

2. The atoms vibrate more as the temperature goes up. So, even though they stay joined together, they move slightly further apart, and the solid expands a little in all directions.

3. Unlike other liquids, when its temperature falls below 4 °C, water begins to expand again, and becomes less dense.

4. Firstly, we don't have to allow the gas to expand if it gets hotter; if we put it in a sealed container then we can just allow the pressure to increase instead. Secondly, if we do allow a gas to expand, then it will increase in volume much more than solids or liquids do as it gets hotter. Between 0 °C and 100 °C it will expand by a third, so 300 cm³ of gas will become 400 cm³.

Page 140

1. Volume of a liquid: mercury-in-glass or alcohol-in-glass thermometer; length of a solid: bimetallic strip in a thermostat.

2. The melting point of ice, defined as 0 °C, and the boiling point of water at standard atmospheric pressure, defined as 100 °C.

3. Large response to a small change in temperature.

4. EXTENDED The thermocouple is based on the fact that any two metals in contact generate a tiny voltage (actually a tiny e.m.f.). In order to measure this voltage with a voltmeter, the two metals need to form a circuit, which, as in Fig. 2.18, means that

there must be two junctions. If the junctions are at the same temperature, there will be no voltage because the two voltages will cancel out, but if the junctions are at different temperatures, the difference between the two voltages can be measured with a voltmeter. One junction is placed at the point where the temperature is to be measured. The other junction is kept at room temperature, or for accurate work it is placed in a beaker of melting ice to take it to 0 °C.

Page 143

1. By transferring energy to them.
2. Its internal energy has increased.
3. The ability to store internal energy.
4. The high thermal capacity of the walls causes the house to warm up slowly during the day and to cool down slowly at night.

Page 148

1. There is energy input without change of temperature.
2. At this temperature the molecules have enough energy to leave the liquid in large quantities, even those inside the liquid. These molecules collect to form large bubbles of vapour and cause the liquid to bubble violently.
3. When a liquid evaporates it loses molecules from its surface. This will occur in an open container of water at any temperature. For example, water from a hot drink left in a cup will eventually evaporate. The molecules of water in the cup will have a range of energies, and even at room temperature the molecules with the highest energies will leave the surface.

Transfer of thermal energy

Page 155

1. They contain released electrons that can move freely and transfer energy.
2. There are no particles in outer space to transfer energy by colliding with each other.
3. Vibrations of the particles are passed on through the bonds between the particles.
4. Some wax is put on one end of a metal rod. The other end of the metal rod is heated until the wax on the other end melts.
5. EXTENDED Use petroleum jelly to attach drawing pins at regular distances along the copper strip. Heat one end of the strip and measure the time it takes for each drawing pin to fall off. Plot a graph of time until the drawing pin falls off against distance from the point that is being heated.

Page 156

1. The particles are free to move.
2. Warm air expands which makes it less dense. Less dense air floats up above more dense (cooler) air.
3. Heat some potassium manganate(VII) crystals in water or show convection currents using smoke in air.
4. Fibres in the insulation create air pockets. This restricts the movement of the air and so convection currents cannot form.

Page 158

1. It can travel through a vacuum.
2. A hot object.
3. Two from: temperature, type of surface, area of surface.
4. EXTENDED The dull, black side.

Page 160

1. Convection.
2. The top of the room.
3. a) Vacuum has no particles to connect.
   b) Vacuum has no particles to form convection currents.
   c) Silver surfaces reflect the energy and do not absorb or emit it.
4. The flask reduces energy transfer in both directions, so hot drinks do not lose their energy and cold drinks are not warmed by energy entering from outside.

Page 163

1. More than half the energy wasted is through these two features.
2. Trapped air in the walls, roof, windows, etc.
3. Air is a bad conductor (good insulator) so keeping a layer near the body reduces heat loss by conduction. Keeping the layer trapped reduces heat loss by convection.
4. In hotter climates, you may want to lose heat, so loose clothing allows the air to move and transfer heat away from the body.

SECTION 3 PROPERTIES OF WAVES

General wave properties

Page 175

1. a) The waves travel by vibrations in the direction of travel of the wave.
   b) The waves travel by vibrations at right angles to the direction of travel of the wave.

2. **a)** The distance between consecutive peaks or troughs of the wave.

   b) The number of peaks/troughs that go past each second.

   c) The size of the vibrations.

3. 15 m.

4. Energy.

Page 178

1. $v = f\lambda$, f is constant, so if v is reduced so must λ.

2. The density of each medium.

3. They must be comparable.

Light

Page 187

1. The light from the bottom of the pond is refracted away from the normal as it leaves the pond, so it enters your eye at a shallower angle. Your brain is fooled into thinking this shallower angle is the true angle of the bottom of the pond and so the pond looks shallower than it really is.

2. Being more dense than air, the carbon dioxide in the balloon will slow down the sound wave. This will tend to focus the sound together, like a lens. (A balloon filled with hydrogen will do the opposite.)

Page 188

1. EXTENDED 30.7°.

2. EXTENDED 36.3°.

3. EXTENDED 1.43.

4. EXTENDED **a)** More slowly.

   b) In diamond; because the speed in the material is inversely proportional to the refractive index, slower speed = higher index.

   c) Air: 2.99×10^8 m/s; water 2.25×10^8 m/s; glass 1.97×10^8 m/s; diamond 1.24×10^8 m/s.

Page 191

1. The angle of incidence at which the angle of refraction becomes equal to 90°.

2. 45.6°.

3. 1.29.

Page 199

1. The white light incident on the prism is split into its component colours by the prism – each component colour has a different wavelength so is refracted by a different amount.

2. 3×10^8 m/s.

3. X-rays.

4. Gamma, ultraviolet, visible, infra-red, microwaves.

Page 201

1. Gamma rays, which as you see in Fig. 3.41, are the electromagnetic waves with the shortest wavelength, and therefore the greatest frequency and energy, are produced by radioactive nuclei; X-rays, which have the next highest energy radiation after gamma on the electromagnetic spectrum, are produced when high-energy electrons are fired at a metal target.

2. By exciting the atoms in a mercury vapour.

3. A photograph taken to show the infra-red radiation given out from objects.

4. Water particles in food absorb the energy carried by microwaves. They vibrate more, making the food much hotter. Microwaves penetrate several centimetres into the food and so speed up the cooking process.

Sound

Page 211

1. Longitudinal.

2. Small differences in air pressure.

3. 20–20 000 Hz.

4. Sound with frequencies above the range for human hearing.

5. A sound source and two microphones are arranged in a straight line, with the sound source beyond the first microphone. The distance between the microphones (x), called microphone basis, is measured. The time of arrival between the signals (delay) reaching the different microphones (t) is measured. Then speed of sound = x/t.

SECTION 4 ELECTRICITY AND MAGNETISM

Simple phenomena of magnetism

Page 223

1. They attract each other.

2. They repel each other.

3. It will line up approximately north–south.

Page 224

1. Magnetically hard materials retain their magnetism; magnetically soft materials lose their magnetism if the outside magnetic influence is removed.

2. An alloy is a material composed of a mixture of metals. A ferrous material contains a high proportion of iron.

3. A permanent magnet that is made of magnetically hard materials.

4. In electromagnets and relays.

Page 225

1. It will be attracted. It has had magnetism induced in it; it has become magnetised.

2. The south pole.

3. Soft magnetic materials will attract a known. magnet, but only magnets will also repel magnets.

4. Same poles facing each other.

Page 226

1. A region of space in which magnetism affects other objects.

2. The path that a free north pole would take.

3. Place a bar magnet under a thin sheet of plastic, and sprinkle iron filings on to the top of the plastic. The iron filings will arrange themselves into strings of filings along the field lines. Place a small compass (known as a plotting compass) on the plastic in place of the iron filings. If you move the compass in the direction that its north pole is pointing it will follow a field line.

Page 229 top

1. The magnetic field lines radiate out from the north pole and go round to the south pole.

2. They attract each other and the field lines go from a north pole to a south pole.

3. The field lines go from a north pole to a south pole, not between like poles.

Page 229 bottom

1. Magnetic field lines show the direction of a force (on a free north pole); if field lines crossed it would indicate a force in more than one direction, which makes no sense.

2. Even, the same strength at all places.

3. Between the poles of a U-shaped magnet, or when opposite poles of two magnets are placed close to each other.

Electrical quantities

Page 236

1. You are the insulator. You will have rubbed electrons either onto or off yourself, perhaps by sliding your feet over a carpet. The metal handrail is a conductor – when you touch it, it allows the electrons to move to restore the balance and this is what you feel as a shock.

2. Negatively charged.

3. Positively charged.

4. The key idea is friction – water droplets rubbing against each other, bits of dust, etc. Although water is a conductor, in a cloud it is isolated from the ground so the charge can build up.

Page 238

1. Electrons are extremely small and negatively charged. Electrons are also around the outside of atoms. These key ideas make it much easier for electrons to be moved about (than the positively charged parts of the atom) to account for all the electric effects we know.

2. The electron clouds in your feet repel the electron clouds in the floor. The force of repulsion is easily enough to stop you falling through.

3. a) Polythene rod should be negatively charged and cloth positively charged. Perspex rod should be positively charged and cloth negatively charged.

   b) They will be equal and opposite.

Page 243

1. **EXTENDED** a) 15 C.

   b) 20 C.

   c) 92 C.

   d) 45 C.

2. **EXTENDED** 0.5 A.

3. **EXTENDED** 120 s.

Page 246

1. 10 V.

2. 6 Ω.

Page 251

1. The longer the wire, the further the electrons have to travel through the wire.

2. The thicker the wire, the more routes electrons have to travel through the wire.

3. **EXTENDED** 3R.

4. **EXTENDED** 1/3R, or R/3.

Page 252

1. **EXTENDED** 220 W.

2. **EXTENDED** 12 V.

3. **EXTENDED** 0.11 A.

Page 253

1. **EXTENDED** No, because the voltage is not high enough from the mains.

2. **EXTENDED** 2160 J.

3. **EXTENDED** 3.3 A.

4. **EXTENDED** 218 s.

5. **EXTENDED** 12 V.

Electric circuits

Page 262

1. There is no current when the circuit is not complete.

2. In parallel each bulb takes the same energy from the battery, so the battery has to deliver twice as much energy as it would if the bulbs were in series, where its energy is shared.

3. Can be switched on and off independently.

4. In series dimmer because battery energy shared between two bulbs, in parallel full energy of battery given to each bulb.

Page 265

1. It is the same.

2. Each appliance can be designed to work with mains voltage supply; appliances can be switched on and off individually.

3. 122 Ω.

4. **EXTENDED** 88.1 kΩ.

Page 268

1. The output of a potentiometer can be set to zero.

2. 6 V.

3. High.

4. Since $V = IR$, and I is the same in both R_1 and R_2, then if $R_2 \rightarrow R_1$ then $V_2 = V_{out} \rightarrow V_1$.

Page 269

1. A material that does not conduct electricity as well as a conductor such as copper but better than an insulator such as plastic.

2. In brighter light, the resistance of the LDR decreases, so the current in the circuit will increase. The ammeter reading will therefore increase in brighter light.

3. Increasing the temperature reduces resistance.

Page 273

1. A device that transfers energy from one form to another; LDR and thermistor.

2. Between the two plates.

3. Electromagnet.

Page 277

1. **EXTENDED** The diode only allows the current to flow for half the cycle of a.c.

2. It smooths out the output p.d. because the capacitor is charged up by pulses of electricity and delivers a steady forward current through the resistor even when the e.m.f. is reversed.

3. Input: base and emitter; output: collector and emitter.

4. **EXTENDED** If the input to base is below 0.6 V then almost no current flows in the output circuit, but when the input to base is raised above 0.6 V then the current flows in the output circuit.

Page 281

1. The combination of signals at the inputs.

2. High.

3. Initially both inputs are low, so the output is low. The set input then goes high, so the output goes high. The set input goes low but the output remains high (latched on). The reset input goes high, so the output goes low. The reset goes low and the output stays low – latched off.

4. Switch and resistor.

Dangers of electricity

Page 290 Extended

a) 1.6 A, 3 A fuse.

b) 0.35 A, 3 A fuse.

c) 0.43 A, 3 A fuse.

d) 9.1 A, 13 A fuse.

e) 3.9 A, 5 A fuse.

Page 291

1. Brown wire: live, connected to fuse. Blue wire: neutral wire. Green and yellow wire: earth wire.

2. It melts if the current gets too high.

3. The student should not choose the 'nearest' fuse, but the 'nearest above'. If the appliance requires 6 A, the 5 A fuse will melt when the appliance is used.

4. The earth connection needs to be a low resistance path. This means that, in the event of a fault occurring, a high current will pass through the wire and this will melt the fuse (or trip the circuit breaker).

5. The casing cannot become live because it is not a conductor.

Electromagnetic effects

Page 297

1. An e.m.f. is created in a wire in a complete circuit when:
   - the wire is moved through a magnetic field ('cutting' the field lines)
   - the magnetic field is moved past the wire (again 'cutting' the field lines)
   - the magnetic field around the wire changes strength.

2. No, it needs to move relative to the field.

3. EXTENDED The magnitude of the induced e.m.f. depends on the field strength and the speed with which the wire is moved.

Page 299

1. Via slip rings.

2. To maximise the effect, increase the rate of rotation, increase the strength of the magnetic field, increase the number of turns on the coil. The output is an alternating current because the relative motion between coil and field reverses each half-turn.

Pages 301–302

1. When the secondary coil has more turns than the primary coil, the voltage increases in the same proportion. This is a step-up transformer. A transformer with fewer turns on the secondary coil than on the primary coil is a step-down transformer, and produces a smaller voltage in the secondary coil.

2. 20 V.

3. 6.0 V.

4. a) 24 V.

   b) 2 A.

   c) 24 A.

Page 304

1. High voltage transmission reduces power loss.

2. The voltage is stepped up at the power station for high voltage transmission then stepped down again before use.

3. a) 25 600 W.

   b) 0.64%.

Page 307

1. Your sketch should match Fig. 4.102. It should be a similar shape to a bar magnet pattern – 'fanning out' at the poles; 'loops' along the sides, etc.

2. The field at the centre of the coil is most nearly uniform.

3. a) Your sketch should match the right-hand part of Fig. 4.97.

   b) Sketch should match left-hand part of Fig. 4.97.

Page 312

1. The current in the coil creates a magnetic field around it. This interacts with the magnetic field from the permanent magnet, producing forces in opposite directions on either side of the coil. Putting the coil on an axle allows these forces to spin the coil.

2. The commutator reverses the direction of the current in the coil each half-turn and therefore reverses the direction of the forces on the two sides. This allows the coil to maintain its motion in the same direction.

Page 313

1. See Fig. 4.104: thumb = movement; first finger = field; second finger = current.

2. Increase the current or increase the strength of the magnetic field.

3. Change the direction of the current or reverse the magnetic field.

Cathode-ray oscilloscopes

Page 320

1. A stream of electrons.

2. By thermionic emission from a heated cathode

3. The positive plate: they are negatively charged electrons.

Page 321

1. EXTENDED The coating on the screen absorbs energy from the electrons and releases energy as light, so a dot appears on the screen.

2. EXTENDED By controlling the voltages on the x-plates and y-plates.

3. EXTENDED A circuit that moves dots across the screen from left to right at a constant speed and then returns the dot very quickly to the start.

SECTION 5 ATOMIC PHYSICS

The nuclear atom

Page 334

1. EXTENDED Most alpha particles were unde-flected, indicating the mass of the atom is mostly concentrated in a small region. It must be a positively charged nucleus to repel the positively charged alpha particles. Knowing the mass of the atom and the size of the nucleus, it follows that the nucleus must be very dense material.

2. EXTENDED If electrons formed part of the nucleus it would have no overall electric charge and would not repel alpha particles at all, even those which came close to the nucleus.

3. EXTENDED If electrons had a mass similar to the alpha particles the electrostatic force between them would have a much more noticeable effect on the alpha particles.

Page 335

1. Protons, neutrons, electrons.

2. They have the same number of positive protons as negative electrons.

3. The proton number is the number of protons; the nucleon number is the number of protons and neutrons.

4. **EXTENDED** Because they have the same number of protons, isotopes of an element have the same number of electrons, and it is these that determine the chemical behaviour.

Radioactivity

Page 341

1. The emission of particles and/or energy from an unstable nucleus.

2. Unstable.

3. Alpha particles are relatively large, so as they travel they collide often, reducing their energy quickly, so they cannot travel very far. Beta particles are smaller and travel more quickly, having fewer collisions and losing less energy each time. This means they will travel further before losing all their energy. Gamma radiation, being electromagnetic waves, only interacts weakly with matter so it has a much larger range.

4. Alpha and beta particles are charged and so are deflected, but gamma particles are uncharged and so are not deflected.

5. In the Rutherford scattering experiment a beam of alpha particles was fired at a piece of gold foil to investigate how they scattered from its constituent atoms. Alpha particles can only travel a few centimetres in air – in that distance their energy is absorbed by air molecules. So in order for the alpha particles to reach the gold foil in the chamber of the apparatus without loss of energy, the chamber had to be evacuated.

Page 343

1. Two protons and two neutrons are emitted. Atomic number reduced by 2 and mass number by 4.

2. A neutron changes into a proton. Atomic number increases by 1. Mass number not affected.

3. No change to the number or types of particles. There is a reduction in energy however.

4. Emitting alpha or beta radiation changes the number of protons in the nucleus. This means the number of outer electrons will also change, changing the chemical behaviour – it is a different element.

Page 344

1. Half-life is the time taken for half the active nuclei in the sample to decay, i.e. the time for the activity to reduce to half its current level.

2. Activity is 800 Bq now, so in 8 hours it will be 400 Bq; 8 hours later it will be 200 Bq and a further 8 hours later the activity will be 100 Bq. This gives a total of 24 hours, three half-lives.

Page 349

1. Radioactive emissions are ionising radiations – they can ionise cells in the body, which may destroy the cells or damage them (particularly hazardous is the damage involves mutations to the cell which can lead to cancerous changes).

2. Sterilising medical equipment, radiotherapy, radiocarbon dating, smoke alarms, tracers.

Index

A

absolute zero and the Kelvin scale 129

AC generators, electromagnetic induction 297–9

acceleration 20–1

acceleration due to gravity, falling objects 25

alpha (α) particles 333, 339–43, 346–7

alternating current 274, 291–2, 299

ammeter, measuring current in amperes 242

analogue and digital signals, digital electronics 278

angles, of incidence and reflection 184, 186–7

atmospheric pressure 101–2

Atomic Physics
  introduction 330–2
  nuclear atom 332–5
  radioactivity 338–53

B

balanced forces 55, 62–3

barometers, mercury 101

Becquerel 343

beta (β) particles 339–43, 346–7

bimetallic strips 135

bistable circuits, logic gates 280–1

boiling point 148–9

Boyle's Law 124, 127–8

Brownian motion, kinetic molecular model 126

C

capacitors, circuit components 271–2

cathode-ray oscilloscopes
  electron beam 319–20
  introduction 318
  thermionic emission 319
  time-base circuit 321

centre of mass 63–4, 65

centripetal force 60–1

CERN (European Organisation for Nuclear Research) 48

checklist
  cathode–ray oscilloscopes 322
  density 43

electric circuits 282–3

electrical quantities 254–5

electricity 293

electromagnetic effects 314–15

energy, work and power 93

forces 68–9

kinetic molecular model 130

length and time 14

magnetism 230

mass and weight 34

nuclear atom 336

pressure 107

radioactivity 350

sound 215

speed, velocity and acceleration 28

thermal properties 150

transfer of thermal energy 164

wave properties 179, 203–4

circuit components 265–77

circuit diagrams, symbols 259–60

commutator, D C motor 311

compression 46

conduction
  thermal conductors 153–5
  thermal insulators 153–5

conductors and insulators
  comparison 234
  electron cloud 233

conservation of energy 77–8

convection, convection current 155–6

conventional current 243, 309

converging (convex) lenses
  focal length 192–3
  real images 194–6

coulombs 236, 242

D

D C motor 311–13

density
  examples 38
  formula 37–8
  introduction 36
  investigation 39
  irregular objects 41–2
  liquids 40
  regular objects 38

diffraction
  loudspeakers 178
  waves 177

digital electronics
  analogue and digital signals 278
  logic gates 279–81

diodes 260, 275

direct current 274

dispersion of light 197, 198
  visible spectrum 198–9

distance/time graphs 19–20

dynamos, electromagnetic induction 297–9

E

Earth
  age of 348–9
  energy transfers 76

echoes, measuring speed of sound 212–14

elastic behaviour 50, 52

electric charge
  charging by induction 238–9
  charging insulators by friction 234–6
  conductors and insulators 233–4
  electric fields 236–7

electric circuits
  circuit components 265–77
  circuit diagrams 259–60
  current in circuits 263–5
  digital electronics 278–81
  introduction 258–9
  series and parallel circuits 261–2

electric current
  conventional current 243, 309
  in series circuit 241–3

electrical quantities
  electric charge 233–40
  electric current 241–3
  electrical energy 75, 251–3
  electromotive force (e.m.f.) 243–4
  introduction 232–3
  potential difference (voltage) 244–5
  resistance 245–51

electricity
  electrical hazards 287–8
  insulation, fuses and circuit-breakers 288–91
  introduction 287
  mains electricity 291–2

electricity (*continued*)
  residual current circuit breaker 290
Electricity and Magnetism
  electric circuits 258–87
  electrical quantities 232–57
  electricity 287–94
  electromagnetic effects 295–317
  introduction 220–1
  magnetism 222–31
electricity transmission, energy losses in cables 302–4
electromagnetic effects
  cathode-ray oscilloscopes 318–23
  electricity transmission 302–4
  electromagnetic induction 296–7
  introduction 295–6
  magnetic effect of current 304–17
  transformers 299–302
electromagnetic induction
  AC generators 297–9
  dynamos 297–9
electromagnetic radiation
  gamma (Γ) rays 199
  infra-red radiation 200
  microwaves 200
  radio waves 200–1
  ultra-violet radiation 200
  X-rays 199–200
electromagnetic spectrum, waves 197–8, 202
electromagnets 307–8
electromotive force (e.m.f.) 243–4
electrons 333
electroscopes 239
electrostatic
  charge 234–6
  forces 47, 237–8
  hazards 241
energy
  conservation of 77–8
  different forms of 74–5
  efficiency of transfer 84–6
  introduction 71–2
  potential energy 72–3
  resources 79–83
  transfer of energy 75
  transfer of 81–4
  work and power 86–93

equation triangle
  angle of refraction 188
  electric charge, current and time 243
  force, mass and acceleration 58
  force, pressure and area 99
  Hooke's Law 54
  mass, density and volume 38
  power, current and voltage 251
  speed, wavelength and frequency 175
  voltage, current and resistance (Ohm's Law) 245–6
  weight, mass and acceleration 32
  work, power and time 91
equilibrium 63, 64
evaporation, kinetic molecular model 126–7, 148
exam-style questions
  electricity and magnetism 324–9
  general physics 110–17
  particle model and thermal transfer 166–8
  radioactivity 354–7
  wave properties 217–19
examinations
  objectives 358–9
  techniques 359–61
expansion of solids, liquids and gases 134–7
experimental skills
  handling observations and data 367–8
  observing, measuring and recording 364–6
  organising techniques, apparatus and materials 362–4
  planning and evaluating investigations 369–74

F

falling objects
  acceleration due to gravity 25
  terminal velocity 25
fibre optic cables 190
fiducial mark 13
Fleming's left-hand rule 309, 319
forces
  balanced 55, 62–3
  centripetal 60–1
  effects of 46
  Hooke's Law 51–2

introduction 45–6
  mass x acceleration formula 57–8
  moment of 62–3
  resultant 49, 56
  types of 47
  unbalanced 55–6
  vectors 66–7
forces on an aircraft, investigation 59–60
formulae
  acceleration 20
  density 37
  distance travelled 22–3
  energy, current, voltage and time 252
  force, mass and acceleration 57
  kinetic energy 74
  Ohm's Law 245–6
  potential energy 73
  power, work and energy 91
  pressure 99
  pressure in a fluid 105
  refractive index 187, 188
  specific heat capacity 141
  speed 17
  speed, wavelength and frequency 175
  transformer voltages 300
  work done 87
fossil fuels 79

G

gamma (Γ) ray 199, 339–43, 346–7
Geiger-Müller tube 339, 345
General Physics
  density 36–44
  energy, work and power 71–97
  forces 45–70
  introduction 8–9
  length and time 10–15
  mass and weight 31–5
  pressure 98–109
  speed, velocity and acceleration 16–30
geothermal power 83
graphs
  distance/time 19–20
  resultant forces 66–7
  velocity/time 21–3
gravitational fields, earth and moon 31–2
gravitational force 20, 47

H

Hooke's Law 51–2
  investigation 53
  spring constant 54
hydroelectric power 82
hydrometers 40

I

infra-red radiation 156–8, 190, 200
input transducers, circuit components 269–71
insulation, reducing transfer of thermal energy 162–3
insulation, fuses and circuit-breakers 288–91
internal energy (heat) 75
inverse proportionality, Boyle's Law 124
investigations
  centre of mass 64
  density 39
  efficiency of electric motors 85–6
  electromagnetic induction 298
  electromagnets 308
  electrostatic charge 240
  forces on an aircraft 59–60
  Hooke's Law 53
  infra-red radiation 158
  latent heat of vaporisation 144–5
  magnetic field patterns 226–7
  measuring the speed of sound 213–14
  pressure 100
  principle of moments 62
  radioactive decay 345
  radioactivity 341
  refection of light 185
  refractive index 189
  resistance of a wire 248
  specific latent heat of vaporisation 146–7
  speed/time 23–4
  terminal velocity 26
  thermal conductivity 155
  thermal energy transfer 161
  thermistors 270
  wind power 80
isotopes 334–5

J

Joules, measure of energy 252

K

Kelvin scale of temperature 129
kinetic energy 73–4
  different types 75
  transfer of 78
kinetic molecular model
  Brownian motion 126
  evaporation 126–7
  kinetic theory of gases 122
  molecular pressure 125–6
  molecular structure 121–2, 123–4
  observed features of gases 124
  pressure and volume 127–8
  states of matter 120–1, 122–3

L

Large Hadron Collider 48, 250
latent heat
  of fusion 143
  of vaporisation 143–7
length and time 10–15
Leslie's cube 157–8
light
  converging (convex) lenses 192–6
  dispersion of 197, 198
  introduction 181–2
  reflection of 183–5
  refraction of 186–9
  refractive index 187–9
  total internal reflection 190–1
light-dependent resistors (LDRs), circuit components 268–9
light-sensitive switch, circuit components 276–7
limit of proportionality, stretching 49–50, 52, 54
liquids, density 40
logic gates
  bistable circuits 280–1
  truth tables 279–80
longitudinal waves 75
  compression and rarefaction 172–5
loudspeakers, diffraction 178

M

machines, simple examples 89–90
magnetic effect of current
  current in a wire 304–5
  D C motor 311–13
  force on a charged particle in a magnetic field 47, 311
  force on a current carrying conductor 309–10
  magnetic effect in solenoids 306–8
magnetic materials
  magnetically hard or soft 223–4
  non-ferrous and alloys 223–4
magnetism
  introduction 222–3
  magnetic fields 226–9
  magnetic induction 224–5
  magnetic materials 223–4
  magnetisation and demagnetisation 225
magnifying glasses 195
mass, centre of 63–4
mass, force and acceleration 57–8
mass and weight 31–5
masses, comparing 33
measurements
  accuracy 10–11
  micrometers 12–13
  oscillations 13
  stopwatches 12
  volumes 12
meniscus 11
micrometers 12–13
microwaves
  radar 200, 202
  radio waves 200–2
molecules, kinetic molecular model 123–4
moment, of forces 62–3
motion in a circle 60–1
MRI scanning 250

N

newton
  definition of 57
  meter 31, 33
Newton's First Law of Motion 55
Newton's Second Law of Motion 57
Newton's Third Law of Motion 59
non-renewable energy sources 79
nuclear, power 74, 83
nuclear atom
  Geiger and Marsden's experiment 333
  isotopes 334–5
  nuclear equations 342
  nucleus 334, 342–3

nucleon number, A 334, 342
nuclides 334

O

Ohm's Law, resistance
  245–51
optical fibres, pulse spreading
  191–2
oscillations 13
oscilloscope, displaying sound
  waves 211

P

permanent magnets and
  electromagnets 223, 229
plastic behaviour 50
potential difference (voltage)
  244–5
potential energy
  gravitational 72
  kinetic 73–4
  transfer of 78
potentiometer, circuit components
  267–8
power, rate of doing work 90–1
power rating, Watts 251
pressure
  atmospheric 101–2
  difference in depth 103–5
  in fluids 100–1
  introduction 98–100
proportional behaviour, springs
  51–2
proton number, Z 334, 342

R

radar, microwaves 200, 202
radiation, infra-red radiation
  156–8
radio waves, UHF, VHF short,
  medium and long 201–2
radioactivity
  background radiation 339
  half-life 343–4
  introduction 335, 338
  ionising radiation 339
  radioactive carbon dating 331,
  349
  radioactive decay 339, 342–3
  radioisotopes 346–7
  safety precautions 346
  tracers 347
ray diagrams, the normal 184
reflection, of waves 176
reflection of light
  ray diagrams 184–5

total internal refection 190–1
  virtual images 183–5
refraction, waves 176–7
refraction of light 186–9
refractive index 187–9
relays, circuit components 272–3
renewable energy sources 79–83
residual current circuit breaker
  290
resistance
  combining resistors 264
  for length and cross-section
  249–51
  measuring 246–8
  Ohm's Law 245–6
resultant forces 49, 56
  vectors 66–7
rheostats, circuit components 266

S

scalar quantities 66
Science in Context
  absolute zero and the Kelvin
  scale 129
  age of the Earthy 348–9
  beginnings of plastics 50
  boiling point 149
  centre of mass in aircraft 65
  damage to ears 210
  density in action 42
  direct and alternating
  currents 274
  electrostatic hazards 241
  energy and the earth 76
  Faraday's cage 228
  Hooke's Law 52
  linking fundamental forces 48
  mains electricity 291–2
  optical fibres 191–2
  pressure and submarines 104
  simple machines 89–90
  sunglasses 182
  superconductors 250
  ultra-violet ray dangers 201
scuba diving 102–5
significant figures 78
solar power 82–3
sound
  damage to ears 210
  displaying sound waves 211
  echoes 212–14
  introduction 208–9
  measuring the speed in
  air 210

pitch, frequency and amplitude
  211–12
  ultrasound 209
  wave energy 75
specific heat capacity 141–3
speed, formula 17–18
speed, velocity and acceleration
  16–30
speed/time investigation 23–4
spring balance 31, 33
spring constant, Hooke's Law 54
stable equilibrium 64
stretching, limit of proportionality
  49–50, 52, 54
submarines 104, 332
sunglasses 182
superconductors 250

T

temperature-operated alarms,
  circuit components 277
tension 46
terminal velocity 25–6
thermal insulators and conductors
  153–5
Thermal Physics
  introduction 118–19
  kinetic molecular model 120–32
  thermal properties 133–52
  transfer of thermal energy
  153–66
thermal properties
  evaporation and boiling
  148–9
  expansion of solids, liquids and
  gases 134–7
  introduction 133–4
  latent heat 143–7
  temperature measurement
  137–9
  thermal capacity 140–3
  water 147–8
thermistors, circuit components
  268–9
thermocouples 139
thermograms 156–7
thermometers 137–8
tidal power 81
torsion 46
total internal refection, critical
  angle 190–1
transfer of energy 75, 77–8
transfer of thermal energy
  conduction 153–5

convection 155–6, 158–9
domestic radiators 158–9
introduction 153
radiation 156–8
reducing by insulation 162–3
vacuum flasks 159–60
transformers, electromagnetic
effects 299–302
transistors, circuit components
275–6
transverse waves
amplitude and period
173–4
light waves 183

U

ultra-violet radiation,
electromagnetic radiation 200
ultrasound, uses 209
unbalanced forces 55–6
uniform magnetic fields 229

V

variable resistor 265–7
vectors, resultant force 66–7

velocity 18
velocity/time, graphs 21–3
virtual images, reflection of light
183–5
visible spectrum, dispersion of
light 198–9
voltage (potential difference)
244–5
volumes, units 12

W

water
anomalous expansion 135–6
specific heat capacity 147
water power 81
Watts, power rating 251
Wave Properties
electromagnetic spectrum
197–8
introduction 170–2
light 181–207
longitudinal and transverse
waves 172–4
sound 75, 208–16

speed, frequency and
wavelength 174, 175
transfer of energy and
information 174
wavelength and period 173–4
waves
diffraction 177
reflection 176
refraction 176–7
weighing objects 33
weight, equation triangle 32
wind power 79–80
work
calculation 87–8
definition 86
simple machines 89–90

X

X-rays, electromagnetic radiation
199–200

Notes

Notes

Notes

Notes

Notes

Notes

Notes